Light on the Guru and Disciple Relationship

With kind regards, ॐ and prem

Light on the Guru and Disciple Relationship

Written and Compiled by
Swami Satyasangananda Saraswati

Under the Guidance of
Swami Satyananda Saraswati

Yoga Publications Trust, Munger, Bihar, India

Published by Bihar School of Yoga
    First Australian edition 1983
    First Indian edition 1984

Published by Yoga Publications Trust
    Reprinted 2006, 2011

ISBN: 978-81-85787-40-4

Publisher and distributor: Yoga Publications Trust, Ganga Darshan, Munger, Bihar, India.

Website: www.biharyoga.net
        www.rikhiapeeth.net

Printed at Thomson Press (India) Limited, New Delhi, 110001

Dedication

*In humility we offer this dedication to
Swami Sivananda Saraswati, who initiated
Swami Satyananda Saraswati into the secrets of yoga.*

Dedication

To our guru Sri Swami Satyananda Saraswati
who continues to inspire and guide us
on our spiritual journey.

Contents

Part II

Introduction

This book has been written for the purpose of illuminating the subject of guru and disciple according to the teachings of Swami Satyananda Saraswati. So much has been expounded on this ancient and timeless tradition, but this volume unifies the main areas of relevance for the day to day practical application of the guru-disciple relationship.

The first section was written by Swami Satyasangananda Saraswati, who accompanied Swami Satyananda on all his tours in the 1980s. The second section contains a selection of satsangs and talks given by Swami Satyananda on the guru-disciple relationship and includes a number of quotations from letters written by him to his disciples.

This work is given in the hope that seekers and aspirants may find inspiration and upliftment through the guru-disciple relationship.

My guru has shown me the path.
He desired my body.
I gave it to him unflinchingly.
He asked me for my prana,
I offered it, unhesitatingly.
He said, "Will you give me your mind too?"
I replied, "It is yours forever."
I was left with nothing,
Empty and desolate.
The dark blue sky dotted with stars, and the moon,
That was all I had now.
Then all at once,
The sun burst upon me with a song,
The restless ocean bathed me with its waves,
The thundering clouds burst upon me with rain,
The snow-white swan danced before my eyes,
A flash of lightning illumined my soul.
My Guru came to me once again.
He said, "Will you give me the samskaras
You have collected life after life?"
I looked into his deep brown eyes,
Into the dark and deep abyss of his Being.
For what seemed aeons, he stood before me.
Everything else began to dissolve before my eyes,
To melt and fade away.
There was unity within and without.
It is the grace of my Guru,
He who has extinguished my being,
And absorbed me into himself.
My Guru has shown me the path.

Swami Satyananda Saraswati

Part I

1

Prologue

The following story was told to me by my guru.

One day a rishi came to the court of a king. The king said, 'What can I offer you?"

"Whatever is your own," was the rishi's reply.

"Very well," said the king, "I offer you ten thousand cows."

"But they are not yours," said the rishi, "they belong to your empire. I will only accept something which is your very own."

"Then I will offer you one of my sons," said the king.

"Your son is also not your own," replied the rishi.
The discussion continued, the sadhu declining all the king's offerings on the grounds that he did not really own them.

"All right," said the king at last, "I offer myself."

"What do you mean by that?" asked the rishi. "You do not even know who you are. How can you offer yourself to me?"

"Then I will give you my mind," said the king after some deep thought, "that is my own."

Still the rishi was not satisfied. "If you give your mind to someone, it means that you will think of that person and nothing else, unless it is specifically permitted. What is the point of giving away five hundred gold coins and then spending them on yourself?"

So the rishi left the court. After a few months he returned.

"Tell me honestly and seriously," he said to the king, "whether you are now ready to give me your mind. I don't

3

want to hear about your property, your empire, your queen or your children."

The king thought deeply and replied, "No. I'm not ready yet."

So the rishi went away again, and came back a third time. During his absence the emperor had prepared his mind through yoga.

"I will try to offer you my mind this time," he said. "If I fail, forgive me."

The rishi accepted the king as his disciple, and from that day on the king's mind stopped thinking about everything except his guru. He did not care for his own welfare or for the welfare of his kingdom, he only wished to be with his guru.

The people reported this to the guru, who called the king to come to him. "Now it is time for you to get back to the business of ruling the kingdom. This is my command," he said.

This story illustrates clearly how total surrender forms the core of the guru-disciple relationship. The disciple offers his or her limited self to the guru, completely merging the mind in him, and then receives it back in its fullness. This is the true concept of surrender. But how many of us can hope to achieve it? The life of every disciple should be dedicated towards the attainment of this goal.

2

Necessity for Guru

No matter who or what you are, the guru is a necessity in your life. We are all lost wanderers in the ocean of life. We need a direction, a goal and an aim to sustain us. The entire span of existence is spent searching for a purpose. We look for it in wealth, in status, in relationships, but ultimately realize the illusory quality of these pleasures. And when people reach old age, they feel that life has cheated them. They feel that it was all futile and meaningless. They are left bankrupt.

If you reflect closely on your life, you will find that it has been spent entirely in the search for something. You knock on many doors, and return defeated. You search for eternal love, but it eludes you. You chase after money and status, but it is just a temporary quest. And even after attaining it, you still feel dissatisfied and discontented. Even if you supposedly have all the requisites for a happy and successful life, such as beauty, friends, wealth and success, you still cannot eliminate that nagging insecurity which haunts you in your reflective moments – the fear of losing it all, the fear of growing old, the fear of death. In times of solitude these fears become living realities and you feel shattered.

Human beings remain forever in delusion, clouded by false notions which appease the baser instincts. Many times the circumstances of life shock you out of your delusion in order to help you grasp the truth, but you pay no heed to it.

It is only the wise who recognize what life is trying to tell them, who recognize the symptoms. And they concede that there is more to life than the mere pleasures which have sustained them. It is then that they turn inwards and search for a more meaningful relationship with life. And it is this realization that brings them to the quest of the inner self.

After all, the problem lies not in the world and the qualities we attribute to it, but in ourselves. For we are trying to assign a quality of unchanging and eternal permanence to something which is forever changing and illusory. The world about us is an ongoing process. It is not static, but forever in motion. Creation, sustenance and disintegration are the inherent laws of nature. There is nothing we can do to stop this process.

There is one source, however, which is absolute, infinite and eternal, but this source exists within us. We do not have to look for it in the external world. It is so close, yet so far. On account of delusion and ignorance, we remain forever separated from it. The sages and wise people have described this source as the true self. Not the self which you are accustomed to identify with, but another self which exists within you and is crying for your attention and compelling you to look inwards for eternal happiness.

But what is this true self? Does it really exist and how are we to find it? At this point and primarily for this reason, the guru becomes necessary. The path to the inner self is long and hazardous, narrow as a razor's edge, full of pitfalls. And how are we to know the way? It is not simply a matter of undertaking a long and hazardous journey – we don't even know the destination. So what are we to do? We have to find someone who has traversed the same path, who has, in fact, reached the destination and can lead us towards it.

The sages who devised the guru-disciple relationship had a very clear insight into the limitations of the more mundane and gross relationships. After all, how can we expect someone who has the same level of awareness as ourselves to guide us on the journey? It is a case of the blind

6

leading the blind. Many people who have understood this point clearly have searched for someone with greater wisdom and experience who could lead them to greater fulfilment in life. They have found a guru.

In the scriptures there is repeated emphasis on the fact that one cannot make progress in spiritual life without the guidance of a guru. From all points of view this seems to be a logical claim. Without the help of a teacher, we cannot learn science, history, geography, mathematics, art or architecture. In the same way, for spiritual knowledge we must accept a guru.

Many people have argued that a guru is not necessary, that the real guru is within us. This is true. But how many of us can claim to hear him, understand him, or follow his instructions? In fact, we even tend to doubt his existence. Our mental concepts are limited and gross. The mind is a tumult of turbulent passions, desires and ambitions. Amidst all this commotion, how is it possible for you to hear the voice of your guru, which is the voice of silence? It is as futile as holding a conversation with a person who is hard of hearing in a room where a band is playing at full volume. In order for him to understand any part of what you are saying, the music must be turned off.

In the same way, we have to turn off the tumult within our minds if we wish to comprehend the sound of silence which belongs to our inner guru. But is it possible to do this when we don't even understand the patterns of our mind? We don't know why we feel hate, love, jealousy, anger and passion. So how are we going to eliminate them and stop the terrible din that is going on inside us twenty-four hours of the day? In fact, the more we try to suppress it, the louder it becomes.

To stop this inner turmoil, we require a guru. It is he who has mastered the laws which govern the mind, body and spirit. He alone can show the way to transform the negative patterns of our mind which stand between us and our inner guru. It is he who manifests our inner guru as a part of our personality.

7

It is the living guru who leads us inwards. He serves as a detonator to explode the great power dormant within us. When that is done and we are able to contact the inner self at will, then we may say that we do not need a guru; but not until then.

It seems that those who reject the necessity for a guru do so because of certain mishaps in their personal lives. Although one may understand their scepticism in the light of their experiences, one cannot accept their total negation of the guru-disciple relationship. Simply because they themselves have not been fortunate to experience this relationship positively is no justification for their absolute rejection. A careful study of the lives and histories of people who have denounced the concept of guru will show this to be true.

It is a great error to misguide people because of one's own insecurities and mental limitations. If you have negative reactions in your dealings with a guru, then you may denounce that guru and remove his influence from your life. But you certainly cannot use this one experience as a universal condemnation of all gurus. It is similar to a man whose marriage has failed. He then proclaims to the world that all women are bad and that marriage is futile. Is he justified? Would any reasonable person consider his proclamation as a universal truth? If this man were able to convince others that all women are bad and that marriage is a disaster, he would be seriously impeding the evolution of mankind.

Strangely enough, it is often the same people who denounce the guru and declare that the guru-disciple relationship is not conducive to mental growth who in time seek to acquire the status of guruhood themselves. They claim enlightenment and the power to transmit their knowledge! How can a person who has not been able to fulfil the requirements of a disciple become a guru?

To be a guru, one must be a good disciple. One must undergo the difficulties, pain, ordeals, insults and injuries that a disciple encounters. One has to eradicate the ego and become as humble as a blade of grass that bends with the wind. Only then can one blossom as a guru, not otherwise. We have seen in the past, and in recent times, the dangers that befall those who have attained guruship instantly and have not exposed themselves to the disciplined life of a disciple. It is only in the case of great saints who have been enlightened from birth that this discipline may not be necessary.

Guru is the guiding light. He may be in the physical body, but his spirit soars high into realms unknown. It is our needs, not his, that bind him to earth. His motives are selfless, his desires vanquished – he has no aims and aspirations. Although it may seem to an onlooker that he is very involved and immersed in what he is doing, for him it is all maya. He has the special ability to be a part of everything and yet remain outside as a witness. He can withdraw himself at any moment.

The guru is the fulfilment of your life. He represents purity, peace, love and wisdom, and he assumes the responsibility to draw out these qualities from within you. It is only when you strive to develop this part of your personality that the guru becomes a necessity. All the other relationships you have established in your life cannot inspire or guide you to the attainment of this goal. Just as the innocence and purity of a child inspires you to be loving, kind and gentle, the guru, through the purity of his motives, compels you to grow inwardly.

However, some of you may not wish to know this inner self. Life's experiences may not have affected you deeply, and you may wish to continue your search for happiness in the external world. Even if that is the case, the guru is still an essential part of your life.

You cannot deny that at times you have suffered due to your inability to cope with the circumstances and the cruelties which befall you. You may have enormous wealth, but your poor health does not permit you to enjoy it. You have

9

children, but they fall prey to drugs, schizophrenia and insanity. You have a good job, but you don't derive the mental satisfaction you are seeking. Or maybe your business is not stable. Sometimes the evil and negative influences of an ill-wisher cast a spell on your family. Whichever way you look at it, it seems a losing battle.

You have tried every method to surpass these difficulties, but in vain. You have been to psychiatrists and doctors, even your own efforts have not succeeded. But if you realize that the guru is the simplest remedy for even these afflictions, then you will save yourself a lot of trouble. In India, people go to the guru not only for spiritual knowledge. They cultivate enduring relationships with the guru because they are well aware that the guru can help them through all the difficulties of life.

The guru is there to take care of your practical as well as spiritual difficulties. He can cure your sickness. His positive influence can eliminate any evil spells that are affecting your life. Your children may not pay heed to your advice but they will surely listen to him. If your business is at stake, you may consult him about any imminent dangers.

The guru does not exist in the realm of the senses. He has attained psychic vision and his knowledge has advanced beyond the limitations of time and space. He has developed the power of intuition and, therefore, he can know your past, present and future. Divine powers work through him and, therefore, association with him always brings good results.

His advice is accurate and his judgement sound. He is fully aware of the dangers that may befall you and, if you seek his advice, he can warn you well in advance. But in order to understand him, you must be receptive to his words. You must try to build an enduring relationship with him, so that when you need him he is there to guide and protect you.

Regardless of the role you are playing in life, whether you are rich or poor, happy or unhappy, healthy or unhealthy, old or young, whether you have an evolved consciousness or not, the guru has something to teach you. He has a message for all. Even the person who has never experienced difficulties cannot deny that there have been moments of dissatisfaction, despair and the feeling of being in a vacuum. It is this vacuum in your life that the guru fills.

Come to the House

Slowly friend,
Slowly, slowly.
Come to the house where I live.
None is the way,
And no light to guide you,
Inside or outside only darkness.
Full of faults from the ages past.
Come to the house where I live.

Walk in the border of darkness,
Walk and walk the day and night,
Autumn, spring, summer and winter.
You have caught hold of the robe,
Awaken the truth.
Slowly, slowly.
Come to the house where I live.

Many are the pitfalls along the way.
Many are the difficulties that you will face.
Blind darkness envelops you on every side.
Come to the house,
Slowly, slowly.

Gone are the sins of the past.
With free and fearless mind,
Become the flower of humanity.
Throw your petals of light
To all those who need, but
Slowly, slowly.

Swami Satyananda Saraswati

3

How to Find a Guru

Before you embark on this project, you must determine exactly what the motives are that compel your search for a guru. What are the needs that he will be fulfilling? What exactly has triggered off this quest? Is it a yearning to awaken the inner spirit? Is it simply to include in your life's pattern the wisdom, presence and benevolence of a wise person? Is it because you wish to inculcate the discipline of yoga, and thereby develop a sound mind and healthy body? Or is it because of the need to alleviate the deep frustration within, caused by the difficulties of physical or mental illness, unemployment or financial troubles?

The motive for searching for a guru is of extreme importance and should involve a great deal of introspection. Always remember that the guru you find will be according to your needs. If your need for the guru is sincere, your search will guide you to the right person. For instance, you may wish to experience the highest goal in spiritual life and, being deluded by the intellect and mind, may consider that you are ready for it. But in actual fact you may still be at the bottom rung in terms of evolution. How then can you start at the top? If tomorrow you suddenly have a brainstorm and decide to become a neurosurgeon, would it be feasible to present yourself to a great master in that field with the request that he should immediately begin to train you to operate? No! He would ask you to first learn basic anatomy.

12

This is a common occurrence amongst spiritual seekers. Sometimes we become over-enthusiastic and overnight decide to pack our bags and go to the Himalayas, Rishikesh, or some such place to hunt out a guru and attain enlightenment, only to return after a series of misadventures, sorely disappointed. The path to enlightenment is an arduous one. Very few can tread that path. Therefore, in order to avoid mistakes, accidents and regrets, you have to systematically determine your needs and the guidance you require for your personal evolution.

You may be temporarily passing through a period of great difficulty and sorrow. As is most often the case when we undergo great stress, something wakes up inside us and we view life from a different angle. We feel a sense of disinterest in worldly life. We want to turn away from all that we once coveted, for we see the transience in everything. Driven by these thoughts, we may search for a guru and take sannyasa only to find that once we have overcome the momentary traumas, our desires, passions and ambitions return with greater momentum. We then realize that if we had analyzed our need carefully, the search for a guru would have been directed towards that purpose and no other.

This thought of the transience of material attachments also occurs in the mind of an aspirant who genuinely wishes to renounce the desires and live with a guru. But it is not the outcome of a reaction to the circumstances of the moment. Rather, it is the outcome of profound understanding of the purpose and aim of life. Once the decision is made, there will be no retracing or faltering in the face of difficulties.

So, at the outset, you must be absolutely sure what you are looking for in the guru. Great care must be exercised in ascertaining this point. Your motives and level of awareness play a very important role in determining your guru. A child at primary school cannot hope to relate to a professor at university. The child must find a teacher who can relate to his or her own level of awareness. It is the same for a disciple.

Therefore, the first step in the disciple's search for a guru is to prepare yourself mentally, physically and emotionally. The best way to do this is to expose yourself as much as possible to satsang, discourses, talks and discussions on spiritual matters. You must look for people of great wisdom who can interpret the mysteries and fundamental truths of life as revealed through the scriptures, people who can inspire you to introspect and to question yourself positively.

This practice of being in the company of wise and learned people can be incorporated into your daily life. Whenever you have the opportunity, you should not fail to be in the presence of such people. *Satsang*, literally meaning 'association with the truth', is one of the simplest and most effective means to aid you at the beginning. It is a well-known fact that when we associate ourselves with positive influences, we tend to develop ourselves in that direction.

Together with attending satsang, you should have a personal sadhana or yoga practice that you do regularly. In time you will find that your perception is clearer and your judgement more accurate. You will have a greater perception of your limitations, strengths and weaknesses. But most important of all will be the realization of your aim and goal of life. It will take time according to the sincerity and regularity of your practice, but you must be prepared to wait. And ultimately your perceptive and intuitive powers will enable you to recognize the guru when the time comes.

One point must be emphasized – the guru should not be chosen through limited awareness. It is far better to delay the choice of guru until the awareness is clear of apprehension, worries, anxieties and doubts. These will undoubtedly lead to errors of judgement. Many times you see people who have attained *siddhis*, or great spiritual powers, who are able to give momentary experiences, and you are swayed by your fantasies and emotions. You may even feel a great affinity with such people, but they are not necessarily the guru you are searching for.

14

You must see these people in the light of what they are. You may encounter many similar experiences before actually finding the real guru. You should draw positive influences from such experiences, but not make a real commitment until you are sure. One can only be sure and ready when the perception is refined and has reached a point of great clarity.

There is no point in being hysterical and neurotic about finding a guru. You must prepare yourself through satsang and sadhana. Many yoga teachers can recommend yoga practices to do at home, and there are ample opportunities to attend the satsangs of the wise. You may approach a guru simply for a mantra, or for advice on difficulties that befall you from time to time in your spiritual and material life. When the awareness grows and the perception deepens, you will spontaneously know the right path and the right guru.

Just as there are many stages of evolution for a disciple, the gurus too are at different stages of evolution. There are jnani gurus, who are adept in the scriptures and spiritual lore; yogi gurus, who have mastered all the yoga practices and can teach them with great skill; and tantric gurus, who can remove difficulties, financial and otherwise, through methods that they have perfected.

However, if you are searching for the highest experience, if you sincerely yearn for it and are prepared to forsake everything, then you must search for a guru who is a brahmanishta. A *brahmanishta* guru is one who abides in *Brahman*, or the ultimate reality. Such gurus are rare, and if you encounter one and are able to recognize this quality, then you should know that you have been fortunate. You may have encountered such people many times, but with your intellect and discrimination clouded with doubt and hypocrisy, you may have failed to recognize them. They do not exactly carry a placard on their backs saying, "I am a brahmanishta, follow me!" The true brahmanishta will probably be living a very simple life, avoiding all the trappings of name and fame.

15

The point to be made clear is that there are two fundamental types of gurus. One has knowledge of the absolute and the other has both knowledge and experience of the absolute. You have to decide which you need. If you just require knowledge, then you should seek out a jnani guru, but if you want to have experience, then you will have to turn to a brahmanishta guru or a tantric guru.

Very often we find that it is beyond the ability of the disciple to determine his own stage of evolution and what exactly his needs are. But still he has a strong desire for a guru. In such a case, it is best to approach an enlightened guru, who is able to discern your level of evolution and able to guide you according to your needs. But if you place your faith in him, you must remember that his instructions are final. He may ask you to take sannyasa and stay in his ashram, or he may send you back with instructions about your sadhana. In the ashram you may be given a very responsible task, or you may simply be asked to cut vegetables in the kitchen, day in and day out. None of this should deter the disciple or boost his ego. Only the guru knows why this choice has been made. In the course of time the disciple will discover that the guru, more than anyone else, has been able to discern his or her deeper nature.

Very often the disciple has been with a guru in the past, but in the present life has to undergo certain experiences without any association with the guru. Once he has undergone these experiences, the yearning for a guru begins to grow. It is like a child who is hungry and cries out to its mother for milk. The mother hears, but she knows it is not the right time to feed the child. So there is a right time for the guru to emerge in your life, and when that occurs, you will find him.

There have also been instances where the guru is revealed to the disciple in a dream or during meditation. The disciple then searches for the person whom he has seen. Sri Aurobindo's chief disciple, known as the Mother, saw him in a dream beckoning her towards him. She later became a very important part of the Aurobindo movement.

16

Sometimes the guru may receive a mandate or order to find a particular disciple. But this occurs mainly in the case of evolved disciples who have a definite mission to accomplish.

We have all heard of the stories about Ramakrishna and Swami Vivekananda. Ramakrishna was searching for his disciple and when he met Narendranath, the young aristocratic boy from Calcutta who later became Swami Vivekananda, he knew at once that this was the boy who would carry out his mission. In those days Swami Vivekananda was a thoroughbred intellectual. He could not accept many of the things Ramakrishna said or did. His intellect influenced his thoughts and reactions, but at the same time his heart was irresistibly drawn towards Ramakrishna. The young Narendranath could not understand it and he underwent a great deal of conflict. Ultimately, the circumstances shaped themselves in such a way that Vivekananda had to surrender to his guru, and the rest is history.

Therefore, we have to realize that there is a greater power that guides these events. When the time is right, these events spontaneously begin to take shape. You are automatically guided to the guru who is meant for you. And when you see him, there is a meeting of hearts, of your spirit and his. At that moment all your doubts will cease. When two hearts meet, there are no questions. It is only when we live in the realm of the intellect that we are nagged by questions, doubts and fears.

I too have searched for a guru in my life. I too have asked these questions. I wondered if I would find him, and whether I would recognize him. These questions worried me too because my search for a guru was through the intellect. From my personal experience I have only one answer. Stop the questions. Look inwards. Intensify your practices. Develop into a sincere seeker and, when that happens, there is no power in the world that can keep you away from your guru.

In the final analysis there is no method involved in finding a guru. Guru is not an item to be sought on the shelf

17

of a supermarket, nor can guru be defined. He is beyond the limited, conventional words that we so often use. It is his spirit that we have to communicate with, not by words, not by intellect and not by the senses. Therefore, it is best to prepare ourselves mentally, emotionally and spiritually and, in the course of time, when we meet the right guru, we will know.

* * *

Guru is not a social necessity. He is not a status symbol like a car or a house in the country which can be discarded the moment something better comes along. He is not a dustbin or wastebasket into which all negativity and neurosis can be thrown. He is the pure effulgent spirit, the dispeller of darkness, the epitome of what each individual should aspire to be. His domain is the spirit, and it is to guide us into this realm that he appears in our lives. Once the link with guru is established, time cannot change it nor death eradicate it. It is a permanent union. Guru stays with you life after life.

4

How to Recognize the Guru

If you have any preconceived notions about the physical appearance of the guru, it is better to discard them right away. One may choose a husband, lover or friend on the basis of physical appearance, but in the case of the guru, one has to ascertain and communicate with the spiritual frequencies, not the outer form.

The relationship with the guru is not based on carnality or physical interactions – these ideas must be transcended. Guru is not there to stimulate the senses or appease the passions. That can be done through worldly interactions. Guru's relationship with the disciple is based on the spiritual, psychic and astral planes, and therefore one must judge the spirit and not the physical appearance. Guru may or may not be attractive; that is of least importance. There is no dearth of attractive people in the world, but how many have attained peace within themselves and illumined their souls?

If the guru is to assist you on the spiritual path, he must have an evolved consciousness. If the guru you find has the same limited awareness as you do, he will exhibit the same afflictions, desires, passions, greed and delusions as you. His motives will be tainted and his advice will be unsound. So you have to recognize the guru as someone with a higher consciousness than yourself.

How do you judge the guru's consciousness? It is a very simple matter. If the guru has an evolved consciousness,

19

then his teachings and his life will not contradict each other. His thoughts, words and actions will be in total conformity. His life will be free from hypocrisy and sham. If he does not meet this standard, it is better to withdraw from him. You are all familiar with the adage, "Practise what you preach," and you can have no respect for a guru who has one set of rules for others and another for himself.

A guru who has a philosophy of convenience, who leads a double life, one image for the public and another behind closed doors, can hardly have a stable personality. If his consciousness is awakened and stabilized in the truth, it will reflect deeply in his personality. There will be no erratic behaviour and whimsicality, rather there will be consistent stability.

Such a guru will draw people to himself spontaneously. You will be completely magnetized by his personality, not hypnotized. Hypnotism is a result of infatuation. Once the spell breaks, one is dehypnotized. But magnetism induces a deep and everlasting influence. Just as the inherent sweetness of honey never fails to draw bees, guru, by the magnetism of his personality, never fails to draw people to himself.

In the presence of such a personality, the seeker has no option but surrender. When we approach such a person, a spontaneous link is established. It is something like love at first sight. Once magnetized, the disciple discerns a transformation within. If you have felt this way in the presence of anyone, then you should know that this is your guru. If the guru you have chosen is well-known, very learned and has big institutions, but fails to stir your spirit, then it is time to think again. The fault may be in you, but still you ought to take a second look.

There are large numbers of personalities who pose as gurus. It is human nature to exploit any good venture and some ambitious people have been brazen enough to exploit guruship too. Humbug gurus and false prophets exist in large numbers, and the seeker must be very careful not to fall prey to such people. The western world especially has been ignorant of the sanctity of the guru-disciple tradition and, therefore, has often been impressed by people who display siddhis and pose as very evolved human beings. Anyone who tries to hypnotize people through the use of siddhis cannot have transcended their lower and mundane awareness. They are merely performing a show or spectacle, and can be compared to a magician who hypnotizes large crowds through his antics. Everyone enjoys the show a great deal, but when it is over, you find that you have learned nothing. If one is awed by such people, then one is surely going to become lost in one's search.

There are many seekers who choose a guru on the basis of his behaviour and personality. If he is charming and speaks kind words, they are attracted to him. If he is rude or abrupt, they feel reproached and reject him. You have to remember that you are seeking a guru so that you may outgrow your limitations. Whether the guru speaks to you kindly and gently, or admonishes and reproaches you, he does so with that aim in mind. Therefore, do not judge the guru by his actions but by the purity of his motives. If his intentions are honest, he may use any method to teach us, and we should not mind. The guru who only speaks kind words to disciples and never reproaches them will only lull them into greater complacency and thereby reinforce their egos.

One point must be remembered. The guru to whom one is attracted will be according to one's evolution and attainment. One's own calibre and personality play an important part in the judgement and assessment of a guru. If the disciple is sincere, he will find a sincere guru. If he wants to attain psychic powers, he will run after those gurus who display their siddhis. If the disciple wants affluence, he will run after gurus who are affluent. If the disciple wants to be enlightened, he will find a guru who is enlightened. There is no doubt about it. So, a disciple should try to know himself, rather than trying to know the guru. Therefore, if one wants a superior guru, one must develop into a superior seeker.

5

The Relevance of Guru

Every individual has certain basic and inherent needs. A child of five needs the love of a mother. He does not require intellectual or sexual stimulation; he just requires the warmth of parental love, a few toys and a secure environment to be happy. As he grows to be a teenager, his needs change. He is no longer wholly dependent on filial love, but it is partially replaced by the need for friends. Not friendships on a sexual basis, but rather comrades, buddies, with whom he can share his secrets and adventures.

As he grows older, another need is incorporated into his personality. The sexual appetite awakens and he requires a partner to appease his desires and fantasies. Try to deny him that experience and he is apt to go crazy. As he matures, he no longer thrives on any of these relationships, but there is a growing desire to be a father The filial tendencies are generated and become active. As a teenager, this area or faculty is present but remains dormant, and only on reaching maturity is it awakened.

This process which starts at birth is never-ending. If at any stage you deprive the child, adolescent or adult of his inherent need, he will develop severe blocks and complexes in his personality. Today problems of juvenile delinquency, crime, rape, murder, insanity, etc. occur on account of the deprivations that individuals have experienced during the course of their lives.

Maybe one was brought up by negligent and harsh parents, or in early maturity was not allowed to express their emotions to the opposite sex. Any such event could culminate in a deformity of character. It is so hard to determine. Even the smallest incident in childhood can develop schizophrenia in the adult. Human beings are extremely sensitive to the events and circumstances they face in their lives. Everything is recorded, programmed and stored, and one can never know what shape a particular experience will generate.

There is yet another need which arises in an individual from the time of birth. That is the need for a guru, a spiritual friend, a mentor and a guide. You may not have realized this, but your children are born with a purpose and their life is guided by that purpose. Although they may not be aware of it, and although they may not be able to express this need coherently, they are unconsciously in search of it.

It is therefore the duty of the parent to expose the child to the presence of the guru. This interaction will bring the positive samskaras to the forefront, so that they may manifest as an active part of the child's life. A child may be born with positive samskaras, but in order to fulfil them the right environment and positive stimulation are required. If you deny this facility, these positive samskaras will be suppressed and other samskaras will begin to predominate in the personality, because a child is born with a mixture of samskaras. It is your duty to prepare the ground and give the child the opportunity to express the right samskaras. Even if the child is born without good samskaras, the presence of a guru in his or her life will surely bring about some change and help to overcome the negative forces in their life.

If a child is exposed to a guru from early childhood, he begins to develop an area of his personality which is triggered off by the guru's presence. This part of the personality enhances all other aspects of his life. The personality develops without any complexes and suppressions, and the child will surely achieve the ambitions, desires and passions he is born

23

for. In order to express our true potential, it is so important for us to be free of limitations. Creativity and genius can only flourish if the individual is not stifled by the environment and relationships.

We have not yet been able to truly understand the significance of the guru in our lives. We see him as someone to whom we can turn when we wish to have a mantra, or feel the need to renounce the world. Yes, the guru is important for those events, but at the same time he also has a place in our lives, even if we wish to remain totally in the realm of worldly interactions.

We have to realize that the guru is an asset to us, no matter where and how we live. It is not only a sannyasin or a sadhaka who requires a guru. In India, almost everyone has a family guru who is regarded as a mentor or guide, who is part of the family. They consult him on all matters, such as business, marriage, birth and death. He advises them and is there to help them in times of trouble. These people are not renunciates, they are average householders, but they have cultivated the samskara of having a guru from generation to generation, and they have found it very useful in their lives.

Very often, we find in a family situation that the children do not listen to their parents, or the husband is inconsiderate to the wife, or the wife is creating tension in the family. No matter how much the family tries, the conflict cannot be resolved because no one is willing to accept or concede to the other's advice. But when the guru speaks, all are willing to listen and obey, simply because they know that he is speaking out of love. He has no vested interest and, moreover, he has the wisdom and intuition to know what is the best solution to a problem.

I have seen children who have decided to go their own way and marry someone against their parent's wishes. The parents have tried all kinds of tricks to change the child's mind, but to no avail. Then they approach the guru and ask for his help. If the guru feels it is necessary for the child to think again, he calls him and tells him not to marry the girl.

And the boy obeys. Just one word from the guru is enough to convince the boy. He is sure that the guru will not advise him wrongly. That is the faith and devotion they have for the guru. The guru, in turn, assumes the responsibility of helping those who have faith and obedience to carry out his work and his wishes.

Today, all around us, in every situation, there is anarchy. The father is against the son. The son hates his parents. The daughter has run off with a man much older than herself. The wife is having extramarital relationships. Each one is doing what they please, with no consideration for other members of the family. The family loses its unity and all its members are thrown into the cruel situations of life to fend for themselves.

Sometimes there is an inability to cope, which results in depression, schizophrenia, insanity and nervous breakdown. All these problems are man-made. We have created them for ourselves. Primitive people had no knowledge of insanity or schizophrenia. They did not even understand what these represented. But in our present society these illnesses are rampant, and the cause is the poor structure of our society.

All human beings need someone to whom they can turn in times of sorrow and joy. Someone who is always there, firmly stationed like the rock of Gibraltar. Someone who will not make any demands. Someone who knows only how to give and never thinks of taking. Someone who will pick you up when everyone else has rejected you. Someone with whom you can cry like a child and not be misunderstood. Someone who has the wisdom and grace to help you overcome your afflictions, so that you may once again stand with your feet planted firmly on the ground.

But is it possible to find such a person? The answer is yes. In the guru you can discover all these qualities and many more. You have only to knock on his door and you will find the answer to what you have been searching for life after life.

6

Guru Tattwa

The guru tattwa signifies the guru element. This element exists in each one of us and is known as the inner guru. This inner guru is the witness of all that you do in your life, silently guiding you on the path to knowledge of the higher self. Sometimes you are distracted and obstinate and pay no heed to this guidance. Nevertheless the guru element waits patiently for the day when you will turn inwards and reflect on the deep significance it has on your life.

The guru tattwa is the highest and purest element that exists within you. It is timeless, ageless and indestructible. It does not decay with death, but is carried on from life to life. As it is not limited by time and space, this inner guru is a rather abstract phenomenon, having no form, colour or sound, and is perceivable only to those who have developed their inner vision. For those of us who live in the world of the senses, this inner guru might as well be a myth.

Therefore, in order to familiarize ourselves with this element which exists in each one of us, we have to find someone who is a direct representation or replica of that inner guru. The preservation of the guru-disciple tradition has been maintained simply for this purpose. The living guru symbolizes the guru tattwa in the disciple. The disciple offers himself to the guru and serves him selflessly in the manner the guru wishes because it is only through humble devotion to the guru that one can realize the guru tattwa in oneself.

26

The modern system of teaching cannot be compared to the guru-disciple relationship because it lacks one element – the guru tattwa. In India, the guru is considered far superior to a teacher. When any Indian comes into contact with the guru, he is full of respect and devotion. He accepts the guru in a physical form because he understands that the physical body is only the outer shell of an inner enlightened consciousness.

It is very important to develop a link with your inner guru, which is the centre you have been searching for. All the happiness, joy and pleasures you crave in the external world are only illusions in contrast to the infinite bliss that is contained within your inner guru. In fact, it is your unconscious search for the inner guru that compels you to hunt for pleasures in your worldly life. You are subconsciously aware of the experience that can be had by this contact, but due to your ignorance and due to the veil of maya, or illusion, you search for it elsewhere in the external world.

When you look at a flower, or a painting, or a beautiful person, you experience a certain pleasure. You think that the object is the source of your happiness, but in fact the experience is taking place within you. It is not the object that is the source of happiness. It is your level of perception and awareness which determines the degree of happiness you are able to experience.

Where does this perception take place? Certainly not outside. It takes place inside you. In that moment you have had just a fleeting glance of that infinite source within you, and that is the cause of your joy. However, you relate it to the object and therefore chase the object in order to have that experience again. But this time there is an expectation. Therefore, your perception is conditioned, so the experience is not as acutely joyful and you are disappointed. So you begin your search again.

When you meet the guru, a similar process takes place. However, because the guru is a true replica of your inner guru, the experience is a more permanent one. Your external

27

perception of the guru is directly related to your perception of the inner guru. If your link with guru is heightened and total, then you are simultaneously able to develop a deep link with the guru tattwa in you. Both experiences are parallel and co-exist side by side. As you develop the ties with the living guru, your contact with the inner guru becomes clearer, more vivid and tangible. And, in this way, the guru tattwa begins to manifest.

In the physical body, the guru tattwa is represented by ajna chakra, or the mid-eyebrow centre. It is at this point that you receive the instructions from your inner guru. It is also at this point that your outer guru commands and transmits wisdom. As you become more proficient in hearing your outer guru at ajna chakra, you will be able to discern the subtle and causal form of your inner guru or the guru tattwa. And in time it becomes a living reality. It is then that the true experiences begin in your life.

7

Types of Guru

It is now necessary to elucidate the different types of guru you may encounter. They have been broadly classified as yogi guru, jnani guru, tantric guru and brahmanishta guru. It is possible to find a guru who is a yogi, jnani, tantric and brahmanishta. Or, in some cases, the guru may be a yogi and a jnani but have no knowledge of tantra or any experience of Brahman. Sometimes the guru is a brahmanishta and has the knowledge of yoga and tantra, but does not teach it to others. It differs from guru to guru. Although we propose to deal with each type separately, it is more common to find a guru who has diverse knowledge and experience.

YOGI GURU

A yogi guru is one who has mastered and perfected the science of yoga through long and arduous sadhana. Due to his advanced practices, he may have acquired siddhis, or spiritual powers, but this is not necessarily the case. At any rate, the yogi guru will exhibit keen intuition, a calm, unruffled disposition and balanced judgement.

A yogi guru may or may not be learned, eloquent or philosophical. But he has an intricate knowledge of the laws which govern the body and the mind, and will undauntedly observe the disciplines and live in accordance with these laws. His life is the epitome of discipline and balance, and

29

he expects the same from his disciples. For the yogi guru, the body and mind are vehicles that must be harnessed before there can be any degree of enlightenment or accomplishment in life.

He has a meticulous eye for perfection and will push his disciples to strive for the same. If he finds the disciple becoming slack, lazy, indifferent and complacent, he may use harsh methods to restore their enthusiasm. His whole life is an expression of yoga and this is reflected in his movements, habits, speech and actions.

The yogi guru, who has thorough knowledge and experience of the workings of the body and mind, often develops mental powers. Sometimes he is known to use these mental powers to help and encourage sincere sadhakas.

We need to draw a distinction between the yogi guru and yoga teacher. A yogi guru has controlled the mind, body and emotions. Every action is yoga. The yogi guru systematically uses the practices of yoga, first to discipline the body, then to control the mind, and finally to transcend both body and mind. Often he subjects himself to severe austerities as a discipline that he must undergo on the path to perfection. When he has mastered these techniques in himself, he teaches sincere sadhakas the way. Although he may teach only hatha yoga and simple pranayama, his knowledge is much wider. He imparts his knowledge according to the ability of the disciple.

The yoga teacher, on the other hand, is still in the process of disciplining the body, mind and spirit. His knowledge may be greater than that of the student, but his range of experience is limited. He has not yet mastered the laws which govern the body, mind and emotions, an accomplishment which is so necessary on the path of yoga.

The practices of yoga form the core of your spiritual sadhana. In order to refine your awareness, balance your energy and raise your consciousness, you will have to integrate the yoga techniques into your daily routine. Just as you wash your face and brush your teeth in the morning, you should also regularly carry out your yoga sadhana. Therefore, the yogi guru is a vital necessity for every aspirant. He is an important milestone in your spiritual quest and it is he who gives you the impetus to train your body and mind, thereby paving the way for other advanced sadhanas.

Yoga is not a limited science. It is intricately linked with tantra and other esoteric philosophies. The practices of hatha yoga lead to raja yoga. Raja yoga and kriya yoga are complementary to each other. Kriya yoga leads to the ultimate aim of tantra. Therefore, it is not uncommon to find that the yogi guru has knowledge and experience of tantra and other philosophies, and is perfectly competent to teach them to selected disciples.

JNANI GURU

The jnani guru, as the name implies, is a very learned person who has a thorough knowledge of scriptural lore. Through diverse interpretation of this lore, the jnani guru is able to stimulate and satisfy the disciple's intellect. The intellect is the domain of the jnani guru and through his guidance and inspiration, the intellectual faculty in the disciple is developed to perfection.

What is Brahman? What is the Self? Is there a creator? Is he God? These are some of the questions that the jnani guru can answer efficiently. A jnani guru will delight seekers with his ready wit and an analytical approach to intricate metaphysical questions. He has a deep understanding of the relationship and relevance of ancient truths with modern day existence. This type of guru may or may not have developed sufficient mental powers to influence the sadhaka, but his wisdom and discretion reflect deeply in his personality.

If this description has aroused a mental picture of a grave person with a solemn look, it may be misleading. Some of the greatest jnanis – people of infinite wisdom – although thorough and mature in their knowledge, reveal a special childlike innocence. With wisdom comes humility

31

and reverence for the higher powers which exist in the universe. For the jnani guru, life is a continuous process of learning and he remains forever in the quest of knowledge.

Jnana yoga is one of the paths to enlightenment and it appeals to the predominantly rational human being. It is a long and tedious path, for one can very easily become caught up in intellectual acrobatics. We are often told that to experience the light or truth, we have to dim the intellect, the mind and the senses. But, in this case, we use the intellect to overpower the intellect. Sri Aurobindo said, "Intellect was the helper, intellect is the barrier, transcend intellect."

The jnani guru teaches the disciple to explore beyond the realm of the intellect. For it is beyond the intellect that you are able to discover intuition. In order to allow your intuitive faculty to manifest, he teaches you to decondition your mind. If your mind is overstuffed with book knowledge, then you are conditioned in your responses and experiences. You relate everything to what the books say or to what you have heard. But if you set aside all that you have heard or read and develop the ability to receive knowledge from within, then you experience the higher knowledge or intuition which is inherent in you. The jnani guru has this aim in mind while teaching his disciples.

However, very often you find that you are not able to transcend the intellect. In fact, it grows stronger and stronger, and you are left with a great deal of knowledge, but no experience. Those who find themselves in this state feel a great sense of frustration. This obstacle can be overcome by synthesizing the practices. You should learn as much as possible from a jnani guru through satsang and discourse and, at the same time, have a sadhana of yoga practices designed especially to suit you. In this way, there will be a simultaneous development of the body, mind, intellect and intuition.

A jnani guru may not be able to transmit the experience, but he is the first step towards arousing your interest and teasing your mind to question the deeper mysteries that await you on this path. A jnani guru is known also as a *brahmakshotriya*, which literally means, 'one who is learned in the Vedas (or the source of knowledge)'.

TANTRIC GURU

The tantric guru is often a synthesis of a yogi, a jnani and a tantric. His initiation is commonly performed by a tantric yogini. It is she who initiates evolved souls into the secret and profound practices of tantra and thus makes them her disciples. The evolved souls usually chosen for initiation are yogi gurus and jnani gurus. The entire personality and spiritual dimension of a yogi guru or a jnani guru are transformed by an encounter with a tantric yogini.

It is only after this initiation that their knowledge is transformed into experience, and they then become tantric gurus. The deeper mysteries of the mind and the universe begin to unravel before them and become a significant reality. After the initiation is complete, the yogini may or may not retreat into the background, but not before she has completed her task of guiding the initiated to a very vital experience and transforming him into a tantric guru. A yogi guru or a jnani guru who has missed this experience is not able to transcend time, space and object, but remains in the realm of the mind and intellect. In the case of the brahmanishta guru, this experience is not necessary. His consciousness is already transcendental and he has attained great heights.

The tantric guru is a master of the mind. The mind is used merely as a tool – as one would use an electric light switch. When the light is needed, the switch is turned on; when it is no longer needed, the switch is turned off. That is the ease with which a tantric guru handles the mind. The thought force of the guru's mind can be projected to far and distant lands with the same speed and clarity as when you lift a telephone and speak to someone at the other end of the world.

The tantric guru can multiply his body so that it may appear in more than one place at the same time, or it may simply take an entirely different form. The body can be projected astrally with full awareness of what is happening at any place, at all times. The guru can materialize his form and may appear to one or more disciples, while his actual physical body is in another place.

The tantric guru is capable of totally understanding the disciple's mind and completely absorbing it into his own. During that period, the disciple will act completely in accordance with the guru, maintaining constant and one-pointed awareness of the guru. At that time the disciple is likely to have rare experiences. His awareness is heightened and he may even develop mental powers. The tantric guru can cause events to occur which are normally impossible. He can even create matter out of nothing. All this is accomplished through his mental powers.

However, most tantric gurus rarely display these siddhis. Even though they can control the minds of disciples, they rarely do so. If they do, they act strictly in accordance with the laws of nature and there are many injunctions that they must adhere to. Going against these laws would mean violating the natural order of things, and a tantric guru is very careful not to be anarchical. He is very aware that these siddhis are only a stepping stone to higher states of mind. If they are used irresponsibly, they soon become obstacles and are likely to disappear altogether.

If at some time the tantric guru chooses to overpower the mind of a particular disciple, it will only be done in accordance with the laws that govern such an act. The karma of the disciple is determined; the duration of the possession is fixed. When the fixed time is complete, the disciple's mind is released and allowed to grow independently. Although the guru can obsess the disciple's mind again and again, this will not be done, for there is a grave risk of causing serious damage to both the disciple and the guru.

When a devotee goes to a tantric guru, the guru first examines his karma and stage of evolution. Every individual has certain karmas which can be eliminated immediately, but stronger karmas have to be worked out. So the guru assigns the disciple a particular sadhana. Or, if the disciple is living in the guru's ashram, he or she is given a responsibility according to the karma. Under no circumstances will the guru act against the laws of karma, for he has great respect for these laws. A tantric guru is also known to absorb the karmas of a disciple and discard them without any suffering, provided there is a very strong and deep link on all planes between the two.

The method of instruction used by a tantric guru is transmission. Instruction can be through tuition and through formal teaching, but only if the disciple is not receptive to transmission. Transmission is the primary method of guidance for the spiritual growth of the disciple. The guru constantly transmits thoughts and checks the disciple to see where the obstructions are and why the energy has ceased to flow. He thus prepares the disciple to work as his medium.

The disciple in turn has to realize his responsibility in constantly maintaining a higher level of awareness, so that the guru may communicate easily. The guru needs no words for the disciple who has attained this state of mind. Therefore, such a disciple becomes invaluable. The guru can communicate with him at any time and at any place, even after he has left his mortal body. There is absolute harmony between them.

Just as the brain sends a message to the legs to walk, the hands to feel, or the eyes to see, in the same way, it is the guru's thoughts that cause the disciple to act. However, it is possible for the disciple to misinterpret these thoughts if he does not remain tuned to the guru's frequency. He may then act contrary to his guru's instructions. Imagine the disaster if your brain sends a message to your feet to walk, but your hands respond instead! Therefore, the disciple should always maintain unity with his guru and this is achieved by the practice of unceasing remembrance.

The tantric guru emanates a magnetic quality. One feels drawn to him like iron to a magnet or a moth to a flame. He lives life with freedom of mind and spirit. He is not ruled by the social norms and conditions which ensnare the average person. To understand the word 'freedom' in its truest sense, we would do best to learn the ways of the tantric guru. Our concept of freedom that we are always striving for is limited and related only to the external world, whereas the tantric guru has attained both external and internal freedom. Karmas do not bind him, nor thoughts capture him. The tantric guru is master of them all.

In India, the tantric guru is consulted for marital and domestic problems, physical and mental afflictions, financial and business worries. Through a deep and profound insight into human relationships, the guru is able to discern accurately where the problem lies and to offer sound advice. Often the devotee finds that the guru has helped him through his mental powers.

However, this is not the prime reason for approaching the tantric guru. It would be denigrating the guru's power. The tantric guru is necessary to guide us to gain experience on the spiritual path. This guidance and experience can be transmitted by a mere glance, by a pat on the head, or by a strict and stringent sadhana. It all depends upon your state of evolution.

BRAHMANISHTA GURU

A brahmanishta guru is one who is established in the supreme consciousness. He is a *jivanmukta*, 'liberated while living'. He does not concern himself with teaching, guiding, inspiring or enlightening people. He is totally immersed in his knowledge and experience of the absolute, and that is where he dwells.

If it were not for the devotees and disciples who assume the responsibility of feeding and clothing him, he would go unfed and unclothed. He is uninterested in and unaware of matters concerning the body. Just as salt mixes with the water in the ocean and does not exist as a separate entity, the brahmanishta guru has merged into Brahman, the supreme. It is not possible for us mere mortals to comprehend the world in which he lives. We can never hope to know the depths he is exploring, nor the heights he is scaling.

It is the light of the spirit which illumines his being. When that occurs, there are no ears to hear, eyes to see, hands to touch, or words to comprehend. The brahmanishta lives in total silence, external and internal. He will seldom or never give lengthy discourses and sermons. He is often not even aware of the presence of devotees and disciples who surround him. At times he may utter words which are incoherent or have no relevance at all to onlookers. Only a bird can comprehend the language of a bird, or a Shakespeare the wit and irony of a Shakespeare.

In spite of the brahmanishta guru's behaviour, people flock to him in their thousands. It seems that just to be in his presence and to experience the warmth and glow emanating from his being is a rare privilege. Many miracles have been known to occur in the lives of the devotees and disciples of a brahmanishta. But he is not even aware that these things are happening through him.

The divine power manifests itself in the brahmanishta guru. He is a living example of the inherent powers within everyone. Even though he may be lost in himself, he is able to draw out your faith, devotion and surrender. He is able to evoke the higher qualities of your personality and urge you to look within.

Ramana Maharshi was a true example of a brahmanishta guru. He was born in South India in the twentieth century. He had travelled so deep into himself that very often he did not have any knowledge of his surroundings, yet the people who flocked to him in thousands found an immediate solution to their problems. His transmission of energy was a spontaneous process, although he himself made no effort to transfer the energy to the disciple.

Eventually, these jivanmuktas can lose total awareness of the body and stop eating, even though food is offered to them. They transcend their bodies and are then known as *videhamuktas*. After this, they cannot live for more than ten or twelve days and soon leave this mortal frame.

The brahmanishta guru should not be confused with an *avatar purusha*, who has incarnated to carry out a particular mission in the world. The avatar purusha can best be compared to a junior god. He has transcended the cycle of birth and rebirth. He does not have to evolve, nor is he governed by the laws of karma and evolution. He incarnates in this life to fulfil a divine order. When the mission is completed, the avatar purusha returns to realms unknown.

The brahmanishta guru is the culmination of all stages of spiritual evolution.

FEMALE GURU

No treatise on guru is complete without special mention of female gurus. Due to orthodox intervention, it has not been possible for female gurus to survive in large numbers. Priests, religious heads and clergymen, influenced by the insular and conventional norms of society, have been successful in hindering the growth of women to the status of guru.

In India, women gurus were given a special place. They have been revered from ancient times, especially during the period when tantra flourished. References to their existence are found in the Vedas, Upanishads, and other scriptures. With the advent of certain religions, however, the situation underwent a great change and for a long time the role of women as gurus was restricted. They were no longer seen as public figures. In recent times they are re-emerging and if society is able to overcome its prejudices and complexes, we will once again have the privilege of receiving initiation and wisdom from women gurus.

A female guru is a very powerful force to contend with. Her inherent intuitive and psychic nature enables her to progress very rapidly along the spiritual path. Her thought frequencies are more subtle than those of men and therefore she is able to communicate with the powerful forces of the universe with greater ease.

It has been established that the greatest obstacles to progress on the spiritual path are intellect and ego. To progress spiritually, one must cultivate and maintain the qualities of love, egolessness, compassion, tenderness, childish innocence, faith, devotion and humility. As these qualities form a basic and inherent part of a woman's personality, it is simple for her to transcend the intellect and allow her faith and devotion to flourish. Bhakti, the supreme pathway to higher experience which all sincere aspirants struggle to maintain, is the essence of her nature. This makes it easier for her to cope with the awakening of the great energy.

Men, on the other hand, find it extremely difficult to cope with their ego and intellect. As a result, they are torn by conflicts and eruptions at every stop when the awakening takes place. Perhaps men have superior intellect to women, but in this case it seems that this is not an advantage.

It is not our intention to try to establish the supremacy of women over men, or to prove that women can play the role of guru more adequately than men. But we need to be aware that women are as competent as men in this field. They have played a pivotal role in helping mankind along the spiritual path, but their capacities have not been fully recognized and accepted, and their names have been obliterated from history. Because of the taboos and complexes of society, women have been forced to retire into oblivion, or to assist and guide people anonymously and in utmost secrecy. But one cannot deny their importance.

There is a well-known adage, "Behind every great man there is a woman." We have seen often enough that women have inspired the explosion of greatness in men. Even on the spiritual path the greatest gurus have been blessed at some crucial moments in their lives by the powerful presence of a tantric yogini or female guru who has initiated them into the tantric rites. Many gurus may hesitate to publicly declare this important event in their lives, but it is an undeniable truth.

It is perplexing why women, who have such extraordinary powers and potential to guide humanity spiritually, should not receive due recognition and acceptance. Is it the religion-oriented society that sternly blocks her role as guru? Or is it men's desire to suppress her spiritually in order to exploit her for their carnal objectives?

In tantra, a science as ancient as civilization itself, it is the woman and not the man who plays the role of guru. It is she who initiates him into the practices. It is she who prepares and conducts the ritual. She puts the mark on the man's forehead and tells him on which point he should meditate.

A tantric yogini guru has the capacity to completely overwhelm her disciples. This is why people often take her to be a witch, sorceress, or some kind of demon who resorts to magic to gain control over her victims. This notion is absurd. It is true that she, like any other guru, is on the lookout for worthy disciples to guide and initiate. But it is simply the power of her mind and the magnetism of her personality which draws people to her. A tantric yogini is not a witch or a sorceress. She is a person who has developed extraordinary mental and physical powers through hard work and personal sadhana. Due to her independent nature and allegiance to no one but her own spirit, she exhibits undaunted courage and fearlessness, sometimes living in total seclusion, or in very severe and austere conditions. Her codes of conduct, norms of behaviour and morality set her apart as an individual. Only the bravest of the brave can venture to tread her path which even angels fear to tread.

Externally, she may appear to be an ordinary person, almost always a far cry from the good, holy, pious, virtuous image of gurus which we have fixed in our minds. But mirrored in the depth of her eyes, one can discern the purity of her soul. Just as a goldsmith fashions ornaments out of gold, thus giving it utility, purpose and direction, in the same way the female guru ignites and explodes evolved souls, assisting them on their onward journey of evolution.

Letter to a Disciple

You have to march towards the goal. An initiated disciple cannot afford to lag behind, however slow the motion. A guru is indispensable for sadhana. The sadhaka alone knows and realizes this.

I have already told you something about meditation (dhyana). Any ideal in which the mind becomes submerged is the best. One can also practise meditation on one's emotions and one's inspirational urges. Gradually increase your frequency. Join the connection daily at four a.m. Meditate under a mosquito net to protect yourself from mosquitoes. Increase your practice to shoulder the great task and responsibility you will be called upon to discharge in the future.

The ishta shall be one and so also the mantra. These will never change. One can get water by digging fifty feet at one place but not by digging one foot at fifty places. Such an effort will go in vain. Once he gets into the train, no passenger keeps his luggage on his head, but lets the burden lie in the train. The same train which carries him will carry all his luggage. What then is the good of worrying? Give up brooding and start acting.

41

8

Types of Disciples

Disciple is derived from the word 'discipline'. A disciple, therefore, is one who undergoes discipline in order to develop spiritually. In Sanskrit, a disciple is called *shishya* or 'one who is willing to learn'. Anyone who offers himself to guru in order to discipline himself is a disciple. It does not matter if you relate his teachings to your spiritual welfare or material life. If you are receptive to his wisdom and follow his guidance, then you are a disciple.

For the purpose of convenience, we have classified disciples broadly into the following categories: householder disciple, karma sannyasin, sadhaka disciple, tantric disciple, sannyasin disciple and humbug disciple.

KARMA SANNYASIN

Let us first consider a typical householder disciple, or karma sannyasin. He or she is married, has children, is perhaps in business or an employee. He is actively involved with family, friends, social obligations and financial commitments. He goes to the guru for guidance on personal as well as spiritual problems. His feelings for guru are sincere, sometimes intense. He has great devotion and faith in the guru.

The guru tells the disciple how to handle himself in the situations which confront him. He gives him sound advice on matters concerning business or marital problems. The disciple understands that the guru's advice is based on intuition and practical wisdom. Moreover, each new experience reveals the innate accuracy of his judgement. The disciple develops trust and confidence in the guru and gradually the link between them is strengthened.

The disciple, in turn, offers financial assistance to the guru's mission. This is an important aspect of discipleship. Householders who wish to establish a greater rapport with guru, but feel unable to do so because of social commitments, have to understand their responsibility in a different light. In the guru-disciple tradition, the disciple offers body, mind and soul to guru as a token of discipleship. This is total surrender. But there are some disciples who, due to family ties and obligations, cannot make the total offering. For these disciples, the system of guru dakshina was established many centuries ago, and in India it still continues today.

The word *dakshina* means 'sacred offering'. Guru dakshina is the offering of land, money, houses, food and clothing, as a token of the love, devotion and faith of the householder disciples or karma sannyasins for their guru. They offer a portion of their earnings. This is their surrender. When disciples make this offering with the right attitude, then along with the offering, they are parting with some of their attachments, ignorance and samskaras that they have accumulated in life. This is the real purpose of dakshina. It is for the disciple's own self-purification and spiritual progress.

It is the disciple's duty to develop and strengthen the relationship with guru by allowing him to have more and more influence. The guru need not be present physically, he need not know about or meddle in the daily affairs of the disciple, but once a mental link has been established, the energy is always available to draw upon. Though the guru does not live with the family, he is a part of it.

Devotion and faith are the foundation of this relationship. Faith can be triggered by a chance encounter, or because the guru has helped you or a member of your family through a difficult period, or it may have happened without any apparent cause. You may be attracted to that particular guru simply because it feels right and positive. Some householder devotees have tremendous faith in their guru and will consult him on every venture, business, marriage or acquisition of property. The trust which the disciple places in guru is never abused and never fails. The guru automatically assumes responsibility for the disciple. In time, the relationship can develop into a deep and permanent one. Even though the householder may never in this life actually live with the guru, he is still very close to him and the guru does consider himself responsible for the disciple's welfare.

Although the householder disciple and karma sannyasin are essentially leading similar lives, there is a subtle difference in the path and goal they set for themselves. The path of bhakti, faith and devotion, is the path for householder disciples. Due to their family and social commitments, they may not have inculcated the daily discipline of sadhana. Their sadhana is undaunted devotion to guru and absolute faith in his divine spirit. For householders, the presence of guru in their lives, or as part of their family, is considered enough to eradicate their bad karma or obstacles. They seek only his blessings, his presence and his love, having full faith in the guru's words and guidance. Householder disciples do not necessarily care for spiritual attainments, nor do they seek detachment, dispassion or renunciation of their passions and desires.

Karma sannyasins, on the other hand, are householder disciples who have been initiated into the path of karma sannyasa by their guru. Their life is similar to that of the householder disciple, but their goal or aim is clearly defined. Through their initiation or dedication to the path of karma sannyasa, they slowly develop a higher standard of living. Externally, they live like anybody else, but internally they aim at transforming all situations and events of their life into a base for their spiritual progress. Thus, even while living in the world and interacting with it, their quest or goal is set apart from that of other individuals. Karma sannyasins are fully aware that their lives are an expression of their karma, and in order to prepare themselves for the higher path of spiritual life, they must strive to fulfil their obligations and duties.

During their initiation, karma sannyasins receive a spiritual name from the guru. This name symbolizes a deeper and hidden part of the personality and is an indication of what one should strive to become. They also receive a geru dhoti or unstitched cloth to wear during sadhana.

Karma sannyasins then return to the family environment with new aspirations. They practise their sadhana and develop their inner potential, and along with that they fulfil their duties towards society and family with a higher awareness. So, on the one hand, the karma sannyasin is a father or mother, a husband or wife, an employer and a member of society, and on the other hand, a seeker of the Self. And they should strive to maintain a balance between the two. Their spiritual progress should enhance their worldly life and vice versa. Their life should be an expression of balance and harmony, not contradiction and confusion.

The karma sannyasin or householder disciple can develop into a very important pole of transmission for the guru. Married life and social commitments need not be a barrier. We must realize and accept one important thing. We are all bound by karma, and our vocation in life is an outcome of many past actions. But this should not prove a hindrance, nor is it an obstacle to spiritual growth. The guru realizes this and accepts it, but often householders tend to feel limited and restricted, not knowing how to relate to the guru because they cannot offer themselves as full sannyasins. They should understand that every action, however simple or trivial it may be, is an important step in the right direction if it is directed to the guru with faith and devotion. There are householders who live more in tune with the guru than some sannyasin disciples. In the final analysis, it is not just a

45

question of living with the guru. It all depends on your ability to surrender to him.

Karma yoga is a very important sadhana for the karma sannyasin as well as the householder disciple. Disciples offer the fruit of their labour to the guru. Karma yoga is first practised and perfected at the guru's ashram. Disciples maintain a constant link with the ashram, devoting some of their spare time to selfless work. The ashram environment works as a positive influence on their mind and in time the spirit of selfless service or karma yoga becomes a part of their personality. It is then easier for them to implement it into their daily life and practise it at all times. This will greatly enhance their evolution and progress in spiritual life.

Householder disciples or karma sannyasins should view their life as a commitment to both guru and family. With each initiation, the link between guru and disciple becomes stronger. Gradually, disciples should prepare their mind. When all other duties and obligations are fulfilled and when the time is right, the householder disciple or karma sannyasin should step on to the higher path of sannyasa.

SADHAKA DISCIPLE

Sadhaka literally means 'one who practises sadhana'. In this relationship, the guidelines are set more firmly than in the householder-guru relationship. In that relationship, the attitude of the guru towards the disciple is more or less that of an elder brother or father, who is benevolent and kind, and showers his blessings. A sadhaka disciple's relationship with guru is much more formal.

The guru determines the sadhana best suited for the disciple's individual evolution and gives out the practices in full measure, right down to the smallest detail. The sadhaka disciple practises them, and from time to time consults the guru and receives further guidance. The guru is informed of the progress or any difficulties and he decides what should be added or deleted from the sadhana.

46

To progress in sadhana, the disciple must adhere strictly to the guru's teachings. It is often the case that the disciple accepts a practice from one guru and after a few days finds another guru whose methods seem to be more attractive. Or he may read a book describing other methods which seem more glamorous and promise quicker results. Or friends next door advise him that the practices will not do what they claim, and that perhaps the guru has not mentioned how dangerous they are. The disciple has to be blind and deaf to all of these interferences and pay no heed to them. The guru's instructions should be final, and nothing else should matter. The disciple must be very strict in this matter.

The guru expects the disciple to maintain regularity and consistency in the practices at all times. In this respect, the guru can be a very uncompromising, merciless taskmaster. He makes no allowances for any discrepancies in the sadhaka's sadhana. The guru is very much involved in the sadhaka's progress and state of mind. It is as much an adventure for him as it is for the disciple. He is impatient when the disciple becomes lazy and procrastinates, especially if the disciple has the potential to be a good sadhaka. To get the disciple back on the track, the guru may resort to severe methods, but if the disciple does not reciprocate and continues to be disinterested, then the guru may withdraw his assistance altogether and treat the sadhaka as an ordinary disciple. The guru's interest in the disciple's sadhana is motivated only by the disciple's sincerity.

As the sadhaka progresses through hard work and application, the guru will subject him to many tests. The sadhaka should be prepared for this and not misunderstand the guru's motives. The disciple will be exposed to difficulties to determine physical stamina, firmness of mind and clear judgement, and on this assessment will depend whether the practices are to become more advanced. In the case of sincere sadhakas, the guru is also known to help through mental powers.

The disciple has to maintain one-pointed sincerity in the sadhana, strictly adhering to the rules, be they dietary, or as simple as sleeping six hours instead of seven. The belief that guru knows what is suitable in terms of sadhana must be firmly maintained, even though the practices may not seem suitable.

In the beginning, the sadhana given by the guru may seem too easy or even inconsequential, and the sadhaka may dismiss the whole thing, thinking that the guru is not really interested. For instance, the guru may tell the disciple that the sadhana consists of ten minutes asana, ten minutes pranayama, ten minutes japa and half an hour reading books on kundalini yoga. The disciple may wonder why the sadhana is not more difficult, especially as he is capable of much more. The disciple may be able to do wonderful asanas and continue for an hour or more, but that may be the first test to which the guru is subjecting the sadhaka.

When you approach a guru as a sadhaka, the first thing to learn is to unlearn everything, to start again as a novice. All previous knowledge must be eradicated and a new beginning made. No matter how insignificant the practice may seem, if you do what you are asked, then you are following the guru's instructions without using too much of your own intellect. That is what the guru expects of you.

The disciple should also never try to assess what progress he has made. It is not for him to judge how far he has reached. This must be left entirely to the guru. Trying to judge one's own progress can lead to confusion in the disciple's mind and undermine his willpower.

In this relationship, the guru is the master or instructor, and he sets down the rules which the disciple must follow implicitly. In time, through practice the disciple develops a clear mind, accurate judgement and a great deal of confidence and ability. However, regardless of the progress, the disciple should always maintain loyalty and humility towards guru, without whom little or no progress could have been made.

SANNYASIN DISCIPLE

Throughout the ages there have been some people who, at a particular stage in their lives, have opted out of the set norms and conditions existing in the world to experience higher ideals and standards. They have realized the limitations of material comforts and the transience of the pleasures derived from them, and become aware of a desire to experience life with an attitude of renunciation. The renunciation is of outer and inner conditioning, so that the spirit may be free to reveal itself. This idea of renunciation is a product of higher awareness. It is at this point in life that a seeker takes up sannyasa.

Sannyasa is not a mere ritual of abandoning one's garments and donning the saffron robes, or shaving one's head and changing one's name. It has a deeper and greater significance than that. It is the process whereby one abandons one's ego, one's desires, one's selfish motivations, one's hypocrisies and shames and, above all, one's limited nature. It is for this that the sannyasin disciple strives.

At the proper time he finds a guru and lives at the guru's ashram under his direct tutelage and guidance. Until the sannyasin is established and arrives at a point from which nothing can disturb him, the guru's advice is to remain in an atmosphere conducive to spiritual growth. The sannyasin disciple is fully aware that the mind can create delusions at any time. It can lead to great heights of spiritual ecstasy and then bring him crashing down with unswerving speed. The sannyasin therefore lives and works at the ashram and accepts all difficulties and obstacles as part of the spiritual training.

Sannyasa is not a religious order, it is a philosophy of life, an ideal which certain people have adopted to achieve a higher understanding of themselves and to enable them to experience the bliss of their true nature. In an ashram people from different religions, cultures and status in society live under the same roof, sharing common ideals with equanimity and harmony. It may be argued that if sannyasa

49

is merely an inner attitude, one may maintain these ideals while living in society. One has only to try it to realize how wrong this is. While existing in society, people are so caught up in the commitments and competitions of life that it is like being entangled in a net. There is no way out. The more one struggles, the deeper one is ensnared in the net.

Besides, we are limited by nature. The afflictions of our personality invade us from all sides, completely dominating our actions. We try to overcome these afflictions, but due to the power of maya and our flagging willpower, very often we fail. Therefore, in order to stabilize the personality and mental fluctuations, a sannyasin should live under the guru's care for some time. After all, a sannyasin does not drop from heaven, he has evolved from society, and therefore has the same afflictions as everyone else. The difference lies in the desire for perfection and greater control over the instincts which retard spiritual growth. A sannyasin has evolved out of the normal pattern of life and is seeking a higher path through the life of sannyasa.

The ashram is not a place where sannyasins sit idly and talk of God or Brahman the whole day long. Sannyasins work unceasingly from dawn until dusk. They do all kinds of work, but there is a difference, and that difference is the attitude with which they work. The work they do is not self-oriented or with selfish motivation. It carries no expectation of reward. Once sannyasin disciples have established this attitude and awareness, they can work successfully anywhere.

Sannyasin disciples offer themselves to the guru, fully aware of their limited capacities and their tainted concepts of love, hatred, anger, jealousy and greed. Sannyasin disciples are, in fact, conglomerations of householder, sadhaka and tantric disciples. They have the steadfast devotion and faith of the householder; they maintain the strict discipline and regularity of the sadhaka to the sadhana that the guru gives them; and they offer their ego, will, desires and total self to the guru in absolute surrender, as does the tantric disciple. The guru maintains a constant link with the sannyasins on

50

all planes and guides them through the complexities that befall them. When the sannyasins have reached a point of stability, the guru sends them out to work in other places according to their capacity.

A sannyasin's life is forever dedicated to the loyal service of guru, and through this loyalty and dedication he experiences the truth.

TANTRIC DISCIPLE

The relationship between guru and tantric disciple is one of the most fulfilling in the whole guru-disciple tradition. Most of the disciples who fit into this category have already evolved their consciousness to a great height through sadhana done in previous lives. Gurus are always on the lookout for such disciples and waste no time in bringing them under their guidance. However, only one in a million can hope to reach the standard of such a disciple

The tantric disciple and guru form a complete circle. Their relationship can assume any form under the direction of the guru. They can be father and child, friend and enemy, devotee and God, two children playing with each other. They can even relate as husband and wife. Nothing exists outside this relationship. It is total.

The disciple may live with the guru or at a far distance. This is not important. What is most significant, however, is that the disciple completely surrenders body, mind and soul to the guru. Every act is the guru's will. "Thy will be done" is the tantric disciple's guiding principle.

Guru's instructions to such a disciple are seldom verbal. The guru transmits and the disciple receives and carries them out. The notion of duality disappears. Disciple and guru are merged into one another, and this can only take place if there is unconditional surrender.

But there is a price to pay – the ego! To qualify as a tantric disciple, you have to submit all your whims, idiosyncrasies, ideas of individuality and the many desires

51

and passions that cling to your mind and psyche to the will of the guru. We all know how difficult it is to transcend the ego. Intellectually, we may understand everything. We may be convinced that the ego is a hindrance and must be eliminated. But, in practice, time and again we fail. The ego comes up in so many different ways, often so subtly that we do not even notice that it is the ego which is playing havoc with our minds. This is why tantric disciples are so rare. Only one in a million can overcome the ego completely and such disciples are specifically selected by the guru.

The tasks given to such a disciple are of a very high magnitude. The disciple has no will or mind of his own; his life is lived for only one purpose – to obey the guru's command. All of the energies and mental frequencies are directed towards the fulfilment of that goal. There is great complexity in such a relationship. At every moment there has to be complete unity between guru and disciple. No task is too menial, too dangerous or too daring for the disciple if the guru has ordained it.

Due to the external expression of total surrender, this particular type of guru-disciple relationship has met with a great deal of ridicule. To the onlooker, the guru often appears as a tyrant master and the disciple his personal slave. But this assessment comes from a very limited understanding. The onlooker can never know the depth to which their minds are united, or even guess what is happening between them on the causal or subtle plane. And, believe me, there is much happening in complete and total silence. The guru may never speak a word, but the disciple is going through an unending dialogue with him. The disciple may derive as much knowledge from the guru's look, a quick glance, or just sitting in stillness, as may be obtained from a long series of lectures by the guru. In every realm, on every dimension, the guru is there to coax, cajole, warn, instruct and entice the disciple to greater and greater heights.

Traditional tantric sadhana includes aghora sadhana, kapali sadhana, kumari sadhana, lata sadhana and shmashan sadhana. (For explanation of these, see the glossary.) These sadhanas require great willpower and self-control. It is not possible for an ordinary seeker to accomplish them and they should not be practised except under the guidance of a guru. These practices are extremely powerful and can explode the mind, creating great problems unless the guru is present to supervise every aspect of the sadhana. The guru gives the tantric disciple a sadhana to explode the unconscious and expand the mind. During these practices, the disciple is able to witness and to experience strong emotions and passions which otherwise remain lurking in the unconscious. The disciple thereby learns to control these strong forces which, if not harnessed properly, may be a source of torment throughout his life.

The tantric disciple is in tune with every thought, word and action of the guru. He is constantly alert and aware of every need of the guru, whether it is expressed verbally or on the mental plane. He is able to anticipate the guru's thoughts and transform them into action. But the most significant aspect is that all this is done without the expectation of a reward or recognition. The expectation of a reward would indicate that desires are still lurking in the disciple's mind and, therefore, the predominance of his ego and will. The true tantric disciple simply acts, and the consequences, good or bad, are not for him to judge. To become the medium of the guru, one must develop the attitude of a pet dog or an obedient servant.

A tantric disciple will not question any action of the guru. He has full trust in the guru's judgement and firmly believes that the guru will not betray that trust. This is precisely why one has to choose a tantric guru very carefully. There is little use in being swayed by emotions and making rash judgements about gurus, only to regret it later. One must think clearly and soundly, but once one has accepted the guru, it must be done in totality. Then there is no room for doubt. All questions and intellectual arguments should cease.

When the disciple's surrender to the guru is complete, the guru's energy begins to flow into him and there is a continual process of transmission between them. This is a very important concept, for it is on this that the guru-disciple relationship has thrived for centuries. The guru is like the main transforming station or power house, and the disciple acts as a channel for taking the power or energy to different centres. The important thing is that the disciple should prepare to be a good conductor. Otherwise, if there is too much energy passing from guru to disciple, the fuse will blow, and if there is no fuse, the wire will melt. Many disciples have been destroyed in this way because they simply could not handle the energy. And this is why total surrender of disciple to guru is necessary. If the disciple is not prepared to follow the guru's instructions on the conscious plane, then how is it possible to do so on the psychic plane?

The guru subjects the disciple to a diverse range of experiences and situations. Some are abhorrent, some dangerous, some pleasant and sensual. In this way he slowly delves deeper into the disciple's mind, exposing the conscious, subconscious and unconscious layers. The disciple explores the great mysteries of the mind and with each experience gains new strengths, stronger willpower and greater determination. Finally, they arrive at a stage where the disciple is no longer overwhelmed by fears, passions, anger, greed or jealousy, for he has met them face to face and conquered them. It is then that the disciple can function independently.

So, in essence we find that the guru simply carries the disciple to higher and greater freedom, where he or she can function without limitations and norms, with an unconditioned mind. Once the disciple is stabilized in this consciousness, the guru allows him to work independently. It is never the guru's intention to curb the disciple's freedom or individuality, rather his aim is to develop the disciple's understanding and awareness of his body, mind, emotions and consciousness, and thereby experience them in their true essence.

The tantric guru and disciple can maintain the full level of communication even after the guru leaves the mortal body. In fact, it is mainly for this reason that the guru nurtures such disciples, so that the spiritual energy may continue to be transferred. If the disciple proves fit to receive the energy, then it does not matter whether the guru is in the physical body or not. He is a medium, an extension of the guru, and the guru is able to operate through him, even after his death.

This tradition of tantric guru-disciple has been handed down from generation to generation, and can be claimed to be as old as civilization itself. We have reference to it in the oldest books known to man, the Vedas. In fact, the first tantric guru-disciple relationship can be attributed to Shiva and his consort Parvati. He unfolded the mysteries to her and warned her to maintain the utmost secrecy, to prevent the knowledge from falling into the hands of ignorant and foolish people who may misuse it. However, in spite of this warning, we find that today the tantric tradition has fallen into the hands of many undeserving people who have reduced the knowledge to black magic, debauchery and an excuse for sexual licentiousness. Due to this, tantra has been grossly misunderstood. However, man will have to pay for the error of abusing a valuable science. If we are able to revive this knowledge in its true and proper form, we will find the answers to many of our problems. In India, there are still many wise men and women who have maintained and preserved this knowledge, usually in the utmost secrecy, away from the din and bustle of unnecessary propaganda.

A tantric disciple is an evolved aspirant to whom the guru adds the final touch. Just as one makes a flute out of a hollow bamboo and produces sweet melodies, in the same way, the guru fashions a disciple who has become empty of ego, into a rare gem that sparkles and shines wherever he goes.

HUMBUG DISCIPLE

One day a guru, in order to check out a disciple who had long been professing his faith, sincerity and everlasting devotion to his guru, said to the disciple, "Come along with me, there are a few things I have to do."

So the disciple and the guru set out. The disciple was curious to know where his guru was taking him, but he decided to wait and let things happen. The first place they visited was a prostitute's house. At first the disciple was alarmed, but then he said to himself, "Well, if my guru wants to go to a woman, what harm is there if I do the same?"

In the prostitute's house, the guru ordered some alcohol and proceeded to drink it. The disciple followed suit and soon the two of them were having a merry time. The disciple all along kept justifying to himself that it was all right to do all these things, as he was only following in his guru's footsteps. And wasn't that the duty of a disciple?

Then the guru left the house, and on the way back to the ashram stopped near a railway yard and touched a live high tension wire with his bare hands. The guru waited for the disciple to do the same, but the disciple, who until now had been following all the guru's actions, drew back in alarm and said, "It's all right for you to touch the wire, you are a siddha, nothing will happen to you, but I will surely die." The disciple, who had followed the guru in actions which stimulated the senses, now stepped back in indignation at an act which didn't suit his philosophy of 'eat, drink and be merry'.

This is just a simple example of what happens with a humbug disciple. His faith in the guru is superficial and his love for himself far outweighs the love he professes for the guru. His motivation and dedication exist only as long as the circumstances are to his advantage.

The humbug disciple often serves the guru under the guise of a tantric disciple or as a sannyasin. The life of a sadhaka is too vigorous and disciplined for his sense-oriented and whimsical nature. After all, to practise sadhana one has to wake up at four or five in the morning, if not earlier. Our humbug disciple is oblivious to the world at that hour. Not only will he avoid such disciplines himself, but he will try to convince others of their pointlessness, with the argument that all these practices only induce and encourage body awareness and thereby accentuate the narcissistic tendencies in us. "After all," says the humbug, "the body will perish; it is transient. So why waste time over it? We must reflect on our soul!" Reflection on the inner self gives him an opportunity to enjoy a couple of hours of extra sleep.

Posing as a tantric disciple is a good camouflage for the humbug's extroverted senses and indulgent nature. For haven't the sages proclaimed that sexual interaction, wine and meat are tools to achieve higher states of mind, and that they should be utilized for this purpose? This is a philosophy which can be very conveniently moulded into an excuse for indulgence. And therefore the humbug feels justified because, after all, he is following the teachings which have been recommended by the tantric scriptures!

It is these humbugs who have so grossly misrepresented the tantric science to the people. It is because of these careless, irresponsible people that a valued science like tantra has been criticized, condemned and debased. Tantra is an all-encompassing and systematic science, and although *maithuna* or sexual intercourse is acceptable, it is not the basis or foundation of tantra. The aspirant must fulfil many requirements, one of them being total *vairagya* or dispassionate detachment before he is considered competent to use sex as a means of sadhana.

Sometimes the humbug disciple adopts the sannyasa role to wile away a few years of life. Maybe the situation at home has become unbearable, or the government wants to draft him into the army, or the girlfriend or lover has left him for someone else. Or he is just plain good-for-nothing. What better place can one find than an ashram to pass into oblivion? At the most his friends will say, "So that's what was troubling him. He was having a spiritual awakening." And thus this humbug is elevated to respectability. But when he discovers that ashram life is not all smooth sailing, that he has to pull his own weight, he becomes perplexed and begins to find fault with his surroundings, rather than in himself. Soon he decides to leave, loudly denouncing all gurus, ashrams and spiritual life, for such a disciple can never survive in an ashram.

The humbug disciple often poses as a very learned and enlightened person. He will be seen giving his advice to all, even to those who do not want it. He cannot bear insult or injury and in the hour of crisis he invariably cracks. There is a story that illustrates this.

A man bought a parrot and trained it to say, "Ram, Ram, Ram." After a few days, it became an expert and the whole day the parrot could be heard screeching, "Ram, Ram, Ram." One day the master put the parrot in a cage and left it out in the sun. A stray cat pounced on the cage in an attempt to get at the parrot. The parrot was terrified and began screeching, but in its panic completely forgot "Ram, Ram, Ram" and resorted to its parrot language. This is what happens to the humbug disciple too. Because he lacks sincerity, it only takes a little encounter with maya, not even a direct attack or onslaught, to upset his balance, weaken his willpower and cause loss of faith in the guru.

There is another kind of humbug disciple – the sycophant. He thrives on the status, name and fame of the guru. He will hunt out a guru who is well-known and has big institutions. He becomes insecure if his guru is not respected by others. His security rests on the laurels of the guru's status. He revels in propaganda of any kind. The world should throw open its arms and accept his guru, for it is on that foundation that his shaky, tottering faith rests. He thrives on the assistance of devotees and well-wishers of the guru, maintaining a list of their addresses to be used without the slightest hesitation for the fulfilment of his own personal needs. These disciples suffer from delusions of grandeur, although they have done nothing to merit any respect.

Some of these disciples develop a closed and narrow outlook through obsessive tendencies. They cannot accept or appreciate the wisdom or status of any other guru. They fail to understand that wisdom, knowledge, fame and status are not the birthright of any one person, but are available to anyone who merits them. They fail to understand that a disciple should be open to the teachings of all wise and sincere people, although their devotion and surrender may be for their own guru.

The description of a humbug disciple could fill volumes, but that is not the intention. The aim is to give a glimpse of the tricks which the mind can play. It is not intended to give a criticism but a few useful hints. If we have these tendencies within us, then it is up to us to recognize them and root them out.

The humbug disciple has a very limited life as a spiritual aspirant. Gurus are very alert and quick to detect such disciples, although, because of their compassionate natures, they may expose humbug disciples to situations in which they can realize their shortcomings and grow spiritually. If the disciple persists with the humbug, he will be left to a destiny which is stern and cruel. Such a disciple can only survive under the protection of a humbug guru, for they will complement each other.

9

Obedience to Guru

Regardless of what kind of disciple you choose to be in relation to the guru, you will need to develop faith, devotion, surrender, egolessness, humility, sincerity and complete and total obedience to him. Some people are more fortunate than others, as they are naturally and spontaneously able to act in this way. Others have these qualities inherent in them, but they are shrouded by an external façade which has been built up as a defence mechanism. It is the presence, love and inspiration of the guru that gradually unfolds to such people their true nature. Still others find it very difficult to maintain these ideals; it is against their nature, but they must continually strive to achieve these qualities. If their efforts are sincere, the guru will undoubtedly help them until they succeed.

Disciples must always be aware that they have chosen to serve the guru, not because the guru needs them, but because of their need to grow, to expand and to throw away the fetters that bind them. It is only if they think along these lines that they will be able to follow the guru's instructions, however meaningless they may seem to be. The moment they begin to think to the contrary, they will be in deep trouble. If faith and devotion dissipate, they will begin to question the meaning of being a disciple, and that's where the confusion begins.

The guru-disciple relationship is not based on logic or the finite intellect. It is a relationship based on higher awareness. To one who has ceased to maintain this awareness, every act will seem futile. The intellect will shroud the mind with negative doubts. The wavering disciple will question the purpose of working so hard in the ashram for no money or reward. The mind will fantasize about how the same work elsewhere would earn money and status. Many similar thoughts will even make the life that has been rejected and thought worthless before coming to the ashram seem glamorous and not so bad after all.

These thoughts may or may not occur, and it is entirely up to the disciple how he handles them. If the disciple unceasingly strives to maintain devotion and faith to guru, he will survive the turbulence of the mind. If not, the strength will be dissipated, the willpower will be weakened, and even if the disciple continues to live in the ashram, there will always be a feeling of unfulfilment.

For strengthening the link with guru, total obedience is required, even from householders and sadhakas who do not live in the ashram. Remember, the guru is not insane, he knows our limitations better than we do. If he asks us to do something, we can be quite sure that it has been given a lot of thought. If guru pushes us hard to do things we do not like, it is merely because we have certain obstacles in our personality which need to be removed to allow us to grow in spiritual life.

Therefore, it is very often advised that the disciple should be as innocent and playful as a child. His needs should be simple, his actions pure and his words playful and kind. As adults, we very often lose the innocence and guileless credulity of children and thereby cannot experience the joys and pleasures of just being. We inhibit the pure expression of our minds, and this becomes a great barrier that blocks the great energy which we are trying to release. It is precisely this freedom of mind and expression that the guru wishes the disciple to develop.

The guru does not care if the disciple can read or write, or is rich or poor. All of these are mere outward manifestations, external coverings. Guru is only deeply interested in and involved with the growth of the disciple's spirit, and for that the disciple should not arrest or interfere with the free expression of the mind. Surrender is a natural urge. When the surrender is complete, the disciple's thoughts are one with the guru. Then and only then does every word the guru speaks come true in the disciple's life. If the disciple is disobedient and obstinate, with a personality of his own, the guru can do nothing, even if he wants to. This is the psychic law.

When the disciple has completely surrendered, his mind becomes connected to his guru's mind. Then there is guidance, not only in conscious moments, but during meditation. Through complete and unwavering obedience to guru, the disciple trains his conscious, subconscious and unconscious mind to receive the instructions. In higher states of meditation, the disciple does not have control over his experiences. It is at that time that he needs the guidance of the guru to show him the way. But in order to be receptive to the guru in that state of mindlessness, the disciple has to be obedient to each and every word of the guru. The disciple must remember that if he cannot obey the guru on the conscious plane, he certainly cannot do so on the unconscious plane.

The purpose of surrender and obedience to guru is to become an efficient instrument of the guru on all levels. It is for precisely this reason that obedience to guru is emphasized. It is not because guru is the tyrant master and the disciple is the slave. If the guru is to transfer spiritual power to the disciple and make him or her a medium through which he can work, it can only be achieved through total obedience.

10

Negativity Towards Guru

It is the hour of crisis for a disciple when he begins to feel negative towards the guru. Negativity arises when the faith is broken and doubts and suspicions creep in. Faith is the wealth of a disciple. It is that by which he lives. Just as a wealthy person survives by money, or a scientist by intellect, the disciple is carried through life by faith. If the faith is lost, the spiritual life is jeopardized and the disciple has been reduced to a pauper. Once the faith is destroyed, it is very difficult to regain it. Therefore, the disciple has to guard his faith as a miser guards his wealth.

Some actions by the guru may at times cause the disciple to become negative. The disciple may react bitterly to something the guru has said or done. Very often it is the disciple's confused mind that projects faults on to the guru. But even if the guru is at fault, it is the duty and responsibility of the disciple to rise above the circumstances. Once the clouds are rent asunder, the disciple is bound to realize that his negativity was simply a creation of his wayward mind.

If the disciple has surrendered to the guru, he must overlook and accept many things. That is the disciple's strength and therein lies his spiritual progress. When the disciple chose his guru, it was on the basis of something he saw in the guru, and the disciple should maintain that as his guideline, trying to bypass everything else.

If the disciple is not able to resurrect his faith through his own understanding and willpower, he should approach his guru and clear the misunderstanding. The guru may be able to explain many things the disciple is not able to see. In this way many complications may be smoothed out. However, if the disciple is still not convinced, he should ask the guru what to do. If the guru is sincere and honest, he will realize that he can no longer help the disciple spiritually and may ask him to find another guru. In some cases he may even suggest the right guru.

At this point it is important that the disciple does not react. Most do, and they convince themselves that a guru is not at all necessary. The disciple should not fall into the trap. He should sit down calmly and assess the situation. He should realize that his spiritual life is in critical danger. If he loses his vision of faith completely, there is absolutely no chance of reviving his spiritual life.

When negative thoughts come, it is important for the disciple to remember that it is all either a trick of the guru or the maya of his own mind. If his faith is undaunted, he can overcome this maya. At times the guru may also create many circumstances to test the disciple's faith. The drama which he enacts seems so authentic, that even the sincerest disciple can become confused. He exposes the disciple to every kind of treatment in order to make the disciple aware of his personal limitations, so that he may overcome them. His motive for doing this is his love for the disciple and his desire to see him grow.

But in spite of the purity of the guru's motives, very often the disciple misunderstands his actions and reacts negatively. He becomes bitter, and feels that the guru is unjust and unkind. It is the disciple's own misfortune if he fails to recognize the guru's love. It should not matter to the disciple whether the guru is kind or cruel, pleasant or unpleasant, attentive or indifferent. His faith and love should remain unscathed under any situation, because he is so sure that the guru is his only true friend and guide.

The disciple should lay his heart and soul bare before the guru in total faith. Faith is not a belief, it is a much stronger force than that. If one's faith is strong, one can overcome any obstacles in life. A miracle is a creation of one's faith.

To a disciple who is an earnest seeker, it should not matter what circumstances the guru creates. No negativity should be shown. By maintaining utmost faith, the disciple cannot be deterred from spiritual progress. However, if he revels in his negativity, nothing can bring him out of the mire. He will sink in his efforts to evolve spiritually, and the loss is only his. No one else is affected.

Letter to a Disciple

One indispensable qualification of a great disciple is that he should carry out immediately and spontaneously the commands of the guru. If in this sphere he acquires that good quality, then in the next sphere also the same happens. When the entire individuality of the disciple becomes obedient to the commands of the guru, only then unforeseen success comes in the sadhana performed according to the guru's instruction.

11

Ego in the Disciple

The disciple's ego stands as the main obstruction between him and the truth. It is the ego which causes him to stumble time and again on the spiritual path. It is the ego which causes him to lose his faith, devotion, humility and one-pointed dedication. Ego is the root cause of all ignorance. It is the maya or web that has been cast upon human beings. If this ego is not checked by the disciple, it will spread like a cancer and overpower him. In spiritual life there is no place for the ego.

In worldly life, we use the ego to counteract the influences of other people. In fact, if we did not possess an ego, it would be difficult to survive. In our day to day life we encounter many people who have only their own progress in mind, and they do not hesitate to exploit others for their own benefit. We use our egos to counteract such encounters. It is because of our sense of individuality that we react. If we did not have an ego, we would not care if someone was dishonest and cheated us, we would simply accept it. If this were to happen while interacting with the world, the egoless person would be crushed.

The ego is present to be used as a brake. The brakes in the car are to prevent accidents and to keep it under control, but if one never takes one's foot off the brake, the car will not move. Therefore, in order to progress in spiritual life, it is necessary that this brake, the ego, be used as little as possible. In interactions with others, disciples should suppress the ego and remain a witness to all that is going on inside. In this way, they will become aware of the ways in which the ego operates, and become accomplished in combating it without doing any serious damage to themselves.

However, in their relationship with the guru, disciples must eliminate the ego completely. There is no place for ego before the guru. What is the point of using your ego towards someone whose only interest is your spiritual upliftment? Guru's motives are not guided by base and vile intentions; he wishes only the best for his disciple. The disciple may misunderstand the intentions, but then the fault lies with the disciple, not the guru. If the disciple allows his ego to get the better of him in his relationship with the guru, then the relationship will be seriously damaged. Using ego to combat the guru is tantamount to burning a rope, mistaking it for a snake.

The guru is fully aware of this discrepancy in the disciple's personality and often performs what could be called an 'egodectomy'. Just as a surgeon performs an operation to remove a cancerous growth from the patient, in the same way the guru operates on the disciple's ego. The success of the operation depends upon both guru and disciple. The guru must be very skilled and the disciple must possess the ability to regain strength and faith after the operation.

Another danger that awaits every disciple is the sense of superiority which many develop because of their success in carrying out their guru's mission. Very often disciples become arrogant and conceited and think that the success is due to their own efforts. They forget that it is only due to the guru's guidance that they have been able to evolve their consciousness, which in turn has enabled them to act positively and successfully. At times, they may even believe that they are greater than the guru. If they continue to hold these beliefs, they are soon crushed by their ego, and fall victim to the maya.

Ego is a very subtle element. It is difficult, almost impossible to grasp or understand the ways in which it spreads its tentacles. To combat it, disciples must be very alert at all times. It will overtake them if they are caught napping. Disciples must remain forever a witness to their mind. They must assess their reactions, their motives, their circumstances, with the same detachment a coffin bearer would have for the coffins he carries all day and night.

The ego can rear up in the strangest circumstances. Even the act of renunciation could be an act of the ego. There is little purpose in renouncing your material pleasures for sannyasa and then developing the same attachment, neurosis and fixation in your attitude towards spiritual life. This is why it is often said that true renunciation comes from within. Ultimately, one has to renounce even the act of renunciation.

In the traditional sannyasa ceremony, the disciple chants mantras and pledges to renounce, not only the manifestation of the ego in the gross body, but the threefold ego which exists in the gross, subtle and causal form. Ego is the seed of individuality which separates the guru and disciple.

12

Surrender

In order to unite with the guru, the disciple has to surrender totally to him. When you surrender yourself totally, you merge completely into the guru. In total surrender lies the answer. Then you need not practise any asanas, pranayama, or kriya yoga. Who is going to practise what, because you have ceased to exist.

How does this surrender happen? How can the seeker arrive at the path of surrender? In truth, there are no methods for surrender. In the path of surrender, surrender itself is the method. In other paths there are methods and techniques. In order to progress you are required to follow these methods and techniques. You make a significant effort to manipulate and balance your energy through these methods. But in the path of surrender, there is no effort. It is spontaneous or not at all.

The moment you develop a technique for surrender, it ceases to be surrender. Because then you have created a facade, a deception, and the moment you create a deception, you separate yourself from the experience. You are not totally involved or immersed in the act of surrendering. While using techniques, you still exist as a separate entity, but in surrender your existence is annihilated. The moment you ask yourself, how can I surrender, you are defeating the purpose. How can you ask yourself how to love? Either there is love or there is not. You cannot teach yourself to love. It is a spontaneous ongoing process. Love is being totally open, totally vulnerable. In true love, there are no securities that you can cling to. You have given up everything for the sake of love.

The same happens in surrender. Love and surrender are deeply one. They go hand in hand; they co-exist with each other. Where there is love, there is surrender. We think that we love each other, that we love our friends and parents and husbands and wives. But is there total surrender? Have you ceased to exist before the person you have surrendered to? If not, then your love is subject to conditions, and therefore is cannot be love.

With the guru, too, very often the disciple is deluded. He thinks that he loves the guru and that his surrender is complete, but the conditions remain. The love is a technique and the surrender a facade. In total surrender the disciple has no mind. He loses awareness of 'I am-ness' in relation to the guru. He is totally vulnerable, open and guileless. The disciple has no choice before the guru. He is a servant, a slave, and he exists only for the guru.

It is only then that the true grace of the guru begins to pour into the life of the disciple because he has emptied himself; because he is ready to receive; because he has given everything and is left with nothing. He exists like a child with no barriers or facades. The guru, in transmitting his energy into such a disciple, transforms his life and personality.

So it is good to surrender, but at the same time it is difficult. It is the most difficult thing in the world. Asanas, pranayamas, japa and kriya yoga are easy because they entail methods. And you can easily train yourself to adopt any method. But for surrender there is no method, no training, no technique.

The question now arises, what is it that stands between the disciple and total surrender to guru? What is this barrier? And why is it so difficult? Each of us, no matter who we are, lives with the ego, centred in the ego. We traverse life with this sense of 'I am-ness' tucked safely up our sleeves. It is a defence mechanism which we use to safeguard ourselves. Without a sense of identity, we are hopelessly and miserably lost.

This sense of identity may be relevant in your day to day worldly life. But in relation to guru and in relation to your spiritual life, it is the greatest obstacle. It is this ego which stands between you and total surrender. Your ego tells you not to surrender. The ego in you does not want to die, and with surrender it will be totally mutilated. Therefore, your ego will always auto-suggest to you the dangers of total surrender. And because you are so intoxicated and totally captivated by the sense of 'I am-ness', your ego gets the better of you. You surrender to your ego. So there is a constant battle between surrender to the guru and surrender to your own ego.

But if you can become aware of this defence measure in you; if you can become conscious of the workings of the ego, then it automatically begins to dissolve. It begins to disintegrate because the moment you focus your awareness on a problem, it begins to solve itself. With continued awareness, this ego which is inherent in you gradually becomes weaker and weaker. And if you are very careful not to give the ego any opportunity to strengthen itself, one day you will come to feel that you do not exist. The moment you feel 'I am not', surrender happens. Surrender happens only when you are no longer living in the realm of ego.

When you surrender to guru, you become like a valley, a vacuum, an abyss, a bottomless pit. You acquire depth, not height. This surrender can be felt in many ways. The guru begins to manifest in you; his energy begins to flow into you. The guru's energy is continuously flowing, but in order to receive it you have to become a womb, a receptacle. You have to come down. You have to bow down. If you are above him, that flowing energy cannot come to you. You will miss it. So bow down to guru.

Even in a minor surrender to guru, energy begins to flow. Suddenly you become a vehicle of that energy. We

71

have heard hundreds of stories about how with just a touch or a look someone became enlightened. This is possible and it has happened innumerable times in history. Even a look into your eyes from guru can transform your whole being; but for that your eyes must be vacant, not filled with prejudices and complexes. In order to absorb the look of the guru, you have to be empty.

Living with the guru is perhaps the only way in which the disciple can become aware of the subtle workings of the ego. In all other situations of life, the ego is reinforced. We cannot accept injury, loss, unhappiness or misery. Besides, we do not even want to accept these afflictions because we do not feel the need to surrender to anyone. We are scared of being exploited, misused and abused by other people.

But if you are living with the guru, he constantly prepares you for surrender. That is his work, his responsibility. He trains your conscious and subconscious mind to function, without strengthening the ego. He creates situations and events whereby the disciple is able to recognize how his ego has completely dominated him. Gradually, in time, the disciple becomes more aware of this barrier of ego between him and the guru.

The disciple, at times, is able to subjugate the ego temporarily and experiences minor surrender towards the guru. During those moments, faith and love for the guru are awakened. The disciple realizes that through surrender to the guru, he has received something unbelievable, unexpected and unknown, some greater power which he could never have dreamed of. And then he is ready for total surrender. But in order to experience total surrender to the guru, a disciple must live in the guru's ashram and allow the guru to work on his ego in whichever manner the guru considers necessary.

Very often disciples are apprehensive of being exploited by the guru. They fear what will become of them if they surrender totally to the guru. Will the guru take advantage of them, ill-treat them and abuse them? These doubts should

have no place in the mind of the disciple who wishes to surrender. Apart from being untrue, they will completely misguide his actions towards the guru.

Disciples should remember that in total surrender, it is they who have the advantage. Even if the guru wishes to exploit the disciple, a disciple who has surrendered is safeguarded by the laws of nature. His karmas will rebound on a guru who has cheated and exploited him, and the disciple will remain unscathed. Besides, a guru will never cheat or exploit a sincere disciple.

13

Transmission

Transmission is the basis of a guru-disciple relationship. It is the guru's method of teaching the disciple. In ordinary life we are so dependent on words. Without words, we cannot communicate. The teacher instructs the student verbally or through books and lessons. This is formal education. For those who are deaf, blind or dumb, education or instructions become a problem. This is because the system of education is so reliant on the medium of the senses to convey knowledge.

However, between guru and disciple there exists another faculty of awareness. This dimension of awareness far supersedes any of the outer organs of knowledge which are present in everyone. It transcends the barriers of time and space. The guru and disciple can communicate with each other even though they may be thousands of miles apart. They simply tune into the same frequency and the messages start pouring in. If you have ever seen a telex machine working, you will get an idea of what I mean.

Ordinarily, we perceive through the senses. The brain assimilates and decodes the information and certain knowledge is deducted and stored. However, the knowledge that is gained is influenced by and subject to our past impressions and the way in which we are able to perceive and comprehend. In other words, the knowledge we gain is relative to our level of perception and the quality of our

74

intellect. If our intellect is dim, the knowledge is clouded and lacks clarity.

In the method of transmission, the disciple has to jump over the intellect. He has to live in the plane of pure consciousness. On that plane there is no logic or reasoning. In that state one plus one need not necessarily add to two. The disciple is open and receptive. His mind is not conditioned by his senses or by book knowledge. What the books say may be absolutely correct, but the disciple has transcended that knowledge. He has deconditioned the mind. One plus one may be equal to two, but he will not believe it simply because the books say so; he will believe it only after personal experience.

When the disciple has deconditioned his mind and rendered his higher awareness free of its limitations, then his intuition begins to function. Intuition is the highest form of knowledge. It is intuition that creates geniuses in every field, such as art, science and music. Therefore, from this we can see that knowledge gained through intuition and transmission is far more accurate.

In spiritual life too, it is when the intuitive faculty begins to manifest that the disciple becomes complete. It is at that time that the guru is able to transmit higher knowledge to the disciple. It is then that he uses his disciple as a medium to spread his mission far and wide. But in order to prepare himself for this stage, the disciple has to live very closely with the guru. He should try to raise his awareness to that of his guru. He should make his mind empty, so that the instructions can be received. He has to become a good conductor of the guru.

Just as electricity is transmitted from the generating station to various places, in the same way the guru is the powerhouse, a vast reservoir of energy, transmitting this energy to various disciples. If the disciple is a good medium or good conductor, he will carry the load easily. But if he is a bad conductor, or let us say, if his channels for conducting energy are blocked or weak, he will have a breakdown due to

75

overload. Just as the fuse blows when the voltage is too high, or if there is no fuse, the television breaks down, in the same way the disciple, who is not yet ready to receive the energy has a breakdown.

When the disciple is not sufficiently evolved, the guru prepares his mind and emotions through a systematic way of teaching. But if the disciple is sufficiently evolved, then it is not necessary to teach him anything. Then the inner communication between both of them begins to take place spontaneously. As soon as the disciple is in tune with the guru, the energy begins to flow towards him.

For transmission, there should not be any mental, physical or spiritual block in the disciple. Guru and disciple should operate on the same plane. Physically, they occupy two bodies, but spiritually they are one. There is no place for individuality. The disciple's ego is completely dominated by his surrender to guru. That is precisely why surrender is so important in the life of a disciple; so that he may commune with the guru in higher states of awareness and receive his knowledge, grace and wisdom.

The concept of transmission is based on the theory of the universal mind. Each one of us has a mind of our own which is called the individual mind. This is linked wholly to a larger component called the universal mind. Each one of us is a part of that universal mind. The idea of individuality is present only on account of ego. Once the ego is removed, the universal mind becomes functional. If we are all a part of the universal mind, then we are all linked to each other by an unseen cord. Then I can transmit to you and you can transmit to another person without the slightest difficulty.

But due to *avidya* (ignorance), ego and karma, we are all bound to the sense of individuality and therefore we are not able to operate on that plane. The guru, however, has developed the universal mind. He is not subject to laws which govern the individual mind. Therefore, he is able to transmit his thoughts anywhere, because the universal mind is able to unite with every mind at any time and in any place.

76

You have to understand this properly. Two individuals who are spiritually linked can always communicate with each other because they have the same mind. The disciple who has surrendered to guru is a part of the universal mind. Therefore, he and the guru are one. Their minds are united. Then it is not a matter of transmission, but of communication and inter-union.

Very often the disciple lives in the quagmire of individual mind. Every now and then the guru sends him messages to check him out, but they fall on deaf ears. Sometimes, in a rare moment, the disciple's awareness is heightened and he becomes receptive to the guru's transmissions. But when the awareness falls, again the receptivity is dimmed and the disciple is governed by his own mind. Naturally, the guru cannot rely too much on such a disciple whose state of mind is continually fluctuating. It is for this reason that the guru is always very selective when choosing a disciple who is to be his medium. Not everybody can be a good conductor; only the disciple who can transform the guru's thoughts into actions is fit to receive them.

When one becomes a disciple, this connection with the guru should definitely be established. It is a much more powerful way to live with the guru. Spiritual life does not consist of teaching alone. There should come a time in the life of a disciple when all questions and doubts should cease, and a relationship with the guru should be developed on the basis of transmission and contact.

The guru may or may not give lectures and satsangs. He may seldom meet the disciple, but it is important that the guru and disciple are transmitter and receiver. This is the real relationship between guru and disciple. Then the disciple is able to communicate with the guru even after the guru leaves his mortal body. He can commune with his guru as easily as if he were still on the earthly plane. He can receive commands and instructions from his guru, and become the medium for the guru's mission after the guru has gone. It is for the achievement of this purpose that every disciple should prepare. This is the highest kind of discipleship.

14

The Grace of Guru

Guru's grace is a most difficult thing to comprehend, and even more difficult to explain. It is tangible only to those who are receptive to it. In India, there is a phrase which is commonly used to emphasize the importance of guru's grace in the life of a disciple: *'Guru kripa hi kevalam'*. This means that the guru's grace alone can liberate a disciple.

A disciple, aspirant or sadhaka should be fully aware that once he is initiated into any practice of yoga – karma yoga, jnana yoga, hatha yoga or bhakti yoga – the most important and perhaps the most difficult thing he has to achieve is control of the mind. This is the greatest obstacle most disciples will face. They may succeed in combating the turbulences of the mind temporarily, but sooner or later they will encounter them again, perhaps with greater force. When this happens, even the most aware and cautious disciple may become unbalanced and lose control, and the aspirant who is still uncertain may be completely shattered.

It is almost impossible to control the patterns of the mind, especially the negative aspects such as anger, jealousy, greed and passion. They invade the mind from all sides. It is our misfortune that we are not able to recognize them for what they are, and succumb to them. This is a great obstacle and we must find a way to overcome it before we can make spiritual progress. No one is immune; at some time or other, all of us are caught. Even the sincerest and most devoted disciple is subject to the storms and tempests which stir and shake the mind.

Sometimes we are temporarily able to waive the onslaughts of the mind. But if we carefully analyze the situation, we will find that we have only managed to suppress our traumas. In actual fact they remain lurking somewhere at the back of the mind, and it only takes a tiny spark for them to flare up again. If we suppress these onslaughts time and time again, they may erupt as illness, affecting our physical bodies.

So how are we to combat the mind? It is the guru's grace alone that can liberate us from this bondage of the mind. It is he alone who can give us the strength and equanimity to survive the invasions of our mental patterns. It is his grace that helps us through the severest trials. Without it, we can be crushed and torn in pieces. It is with his help that we can hold our heads high and walk along the path once again.

But guru's grace is not achieved so easily. To receive it, we must be sincere and totally his. We must belong to him, body, mind and soul. Then when we encounter difficulties in our internal and external lives, he will come to our side and assist us. But not otherwise. Why should the guru shower his grace on us if we are not fully qualified to receive it? To receive the true grace of the guru, the disciple should have no mind of his own in relation to the guru. The guru thinks and the disciple acts. The disciple does not judge the guru's thoughts. He accepts them as if they were his own. Only such a disciple can receive the true grace of the guru.

However, sometimes even if we are not yet ready to receive guru's grace, he may still help us through some of our difficulties, to alleviate them in a small measure. This too is his grace, but it is not the full force of the grace. The full grace is that which liberates us from the bondage that curbs our growth as individuals. It is that grace which we should aspire for and prepare ourselves to receive. But that grace is available only to one who has no expectations.

We often tend to approach the guru full of desires and expectations. Some of these expectations are more obvious, and others are latent. But nevertheless they exist. They may be gross, rajasic desires, such as acquisition of wealth, name and fame, good health and happiness, or they may be more subtle or sattwic, such as enlightenment, progress in sadhana, mental powers and siddhis. No matter what these desires are, we must strive towards eliminating them. Then and only then will the guru pick us up and carry us along.

Very often the guru showers grace on the disciple, but the disciple does not have the eyes to see. Guru's grace can manifest in many ways – it may be pleasant and sweet, or severe and unpleasant. Most disciples believe that when the guru speaks with kind and soft words, he is bestowing a blessing and the more pleasant and charming he is, the more grace is being bestowed. But this need not be true. Guru's grace can be very unpleasant at times.

The guru is like a carpenter who chops and cuts a piece of wood down to size, not showing the least mercy until he has made something from it. Before he started, the carpenter had a clear vision of what he wanted to create. In the same way, the guru chops, saws and cuts the disciple's ego with a clear vision of what he is trying to achieve, and shows no mercy until he has the finished product. As the carpenter transforms the wood into an object of utility, purpose and beauty, the guru transforms the disciple into a liberated being, to be the guiding light of many. But this can only take place if the disciple, like the piece of wood, remains calm, quiet and egoless, allowing the guru to transform him totally.

To understand the guru is not an easy matter. Guru is able to penetrate deep into our personality and judge us for what we really are. He is able to weigh our strengths and weaknesses, even the ones we did not realize we had. He will use the severest methods in order to make us aware of our limitations. This too is his grace. In fact, if a disciple has not experienced this, he has not really known the guru. In order to receive and understand this grace of guru, one has to approach the guru with sincerity and dedication, expecting

80

nothing, receiving whatever one gets with humility and always striving to maintain unity with guru.

Swami Satyananda's words on this subject are appropriate here. He said, "All over the world there is this tradition of guru's grace in the life of a disciple. The disciple to whom the grace of guru is earmarked is rare, and I often wonder why Swami Sivananda chose me. I think it could only be for one reason. During my life with him, there was not one point where I was not in rapport with him. I always followed him keenly. I noted each and every word and expression. I observed every movement of his life. Even an ordinary act of his meant a great commentary to me. There were times when I knew exactly what he was thinking, and on other occasions I could predict what he was going to do. A disciple has to understand his guru's thoughts before the guru can act. That kind of unity has to be established between guru and disciple, then the grace flows automatically. Therefore, I came to the conclusion years ago – unite with your guru, become one with him, just as sugar dissolves in milk. They become one and do not remain as separate entities. The milk becomes sugary, the sugar milky. They adopt each other's qualities. That kind of unity has to be achieved and then the grace of guru is always present."

15

Guru as Father, Mother, Friend

Disciples are often confused about how they should relate to the guru. They wonder whether they should regard the guru as a kind, benevolent father whom they can run to for love and protection. Or should they simply treat him as a loving friend with whom they can share their innermost secrets and afflictions. We see the guru as an epitome of love and joy. We want to reach out to him, to feel one with him and to relate to him. But at the same time, when we try to do so we feel blocked in the process and are unable to convey our sentiments, thoughts and emotions.

We have to first of all understand that the relationship between guru and disciple is not based on logic. In fact, if you begin to analyze and reason this relationship, you may end up negating it altogether. The philosophy behind this relationship is abstract and intangible, the treading ground insecure and uncertain, and the reasons and motives for developing the relationship are purely individual and on a personal basis.

To a true disciple, guru encompasses everything one can perceive in the world. He is father, mother, friend, relative, husband, wife, son, daughter, even God. He is the sun and the moon, the flowers and the trees. Well, in short, he is the essence of everything that exists in the disciple's life.

In actual fact, the guru is what you see in him. It is your perception that determines your experiences with guru. If you perceive him as unlimited, infinite and a never-ending experience, then he is that for you; but if you perceive him as an ordinary man, then you will always fail to realize the divinity in him. That does not mean that he is not a divine being. You can't see it, that's all. To a blind man, the sun is always non-existent.

The guru serves as a clear mirror in which you can see your own reflection. In himself, he is pure, shining, effulgent spirit. Anything that is pure and free from reflection will reproduce the image that is focused on it. Therefore, what you see in the guru is merely a projection of your own personality. However, on account of his physical presence, we are often unsure of how we should develop the relationship with guru. For this purpose, in the Puranas and other scriptures of India there are a few examples which can serve as a guideline to disciples, so that they can streamline their emotions and energy towards guru and in time develop one-pointedness.

The basis of the guru-disciple relationship is devotion. That is the underlying principle. Without devotion, you cannot relate to the guru in full measure. However, in order to generate this devotion and make it a reality, the disciple can utilize one of four *bhavas* or attitudes which are outlined in the scriptures. These bhavas or attitudes relate to feelings and sentiments which are a common occurrence in our daily lives, and therefore are easier to express.

The first is known as *dasya bhava*. *Dasya* means 'servant'. Therefore, the disciple is the loyal, obedient servant and the guru is the master. Just as a dedicated servant has only one aim in mind, to accomplish with perfection the task given to him by his master, similarly, the disciple dedicates himself to his guru's work. There is no task too arduous for the disciple. He cares not whether the guru is kind and loving in return, or whether he is strict and admonishing. His duty is to serve, and that is all he knows and cares about. This example is exemplified in the famed epic, *Ramayana*, in the relationship between Rama and his most trusted aide

83

Hanuman. The servant-disciple does not question the motives or judgements of the guru, he simply obeys the order, leaving everything else in the hands of the guru.

The second is *vatsalya bhava*, or the attitude between father and son or father and daughter. We are all deeply ingrained with filial tendencies from birth. They arise as a natural response in us, and therefore this attitude does not need much elucidation. However, the prevalent attitude between parents and children in India is very different to what it is in the West. In India, the father stands as a symbol of wisdom, knowledge and experience, and the son pays him due respect, love and loyalty. The father's words are considered sacred and the children do not go against his wishes as a token of their love and surrender. Once again, we can draw a parallel example from the *Ramayana* by reading about the relationship between King Dasharatha and his son Rama. Even though Rama was the legal inheritor of the throne, and his father had unjustly banished him to twelve years exile, thus denying him the kingdom, Rama did not disobey his father. He simply said: "What is a kingdom; I could give up my life for you."

The third bhava, which is known as the *ishvara bhava*, is the relationship between devotee and God. The guru represents the unattainable divinity and the disciple is his humble devotee. As devotee, the disciple throws himself at the feet of the guru and seeks his love and protection. Here the disciple takes on the role of a *bhakta* or devotee and practises bhakti yoga towards the guru. The disciple worships his guru as a transcendental being and, ultimately, fully merges with the guru. This was seen in the case of Sri Ramakrishna and Kali. Ramakrishna loved Ma Kali as his Mother Goddess. He bathed her statue, danced before her, lit incense, offered her food and cried in front of her like a little child. Ultimately, he was able to transcend awareness of his mortal self and become a part of her.

The fourth bhava is *madhurya bhava* or *sakha bhava*. It is the feeling between two friends who have attained complete unity due to their love and attachment for each other, such as in the case of Radha and Krishna, Arjuna and Krishna, Krishna and the gopis. Krishna and the gopis would play like little children, but they were totally immersed in each other. Radha met Krishna only once in her life, as a child, but that memory remained so deeply ingrained in her consciousness that she could never forget him. And even today in India they live eternally as one. We never think of Krishna without Radha.

Now, in the relationship with guru, the disciple chooses one bhava according to his own personality and needs, and develops that to its fullest potential. If he feels the need for a friend, he should regard the guru as his friend. Or, if he has been lacking parental love, the guru can be his mother and father. If the disciple wishes to totally surrender to the guru, then he can regard himself as the guru's slave. It all depends on your own basic need and which area of your personality is the most powerful and easily expressed. However, no matter which attitude you choose for yourself, it should be a spontaneous expression, a natural outlet for your emotions and personality.

These bhavas are relevant to all categories of disciple except the sannyasin disciple. To the sannyasin, the guru represents the all-pervading reality at all times. The guru is a replica of the highest truth which he is striving to experience.

So the disciple utilizes a particular bhava or attitude as a tool to strengthen his link with the guru. The attitude which he adopts corresponds to his worldly personality and therefore he finds it easier to conceive and express. However, although the disciple uses this as a tool, he has to be careful in maintaining a selfless attitude with no expectations from the guru.

The guru may or may not respond to you in the manner you want him to, but nevertheless your love, devotion and selflessness towards him should not be in the least affected. Just as a child loves his mother throughout his life, regardless

85

of how she behaves towards him, because his bond is deeper than an external link, in the same way the disciple strives to maintain his attitude to the guru, not relying on any external interaction between them.

Sometimes, in adopting a certain bhava towards the guru, disciples tend to transfer their complexes and neuroses too. If they have become insecure due to the suffering meted out to them by harsh parents, then in their relationship with guru too they feel insecure. This should not happen. The disciple has linked himself with guru in order to transcend the base and negative qualities in himself and not in order to remain steeped in them. Therefore, a disciple has to remain alert on this point.

The guru symbolizes a person to whom you can direct your surplus emotions in order to channel them into higher and positive experiences. The idea is to free you of your limitations, not to bind you. The guru has no barriers of expression. If the barrier or block is there at all, it exists in you and you have to strive to eliminate it with the help of your selfless love towards the guru.

Even in your meditation practices you can develop a picture of the guru as you wish to see him, as a father, friend, master or God. You can talk to him in your meditation; you can fantasize and build up the relationship as you want to in your mind. The guru becomes the symbol of your consciousness, gradually raising your awareness to greater and more sublime heights.

Each one of us has surplus emotions. If they are not used constructively, in time they tend to dissipate and become a source of frustration and depression. However, if you direct these emotions towards guru in the manner explained above, then you will be channelling, transforming and sublimating your energy towards a higher experience, that of union with the guru.

16

Initiation

It is the desire of disciples for spiritual grace that leads them to various spiritual masters. They listen to their wisdom and knowledge with keenness of mind and soon single out one guru whose teachings and personality appeal the most. They then approach that guru and thus their spiritual courtship begins. The disciple expresses his sincerity and desire to delve into spiritual life. And the guru, in turn, assesses the spiritual qualifications of the prospective disciple, his inner nature and situation in life. At the appropriate time, the disciple asks for initiation.

Initiation or *diksha* is the guru's formal acceptance of a disciple. Until the disciple is initiated or receives diksha from the guru, he cannot advance in his sadhana. In all the ancient scriptures, great stress is laid on the importance of initiation in the disciple's spiritual life. The word diksha is derived from a combination of two words: the root *diks*, which means 'to consecrate, dedicate', and the root *daks*, which means 'to grow, to become strong, to expand'. The yogic term diksha means both 'to give' and 'to receive'. It is personal experience that gives the power to transmit spiritual insights and to receive them. In India, however, the word diksha has retained its connotation as 'spiritual initiation'.

If you happen to refer to the ancient scriptures, you will find that the tradition of initiation by the guru has been a longstanding one. There is repeated emphasis that without the guru's initiation into the spiritual practices, an aspirant's or disciple's spiritual life is incomplete. In fact, it is even said that without initiation, one's sadhana will not bear the desired results. The dangers that befall an aspirant who is treading the spiritual path without the guiding eye of a guru are also stated in great detail.

Initiation or diksha has to be understood in the light of a common dedication, or bond, between guru and disciple. If you are dedicating your devotion and faith to the guru, the guru in turn is assuming the responsibility of being your spiritual guide, the one to lead you from darkness to light, from bondage to freedom. Initiation is not just a mere ritual, although it does have an air of being a special and auspicious occasion. The external rite is a means and not an end. It generates a changed atmosphere and prescribes powerful practices. These practices give the newly initiated aspirant the chance to see for himself the truth behind the symbols. The guru does not reveal the truth in absolute terms; the novice has to discover it for himself. The guru simply motivates him to start the quest or journey towards the truth.

During initiation, the guru transfers his spiritual energy to the disciple, thus inspiring the disciple to aspire for greater heights in spiritual life. In the case of highly evolved gurus, it may not even be necessary for the guru to directly initiate the aspirant in a formal manner. He is able to transmit the initiation through his mental powers.

Diksha is a spiritual, energy-charged communication between guru and disciple. Though it is an external event, it is not restricted to the laws of the physical. It is not limited to the time or space of the ritual, but it is an ongoing process that engages your whole existence. It awakens the willpower or ability in an aspirant to perform the sadhana prescribed, and to thereby manifest all his dormant potential. Therefore, diksha is not just for those who are well-advanced on the spiritual path. Diksha is for all of us, for the spiritually weak as well as the strong, to make us whole and active in our spiritual life.

88

Diksha initiates – it begins. First comes the formal ceremony, then in time come higher and greater forms of awareness. It begins a more intense inner life and sets in motion a whole series of events that will completely transform and re-orient your inner being. Diksha expands the consciousness and allows you to embrace what was unconscious before.

Initiation can be of various kinds. One of the most common initiations is the mantra diksha or initiation into mantra. The guru plants a seed in the form of a mantra in the depths of the disciple's consciousness. In time, this seed becomes potential, germinates, sprouts and blossoms. This leads to illumination in the inner world of the aspirant. Mantra sadhana is considered the foremost sadhana in this present age of Kali Yuga. Every individual should aspire to have a personal mantra. At one level this mantra is mere sound and at the highest level, it vibrates with the energy of the cosmic sound.

There are scores of books on mantras. However, a disciple should not wait until the time of initiation before choosing a personal mantra. An aspirant should receive mantra initiation only from a guru who has attained mantra siddhi. Such a person has realized the mantra and is able to create the same situation in the disciple.

Mantra, the mandala of sound, and yantra, the mandala of form, should be received directly from one's guru. Mantra and yantra are tools of meditation and as such they are related to the psyche. They are not chosen on the mundane level of likes and dislikes. The guru, through his intuitive and psychic powers, is able to discern the exact nature of the disciple's psyche, and chooses the mantra and yantra on that basis.

Other formal initiations such as sannyasa or karma sannyasa follow as a natural consequence. Karma sannyasa is an initiation for householders who wish to include a higher standard of living in their life's pattern. In this initiation, marriage, children and material wealth do not stand as a barrier between aspirants and their dedication to the quest for higher knowledge. Instead, they utilize each and every situation of life as a part of their sadhana. Their participation in life is total, but at the same time they maintain their ultimate goal of self-realization etched firmly in their mind. Karma sannyasa is the path of *pravritti*, or involvement. In this initiation, the disciple receives a spiritual name and a piece of geru or unstiched cloth to wear during sadhana as a symbol of dedication.

Sannyasa initiation is for those people who have chosen to dedicate their lives in search of the highest truth through the path of total surrender to the guru. Sannyasa is the path of *nivritti*, or non-involvement. Here the disciple renounces all personal ambitions, desires and attachments, completely dedicating himself to the service of his guru. The guru then uncovers the inherent potential within the disciple and after training him in the ashram, sends him far and wide to carry out his mission. Through personal sadhana and dedication to guru, the sannyasin evolves and in time serves as a guiding light to others.

In this initiation the disciple shaves the head and receives a new name and two pieces of geru. Sannyasa initiation symbolizes the death of the disciple's previous identity and the birth of the new spiritual being. The sannyasin is born again in the same physical body. In the more traditional ceremonies held in India, the disciple with the help of the guru carries out his own funeral rites, thus discarding all the fetters which previously kept him in the clutches of *samsara* or worldly life. As a newly born sannyasin, he makes a promise to himself that he will always place his spiritual goal first and foremost in his life.

As the disciple progresses on the spiritual path, he may receive initiation into more advanced practices, such as kriya yoga, laya yoga, raja yoga or kundalini yoga. In fact, if a disciple has surrendered to the guru, then it is the guru who decides the exact nature of his sadhana. In the more refined forms of diksha, these initiations need not be formal.

The guru may simply transmit the initiation. However, this sort of initiation can only be given to a disciple who has established a strong link with the guru on the psychic plane. For the average disciple, initiation is almost always verbal and ritualistic.

With each initiation, the link between guru and disciple becomes stronger and more firmly established. The disciple places his life and spiritual quest at the feet of the guru, fully aware that the guru is the medium for the experience of divine energy.

Initiation plays a very important part in the guru-disciple relationship. It is repeatedly emphasized in the scriptures that without initiation, the sadhana of an aspirant will not succeed or bear the desired results. Initiation is like that extra burst of energy which is required to propel you into the infinite space between you and the self.

17

Guru should be One

Continuity is a very important aspect of spiritual life. It leads to stability and is the foundation on which further evolution depends. Continuity should be maintained in all aspects. An aspirant or disciple should stick to one mantra, one sadhana and, above all, to one guru.

In day to day life we often see instability in relationships. Human nature is such that we are easily bored with relationships and material possessions. It is happening everywhere. When the circumstances no longer seem appealing, we become desperate for a change. We search for greener pastures. We change husbands and wives, houses and cars, jobs and businesses, without any stability or consistency. Human beings seem to be driven by an insatiable desire for new experiences, and this thirst is never quenched. On the other hand, it seems to become stronger.

This vagrant mind refuses to remain quiet in spiritual life too. Many disciples accept a guru, remain with him for some time, and when the circumstances no longer seem to be appealing, they leave. This is destabilizing. The disciple must realize that if there is to be any progress, the choice of guru must be ultimate and final. One must not move from guru to guru to obey a whim of the mind. This only confuses and complicates matters. If a disciple can find fault with the first guru, he is bound to do so with the second. Ultimately, he will feel totally lost, dejected and full of despair.

One may receive inspiration from the teachings of all wise people. Often we find solace in the words of great teachers. But, according to tradition, there must be only one guru. Guru is one to whom the disciple has surrendered. Once the link has been established, the disciple constantly strives to become united with guru on all levels. So, if the disciple chooses to have more than one guru, to how many people is he going to surrender? If the disciple chooses to change gurus every now and again, how can there be a successful deepening of the link between him and guru? Obviously, the ties will only be superficial and they will always remain that way. Under these circumstances, how can disciples expect to make progress in their spiritual evolution?

In the disciple's relationship with guru, there is no room for flirtation or prostitution. The guru must always remain the same, and the disciple's surrender must be final.

18

Offerings to the Guru

In India, which is renowned as the home of spiritual culture, the tradition of dakshina or sacred offering to the guru has been maintained throughout the ages. Swamis, saints and sages have always been cared for by society because the people realized that by doing this, they were preserving an ancient knowledge and wisdom, and thereby enriching the culture of future generations.

These swamis and saints are people who have devoted their whole life's energy towards the quest for truth. Not only for their own personal evolution, but in order to bring this knowledge to mankind at large, they have rejected nice comfortable lives to live in abject poverty. They have renounced families, wealth, acquisitions, property, all the luxuries and comforts which the average individual cannot do without. Their goal has far transcended the pleasures of ordinary life. They have lived only for the purpose of spreading and bringing enlightenment to others.

The price they have paid for this inner realization has always been renunciation of material pleasures. They have lived as beggars, sometimes starving, without food for days on end, because they have not had the money to buy food. But they have been prepared to do it because their goal of self-realization has been firmly fixed in their minds.

In order to attain the high states of God-realization, a swami or sage has to be free of the duties that ensnare the average person. His energies, mind, thoughts and body have to be wholly directed to that cause. If he has to worry about worldly affairs, such as employment, money, taxation, property, he will be dissipating his mind, body and spirit, and then he can no longer function as a spiritual guide to the people.

If a guru has to assume responsibility of guiding the spiritual evolution of the people, then he has to be in a position where his personal needs are taken care of by others. Therefore, the people of India, who wished to encourage the noble and selfless work that these spiritually illumined gurus were devoting themselves to, created the tradition of dakshina or offerings to the guru. The disciples of the guru undertook the responsibility of feeding, clothing and helping the guru monetarily, so that his work could continue without any obstacles.

Even to this day the practice of giving dakshina to guru has survived. The disciple offers the best of his earnings or assets to the guru as a pledge of his devotion to the spiritual power of the guru. This offering brings guru and disciple closer, and gradually deeper and deeper links are established. The disciple assumes the responsibility of a son or daughter who cares for their father, seeing to his each and every need.

Disciples should feel that there is nothing in the world which they would hesitate to achieve for their guru. The guru deserves the best of everything because he has pledged himself to the spiritual upliftment of others, be they rich or poor, happy or unhappy, weak or strong, expecting nothing in return. One should not hesitate to serve such a soul.

Many times disciples are reluctant to share their material assets with the guru on account of their limited understanding. They argue that if the guru is truly spiritual, he should not require material wealth. This is a foolish statement. A man needs food to survive, clothes to protect himself from the adversities of climatic conditions and money to exist from day to day. In fact, saints and sages have never proclaimed that we should completely abandon the use of money. Instead, what they have emphasized is the abandoning of our attachment, preoccupation and excessive desire for material wealth. To a sage, money serves as a utilitarian commodity. He does not crave it for his own needs. Otherwise, why would he have renounced it at all?

The notion that in spiritual life one does not require money to live seems a fairly recent one. We have seen amongst the Christians, Jews and Muslims that offerings have always been made whenever there is contact between those who are dedicated to spiritual service and those who are longing to follow them, but are still engaged in worldly service for material gain.

Moreover, in giving and sharing with the guru, disciples begin to receive in full measure and abundance. Their personality becomes whole, they feel complete and there is no feeling of dissatisfaction or discontentment. Rather, they feel as if they are brimming with all that they once aspired for. So, in giving, they are actually receiving. In sharing, they are actually replenishing themselves. And in being selfless in their gifts to guru, they are elevating themselves spiritually.

In India, disciples spare no means in serving the guru. In fact, they offer all they have at the feet of the guru, with the full trust that it is in good hands. They know too that to one who is spiritually illumined, wealth, honour, name, fame and property have little importance. If he utilizes them, it is with one aim in mind: to spread knowledge and wisdom to humanity. And what better way can material assets be utilized?

After all, how long are you going to waste your money on cars and houses and clothes? How long are you going to indulge in pampering yourself? You are only intoxicating yourself into deeper complacency and stagnation. It is better to give to the guru what you have in abundance, so that he may utilize it for a noble cause. And in giving to the guru, you will find that you are receiving back more than you gave to him.

The material assets you have accumulated, the wealth you have amassed, the houses, cars and other gadgets you have collected, have not appeased your dissatisfaction. In fact, you find that ultimately they have caused more afflictions. The more you have, the more you want. Each new acquisition is another reinforcement of your ego. Yet, at the back of your mind there is that fear lurking of losing everything. Maybe it will get stolen or lost. It is better if you understand and accept that one day, you will have to leave everything behind, just like everyone else. Therefore, when the disciple offers the possessions which he holds so dear, he is actually offering his ego.

In front of the guru, you are a pauper. You may have wealth in abundance, or you may have name, fame and status. But in reality you are a pauper if you have not awakened your spirit. The guru cares only for the spiritual wealth in you and if you are devoid of that, then you need his riches more than he needs yours.

The common expectation when we offer something to somebody is that the receiver should be grateful for our kindness and generosity. With guru, it is quite the opposite. You have to remember that a true guru is self-sufficient. He can live in abject poverty or amidst riches with the same ease. In fact, he needs nothing. He can simply disappear into the wilderness and live a life in the forest immersed in his own self. For he has found his centre; he does not need external gratification. Nor does he require the gifts we give him. Therefore, your offering to the guru should be an act of humility, and not an act of arrogance.

The guru is amongst us only because we need him. He cares to teach us out of his love and compassion. Not because we are showering gifts on him and thereby he will become rich. In fact, even whilst he is amidst the world, he prefers to live in seclusion and far away from the hustle and bustle of city life.

Most ashrams are situated in isolated and unexplored surroundings. And they are created in such a way that the life there is naturally difficult. There are often no proper roads leading to the ashram. Nor is there any telephone, electricity, television or running hot water, and the food is simple and sparse. All good ashrams are created in the most austere and severe conditions in order to maintain the constant struggle an aspirant has to undergo as a part of his spiritual training.

The guru's *kutiya* or abode is a simple affair. He does not live ostentatiously, even if he is surrounded by wealth. In fact, very often disciples want to offer comfort and pleasant things to the guru, but he rejects them if they are directed towards his own comfort. He only accepts what he can utilize in his work for people who have dedicated their lives to spiritual upliftment.

Very often the guru is forced to create an ashram, although personally he has no desire to do so, because many thousands of people flock to him for guidance and spiritual shelter. He has to accommodate them somewhere, he has to feed and clothe them, and that is how an ashram is created.

The guru does not create an ashram for his own personal comfort, or because he needs a place to live. The ashram is created for you, so that you may have the opportunity to live with the guru and utilize his knowledge. If the guru travels to distant lands to spread his message, it is only out of love and compassion for you. He does not have any yearning to travel to foreign places and to experience their culture. He simply does it because you need it. Without his guidance, you will never ever find the way. You are lost and you need someone to bring you back on to the path. It is your sorrows and afflictions that draw him into your life, not his desire to travel. He would sooner retreat into his shell and live as a recluse.

The ashram at Munger, which was the headquarters of Swami Satyananda Saraswati from 1963 to 1988, had a very humble beginning. Originally, Sri Swamiji had built a small hut for himself in which he lived, and he did not experience the need for anything bigger or better. But as the crowds flocked to his abode, he was compelled to build a place to provide them with shelter. Gradually, more and more people came and the place expanded. Today the ashram is a large complex of buildings. It can house seven hundred and fifty people, but still there is a lack of space. Sri Swamiji himself had no desire to expand his ashram to such gigantic proportions, but it was the need of the people. Today they come to the ashram in large numbers, afflicted by life, and it is a solace for them to have access to such a haven.

If, at any stage, the guru is reduced to poverty, he will still maintain the same love and compassion, calmness and tranquillity. But in order to propagate the mission for which he was born, he has to live in the world, and it is the duty and obligation of the disciples and of society to help him in whichever manner he requires. Noble work should be commended, not obstructed. How many people are there in the world today who can stand up and proclaim in all honesty that they are truly pledged to the upliftment of humanity? Very few, I can assure you. Therefore, when we encounter such a man, we should consider ourselves fortunate to have the opportunity to serve him.

Indians are very clear about this. They will never turn away a swami, a sadhu or a sage. No matter how poor they are, they will offer him whatever they have. And that is why the gurus have always been born in India, because of the spirituality of its people. In the West, it is quite the opposite. Although the people are more affluent and have far more than they require, they do not know the essence and joy in giving and sharing with the guru.

In India, there is a special day celebrated for gurus as a token of the gratefulness that the disciple feels towards the guru, who has dedicated his whole life to the service of others. On this day, which is held on the full moon in the month of July, thousands of people throng to the guru's ashram to offer him all they have. They do not measure and count their assets. They do not consider what they will be left with if they give their material wealth to the guru. They simply offer with open and loving hearts. No gift is too magnanimous if it is offered to the guru. He truly deserves all that you own because he has pledged to serve you selflessly.

99

19

Mantra

It is the mantra that forges the link between guru and disciple, both in the initial and the more advanced stages of the disciple's spiritual journey. The mantra initiation forms one of the first significant connections between guru and disciple. In bestowing a mantra, the guru is appealing to the disciple's unconscious and subconscious mind. It is in that realm that the mantra lives, breathes and becomes a potential force. The guru chooses a mantra to strengthen the occult personality of the aspirant, and then whispers the mantra in his ear. A mala is given together with instructions for sadhana. Both mantra and sadhana are kept strictly secret to preserve their potency.

The guru who initiates the disciples into mantra is invested with the powers of mantra siddhi. In such a person, the mantra exists as conscious energy, and the mantra the disciple receives from him is a concentrated symbol of realization. After practising it regularly, the disciple is elevated to the same level of consciousness. And the dormant potential of the mantra is ultimately revealed to the adept sadhaka.

Therefore, the first point an aspirant should remember is that he should not receive the mantra from any source other than one who has realized the science and power of mantra in himself. A teacher of yoga is not necessarily invested with this power. It is the siddhas and paramahamsas, who have mastered the science of mantra, who alone are fit to initiate aspirants.

Every individual is made up of a gross, subtle and causal body. The gross body is discernible to the human eye. But the subtle and causal bodies are visible only to one who has attained psychic vision. It is these two bodies which constitute the psyche of an individual. And it is that realm of awareness that aspirants have to unfold before they advance in their sadhana. It is the mantra that unlocks the door to this dimension of our personalities. Therefore, the mantra should be chosen according to our psychic personalities and not according to our gross personalities.

To the average human being, the psychic body exists as a mere abstraction. We know it is present because we have read about it in innumerable books. But we are not able to visualize it or comprehend its essence. To the guru, this subtle, psychic, or astral body is a living reality. He is able to pierce the layers of the gross or outer form. And he chooses the mantra on that basis.

The mantra which is given to an aspirant impresses his psyche and leaves a positive imprint on it. The more we practise the mantra, the greater the imprint or impact will be, until ultimately it transforms the whole consciousness of the disciple. Our whole being reverberates, pounds and resonates with the sound of the mantra. We can hear it echoing in every cell and tissue of our body, even though we are not consciously repeating the mantra, verbally or mentally. It is that moment that the mantra comes alive in the disciple. It is then that we are able to grasp what is called the essence behind the form. We hear the divine sound. From this we are able to comprehend the infinite importance and potential that is inherent in a mantra.

The mantra is a link between you and the cosmos, between you and the deeper mysteries of the universe. Its meaning is purely metaphysical and relates directly with the very core of your existence. Gradually, the mantra takes you deeper and deeper, unfolding the many layers which exist between you and the self. Just as you peel the layers of an onion with a knife to get to the juiciest and tastiest part, in the same way the mantra acts as a knife, scraping first the gross outer skin and gradually delving deeper and deeper to the inherent sweetness and blissful experience that exist within you.

In this process, although the aspirant has the tool or implement to achieve unity with the self, he requires a medium or a guide to show the way. This guide clears any stumbling blocks and makes the journey smooth and certain. Otherwise the disciple may easily sink into the mire, for the pitfalls on this journey are innumerable and very deceptive.

It is the guru who assumes the role of the guide. It is for this reason that the mantra is considered as the link between guru and disciple. This is precisely why the aspirant should receive the mantra from a guru who is able to impress his psyche, so that the guru also travels along with the disciple until the very last step.

It has often been argued that if a mantra is just mere sound, then the repetition of any sound should produce the desired effect. One can easily repeat, "Coca-Cola, Coca-Cola, Coca-Cola" or "tick-tick-tick-tick" to transcend the layers of the mind. To this I say an emphatic "No"! People who advocate such nonsense are still in the realm of the gross pleasures of life, and have no desire to transcend them. Meditation on the mantra "Coca-Cola, Coca-Cola" can hardly divulge the secrets of the universe. At best, it will drag you into an even greater complacency of a robot-like existence. Even a child can comprehend the foolishness of this argument.

As explained earlier, the mantra does not relate to your gross body. Rather, it is the food on which your psychic body is nourished. Just as you eat food and drink Coca-Cola to appease your gross, physical body, in the same way you feed your psyche on a diet of mantra so that it can grow and be nurtured into a living experience.

Every sound has a frequency, and I do agree that the word Coca-Cola must also have a certain frequency. But in

102

order to pierce the layers of your consciousness, you require sounds of enormous and infinite frequencies. Mantras are known to have the ability to produce very high frequencies which can penetrate even the impenetrable.

The exact combination of the sounds and the linking of the words plays a very important part in determining the frequencies of a sound. For example, music is composed of sounds, so also is noise. One may then argue that all noise is music. However, we are well aware that music is a symphony of notes which are combined together to produce a harmonious sound. Any noise that is not able to produce a harmony, a melody or a symphony of notes is not music; it is merely noise. In the same way, any sounds or words which do not attain the high frequencies desired of a mantra, any words which are not related to the psychic and astral bodies of an individual, do not fit into the category of mantra.

A car is produced out of sheets of iron. However, when we see plain sheets of iron, we cannot for a moment imagine that we have a car in front of us. Only when those sheets of iron are welded and linked together in a particular arrangement, in exact coordination and with the right combination of other metals, do we have a car, and not until then. Mantras too are formed only through an exact combination of syllables and words. Therefore, mantras signify sounds of infinite frequencies which have been realized by the sages in deep states of meditation. They have been tried and tested through the ages and handed down from guru to disciple in order to liberate the disciple from the clutches of bondage.

To ascertain which mantra is most suitable for you, you must consult a guru. For only he is aware of the subtle forces that are working in you, and what should be the direction of your spiritual quest. This holds good for yantras and symbols as well. Yantras and mantras symbolize live, archetypal influences that determine your inner personality. And in order to transcend these influences, you should use these two methods as an aid to illumination.

103

However, as mentioned earlier, it is the guru who sows the seed of mantra and yantra in the garden of your consciousness after he has checked the soil. And in order to allow the seeds to blossom and flower into fragrant experiences, you must develop a strong link with the guru on all planes, thus allowing him to check the seed at every stage of its growth and to ward off any imminent dangers which may retard its fructification.

Fill the Cup

I heard a voice from within;
'Siva, wake up
And fill the cup of your life
With this nectar.
Share it with all;
I shall give you strength,
Energy, power and wisdom.'
I obeyed his command.
He did fill the cup,
And I shared it with all.

Swami Sivananda Saraswati

20

Guru Seva

In this chapter we shall deal with the importance of guru seva in the life of a disciple, and I shall attempt to redefine its meaning to give it a total relevance to your spiritual sadhana and daily life. In order to understand this concept, it is imperative that all disciples should understand fully its implications in their life. Especially the disciples who have set a high goal for themselves.

Guru seva has often been defined as serving the guru selflessly in an effort to purify the mind of its gross desires. Although this interpretation conveys some idea of the relevance of guru seva in spiritual life, it is incomplete. The underlying importance and effect of guru seva is far more scientific, as it deals directly with the energy flows in your body.

Existence is energy, the movement of energy in so many ways and so many forms. Energy is never static; it is in constant motion. If this energy is not allowed to flow harmoniously, it will create conflict. If its path is obstructed, it will cause tension. If it is not balanced, channelled and directed properly, it will dissipate and wear you out. Within you there exists a fountain of energy bursting to express itself. It is a part of this energy which causes you to think, to act, to feel, to do. But there is a dormant potential of energy which begins to manifest itself during the course of your natural evolution. This energy is called the higher energy, and represents your total potential.

When this energy awakens and builds up in you, it is as if the walls of a dam have broken and the total volume of water gushes into the ocean. If the path is clear, the force of the water will not do any serious damage. But if there are houses and factories and people, they will simply be destroyed by the outburst. In the same way, when the energy begins to manifest itself, it should always be allowed to flow harmoniously in order to avoid conflicts, tension and serious damage to yourself. If your energy can function harmoniously, then you will feel bliss, but if it is in conflict, if it is antagonistic to itself, then you feel miserable. All misery means that your energy is in conflict and all happiness means that your energy is in harmony.

We have to first of all accept that the awakening of this energy can manifest in any person at any time. However, this awakening is not a sudden process. It is gradual and in many stages. In fact, the reasons why you search for a guru or visit an ashram are because the energy is already awakening in you. The superficial or more tangible reasons, such as illness, mental crises, despair, dejection, failure in marriage or other relationships, are just an excuse. They are the outward manifestations of this internal process that has begun inside you.

Even when you first come in contact with a guru or any spiritual master, a similar happening takes place. There is a spontaneous transference, build-up and explosion of energy within you. You may not be aware that this is happening, but it is undoubtedly taking place. This contact with the guru is so powerful that it can occur just by seeing his photograph or reading his book. You do not need to meet him personally in flesh and blood. You can even receive the energy psychically through dream or thought transmissions, without ever knowing it.

Regardless of how this energy begins to take shape and manifest, you will find a gradual metamorphosis and transformation of your personality. What is most surprising, however, is that this transformation is not always for the

106

better or to your advantage, and therefore you are alarmed. If you are a person with deep-rooted guilts and complexes, they will begin to manifest in you and you will develop neurosis and psychosis to many things, perhaps even to whatever attracted and appealed to you earlier. If you have suppressed a part of your personality which you did not like, it will again rear its ugly head.

Apart from your conscious thoughts, you also have a dimension of your personality which is related to subconscious and unconscious thoughts. Very often these thoughts remain unexpressed and unmanifested. You are not even aware of their existence. But when the energy begins to awaken, they begin to expose themselves, and if they are not pleasant or harmonious, they create conflict and tension in your life. You can manage the conscious, but with an explosion of the unconscious there is insecurity. You will not be able to manage it.

However, there are some people who are able to cope with this situation better than others because to begin with they had been leading a more harmonious life and were more or less free of complexes, guilts and taboos. Therefore, their experiences are those of happiness, creativity, bliss and optimism, as opposed to those who had suppressions and guilt.

In order to understand what I am saying, you have to look at this in greater detail. You have to realize that the energy generated in you assumes the form of your personality which is the most prominent. On account of suppressions, certain qualities of your personality become stronger and stronger over the years. When you have the awakening of any energy, naturally the energy is spontaneously drawn to that channel and expresses itself through that part of your personality.

At that stage, you are no longer in control. There is an upsurge within you, and you cannot be the controller or the one to pull the strings. It is no longer in your hands. The energy will manifest and take the form of whatever you have strongly suppressed, or the strongest characteristic of your

107

psyche. If you have anger, guilt, frustration, jealousy, fear, insecurity and passions, your energy will begin to flow in that direction. But if you have a balanced personality, an equipoised attitude to life and its events, then the energy will manifest positively and become constructive rather than destructive.

I shall illustrate this with a simple example. Electrical energy is first generated at the powerhouse or generating station. It is then channelled or directed to your house. When it reaches your home, it is further broken up and directed to different outlets, the refrigerator, the television, the light bulbs, etc. Every outlet receives as much electrical energy as required. The television set would require more energy than the electric bulb and therefore there is a spontaneous transmission of more energy to that socket. You safeguard that socket with a stronger fuse and better plugs. If there is any obstruction in the flow of the electricity, the fuse will blow or the television set will break down.

In the same way, your body is a powerhouse which is continuously creating energy. This energy flows towards any outlet that is available and plugs into it. The stronger outlets draw the greater quantities of energy and the weaker ones have lesser energy. Therefore, this energy has to be directed and used constructively, otherwise it will create explosions in your personality.

This is the situation that exists as far as human beings are concerned. This is why there is ugliness and misery. Happiness and beauty can come only when your life energy is in movement, in relaxed, unsuppressed, uninhibited, integrated and easy movement. Then every situation of life becomes joyous. Then neither husband, child, parents, nor job can be a source of pain and unhappiness. Then you achieve a total balance.

Otherwise you will feel restlessness, dissatisfaction and inner turmoil. You will feel physically worn out and mentally depressed. You will feel stifled in your environment and sense a desire to run away from the present situation and seek shelter elsewhere. Fears and anxieties develop and you feel an inability to cope with life. This is precisely why marriages fail, families split up, murder, crime and rape are committed, and why you begin to feel hopeless and full of despair.

For example, you are attracted to a man because he has certain qualities which you admire. You feel that his personality is an asset to you and you find it very pleasant to be in his company. It may be due to the fact that these qualities are lacking in you and you have always wanted to be like that. Therefore, you regard it as a positive experience to be with such a person. However, when the awakening of energy begins to manifest, you are caught totally unaware. The same qualities in your partner which earlier appealed to you become the source of conflict between you. You begin to feel dejected in his company; you feel anger and hatred and jealousy. And you are amazed at yourself. You wonder how it has happened.

But you have to go deeper. If you had been a person who was relatively free of mental and physical limitation, free of suppressions and complexes, the energy awakening would have enhanced your state of mind. You would have regarded your partner's qualities more positively and truly learned something from him. But instead, all along, although you claimed you admired certain qualities in him, it was only on account of suppression of your guilt and complexes. So when you generated the energy, all those suppressions were exposed and revealed as a part of your personality.

So, the problem lies not so much in generating the energy, but in the direction, channelling and expression of that energy. You are constantly creating new energies. That is what is meant by life, the ability to go on creating the life force. This is the paradox. You go on creating energy, and you don't know how to utilize it creatively. The moment this energy or force is not created you feel ill, but when it is created you again feel ill. The first illness is that of weakness, and the second illness is of energy that has become a burden

109

to you. You are not able to harmonize it, to make it creative and balanced.

Therefore, in order to understand and eliminate our problems, we have to find a method to balance this energy, to channel it to the proper outlets and to allow it to express itself constructively. This is where the guru and the practice of guru seva play an important part in your life.

When you first come in contact with the guru, there is a break-up and re-orientation of your energy cycle. You may not recognize the symptoms, but transformation has begun to take place. The energy is being broken up and restructured. Very often when you meet the guru, you become emotional and depressed. You may become excessively elated and dance with joy or, on the other hand, you may feel absolutely negative.

The meeting with the guru serves as a detonator. Everything that is in you comes surging to the surface. The experience that you have is an outcome of the structure of your psyche and is related to your samskaras and archetypes. Many times these samskaras and archetypes are not known to you, and therefore you are aghast at the feelings a meeting with the guru brings out. I have seen the most die-hard and cynical people burst into tears and cry like children in front of the guru. These people are amazed at their reactions, for it is totally against the idea they hold of themselves. They can't understand it. What actually is happening is that the awakening which carried you to the guru is rejuvenated and reinforced by the contact with him. His presence activates and sparks off a reinforced awakening, and your inner personality is expressed. The guru acts as a mirror, your spirit is reflected in that mirror, and unknowingly you see yourself.

Now with this first contact with the guru, an inner metamorphosis begins to take place. Everything begins to change and for most people, life can never be the same again. More awakenings are bound to take place and more energy is bound to be generated. It is for that you have to equip yourself, and it is at this point that guru seva plays an important, decisive role.

When you do guru seva at the guru's ashram, in actual fact you are balancing the energy flows in your body and channelling them to areas of maximum advantage. The guru is a symbol of selflessness. His goal is the upliftment and further evolution of human consciousness, a purely selfless goal. It is for the achievement of that end that he is amongst us today. And in his presence and by the purity of his motives, we are compelled to perform selfless acts. Moreover, the environment of an ashram is built on the solid foundation of selfless service. There is no place for those with vested interests. They simply will not survive in such an atmosphere and soon leave of their own accord.

So, when you visit the ashram, no matter what your problem is, no matter what difficulty you are undergoing, it is imperative that you plunge into guru seva. This act of guru seva balances the flow of energy in your body and directs energy to the higher centres in you. In time, the higher centres are activated and begin to function, and you find that you are becoming more creative, intuitive and in harmony with yourself. What had gone wrong in the first place was that your energy had awakened, but due to severe blocks in your personality and mental conditioning, its flow to the higher centres was obstructed and therefore expressed itself negatively.

However, when you come to the ashram and serve the guru and work for him, you are unconsciously clearing the path and allowing the energy to proceed on to the higher and more potential centres. As you remain in the ashram and work hard, you find a total transformation in yourself. You feel better, you think with greater clarity and accuracy, in fact, you can once again look at life squarely. Then, when you return home, you are easily able to adapt to your surroundings once again, and you are aware of many things which had not occurred to you earlier.

The principle behind guru seva is selfless work, work without attachment or interest in the rewards. The reason why this practice works so efficiently in balancing your energy is that, due to your selfless motives, your ego is not involved and you are able to bypass your conflicts and tensions without any direct confrontation. They may still be there, but they no longer affect you because your energy is being diverted elsewhere.

Guru seva has to be practised in the ashram. It cannot be done at your home. As explained earlier, the environment of the ashram is conducive to the growth of higher awareness, and this allows your energy to flow unhindered. If you remain in your own environment, you will find it extremely difficult to balance the energies. It is not that the situation where you live is bad or unhealthy. It is just that at that particular time you are not able to cope. Any situation or event will spark off a negative reaction. With the people who are known to you intimately, you are seldom able to rise above hatred, jealousy, anger and other negative qualities. However, in the ashram it is a different situation. Everyone there is trying to develop their internal strength, and you are inspired by the spirit of karma yoga that pervades the atmosphere. Moreover, the positive vibrations of so many spiritual people also help to balance your energy.

Gradually, in time this attitude towards guru seva becomes a part of your personality. It becomes a part of your nature, and you do not have to make any effort at all. You approach all life's situations with the same ease and equanimity. The ups and downs of life do not shatter or overwhelm you. You can handle them. It is then that you can go back to your home and assume your role as a mother, daughter, husband or son.

Awakening of energy has to be handled properly and systematically. There is no point in becoming oversensitive and emotional or negative. Ashram life, simple living, proper diet, karma yoga and the guru's positive energy are so important for you at that time. It is the only cure that can put you back on your feet. No pills, no psychiatrist, no doctor can help you the way a month, or maybe more, doing guru seva at the ashram can help you.

112

21

Guru as God

It is said in the scriptures that if you have the good fortune to see both God and your guru face to face, you must first pay homage to your guru and then to God. For it is the guru who leads us to this experience. It is he who gives us our first glimpse of divinity and guides us beyond the gross and mundane experiences.

The underlying basis of our conception of God is that He is compassionate, merciful, just and possesses infinite wisdom. The devotee or disciple sees guru in the same light. One of the relationships that a disciple may form with the guru is based on the attitude of devotee to God. Guru is the master, disciple is the obedient servant.

However, this should not be taken at face value; we must go deeper to understand the concept. The qualities an obedient servant shows to his master are humility, loyalty, reverence and one-pointed dedication, qualities similar to those one feels towards God. In directing these qualities towards guru, who is the closest thing to God the disciple has encountered, the disciple is simply transforming his mind to enable him to handle the higher experience of relating to God.

Guru reflects the form of whatever one assumes him to be. If one regards him as a liar and a cheat, he is that; if one regards him as wise and noble, he becomes that. Guru can even assume the form of God if one's faith and devotion lead one to believe that he is God. We have to realize that in guru we are only reflecting ourselves. That is why it is said that only those who see their guru as God are fortunate enough to see God face to face.

Today science has made startling discoveries. The concept of God as someone who lives in heaven judging the actions of us mortals on earth has been totally shattered. The emphasis today is on the evolution of man's own consciousness and thus his elevation, not from man to godman, but from man to superman.

Moreover, throughout the ages we have ourselves witnessed the presence of highly evolved and illumined souls. These people have walked amongst us in flesh and blood. They have been subjected to the trials and tribulations of life, as everyone else. And they have proved to us beyond doubt that everyone is capable of attaining the same level of consciousness as they did.

That divine power is present within each one of us. The guru has awakened this divine power within himself and therefore is a direct representation of what you are trying to achieve. The guru is divine energy manifested in a physical body. The purpose of his being amongst us is to regenerate our faith and believe in the supremacy of that divine power which can work through anybody.

Whether you regard your guru as a personification of god or not is a strictly personal matter. It is entirely your own personal faith and conviction that has led you to this conclusion. You cannot expect others to share the experience, and you have no right to impose your opinion on anyone else. My guru may or may not be my God, that is my personal affair. It is not for public consumption. I keep it strictly to myself. To do otherwise is to degrade the concept of both guru and God.

It is absurd to make a public show of deifying the guru. Propaganda and public campaigns should be restricted to the political arena. Spiritual life is not a circus, nor is it a battle to prove the supremacy of one guru over another. Consider your guru as God by all means. It is your right and privilege to do so. But kindly keep it to yourself.

114

22

All that Glitters is not Gold

Today there is no dearth of gurus. In fact, almost anyone who has learned a bit about yoga and is able to convince a few people of their accomplishments is calling themselves a guru. The world is abounding with gurus, sects and cults, each one brandishing their own system or philosophy. Some boldly declare that they can walk on water, or in the air; some declare that they can give a direct experience of nirvana. Others pose as tantrics and entice people to learn the mysterious and occult practices of tantra. Some teach yoga under the guise of Zen, and others teach yoga and tantra as a lost science from an ancient Egyptian civilization.

The mind boggles, and the serious and sincere seeker can be easily duped or misled. After all, the glitter of brass can be easily mistaken for gold by the innocent and the credulous. The seeker is often unaware of the pretences and traps that he may fall into and his quest can easily turn into a nightmare. Therefore, aspirants on the spiritual path have to be careful. There are many who will try to exploit them and draw them into their fold; to entice them with momentary experiences which in the final analysis mean nothing at all.

A disciple grows by his own self-effort. And only the guru who implores you to strive towards perfection is the true guru. No promises, no spectacular displays of powers, no supernatural feats can take you to enlightenment. In

115

fact, if you chase them, they will seriously impede your progress. You will be befuddled and confused.

Remember, enlightenment is not easily achieved. Today we find certain institutions advertising nirvana in a few weeks. What a joke! The title of guru has been reduced to mere tomfoolery. Impostors, charlatans, magicians, pseudo-intellectuals and clowns pose as gurus. And people, lost in their search, follow them.

Many of these gurus proclaim that they can ensure the awakening of kundalini for a few hundred bucks. The innocent and guileless aspirant is duped into believing that a mere titillation of the nervous system is the actual awakening of his kundalini. At this rate, it won't be long before you can walk into a supermarket and buy a special brand of pills to awaken your kundalini!

The awakening of kundalini creates a genius out of an ordinary person. This genius cannot go unnoticed. A person who has awakened his kundalini will stand out amongst the multitude. Then why is it that so many people who profess to have kundalini awakening experiences still exist within the limitations of average human beings?

There are people who pose as gurus to fulfil their own personal motives. Some desire name and fame, others desire wealth. Still others have political ambitions and strive to fulfil them under the guise of a guru. Some make disciples to get services when they grow old. For others it is a business venture like any other. After all, it is a good way to make money and increase one's capital.

It is for this reason that in India, a householder can never rise to the status of guru. Householders who are immersed in family duties and obligations cannot be free of *raga* and *dwesha*, likes and dislikes. Their decisions and actions will be undoubtedly influenced by their loyalty to their near and dear ones, to their wealth and property, because if you have emotional ties with anyone, then the human factor is involved. You become biased and motivated by personal desires and ambitions, and you begin to use

116

your status as guru to fulfil those needs. Then how can such people guide the spiritual welfare of others? Their advice will be tainted by their personal prejudices.

Ladies are an easy target for these householder gurus. If they are simple and credulous, they fall victim very easily to the sweet and kind words of the guru. These gurus try to penetrate into the fold of women and exploit them to achieve their ends. In the scriptures, it is clearly stated that householders do not have the least sanction to make lady disciples, or to give them any form of initiation.

Many so-called gurus find a suitable partner, get married and raise a family. They are not firmly grounded in their beliefs. Even if they had previously advocated the glories of celibacy and brahmacharya, they remould their entire philosophy to suit their new way of life. They are too weak to combat maya and their inadequacies are exposed sooner or later.

Fanaticism is a common trait of these people and their respective sects. A fanatical guru is simply obsessed by his own theories and ideas. His mind is closed to other ideas and therefore has ceased to grow. A fanatic is a fanatic, simply because he expects something in return. He cares only for the enforcement of his views, regardless of whether he has to kill or loot and rape to convert others to his philosophy. Fanatics only breed hatred between their own followers and others.

The aspirant who is in search of nervous titillation and momentary experiences which ultimately have no bearing on his spiritual progress, may revel in the company of such gurus. But what of the innocent, sincere and dedicated seeker? If he encounters such people, he is bound to get disillusioned. These words are a warning to the sincere aspirant of the dangers involved in choosing those who hide their dishonest and vile motives under a covering of gurudom.

They pose as gurus by flaunting their siddhis. The mere acquisition of siddhis does not make one a guru. Anyone can develop siddhis through the practices of yoga. But if you have refined your personality, if you have controlled your conscious, subconscious and unconscious mind, if you have developed the inner spiritual strength and self-realization to transcend those siddhis and not misuse them for personal gain, only then can you be called a guru. Ostentatious living, boisterous propaganda, fanaticism and cheap display of siddhis and supernatural powers have no place in spiritual life. Therefore, anyone who indulges in them cannot be called a guru.

A guru is one on whom the spiritual power has descended through the guru parampara tradition. He is born from time to time as a repository of spiritual force, which he transmits to future generations through successive links of guru and disciple. He has purity of heart and soul. He carries out his work without any selfish motive. His work is performed simply out of love, out of pure love for mankind at large. The only medium through which spiritual force can be transmitted is love. Any selfish motive will immediately destroy this medium, and it is then that fanaticism, egoism and the base and vile motives prevail.

Therefore, seekers have to understand the true picture before setting out on their quest, and then when they choose a path or a guru for themselves, they know exactly what they are getting into.

23

India – a Land of Gurus

What can India offer the world? This is a question which is often asked. In this era of technological advancement, where countries are vying with each other for power, affluence and military superiority, it would seem that India has no role to play. However, there is a growing number of people who are, to say the least, disenchanted with a world that thrives on the miseries of mankind.

These people have realized that although great technological progress has been made, bringing material benefits to many, the inner being has been grossly ignored. The balance between material and spiritual advancement has been destroyed and as a result mankind has found itself in a wilderness of despair. India's strength lies in offering a solution to this problem.

Spiritual and enlightened beings have appeared in the West from time to time, but history tells us of the sad and cruel fate they were often subjected to. They were hanged, tortured, burnt to death and crucified for their innate goodness. To sing of their glories after their death does little to correct the injustices meted out to them.

In India, a man like Jesus Christ would have been revered and treated as God during his lifetime. He would have been honoured like Lord Buddha, Mahavira Jain, and many others before and after them. India has a rich and diverse spiritual heritage, simply because its people are able to recognize and respect the truly enlightened being.

Every nation, like every individual, has one central theme in its life. It is the principal note around which every other note harmonizes. This theme forms the basis or foundation of the life of the nation. Try to change it, and the nation dies. In some nations, political power is its central theme, its vitality, but in India it is the spiritual and philosophical outlook that is the core.

There was a period in history when yoga was a world culture. There is an open-air museum in San Augustin, Colombia, where a series of statues show that the ancient civilization of that country had full knowledge of yoga asanas. In Scandinavian countries, there is ample evidence that the people practised yoga in ancient times. But because of wars, political and religious accidents and the ravages of time, these practices were at first concealed and then completely obliterated.

This happenend in India too, but there were a few people who preserved the knowledge and handed it down from generation to generation. They were the swamis or sannyasins. The people in India realized that these swamis were vital for the maintenance of the spiritual growth of the country, so they were sheltered and clothed until political and religious stability was restored and they could spread their knowledge openly. Because of this, even today India has a rich heritage of spiritual strength.

But human beings are not yet fully ready to use this strength. One wonders what the fate of the second Christ would be if he were to appear again, as has been predicted. I am quite certain that history would repeat itself. His teachings would once again contradict the established systems. A person of truth will certainly speak against the hypocrisy and sham that is being propagated in the name of religion. Naturally, his words will not be well-received, as it happened almost two thousand years ago. The same errors will be repeated. He will be ridiculed, tortured and killed for his wisdom! Then after his death, the same people will revere him. What an irony!

We need to reassess our values. We need to determine why we have been born on this earth. We have to search ceaselessly for a way to develop in all spheres. We have to accept and reject every system until we find the right one. If the existing systems are beneficial to us, then by all means we should accept them. But all around us we can see the failure of the present philosophy and the inability of the average person to express their entire personality. When the awareness of the shortcomings of our lives is awakened, when we realize that our lives lack fulfilment, guidance and direction, when our consciousness evolves to a higher plane, then we will be compelled to seek a guru. And it is in that field that India stands unparalleled. India is the land of gurus.

24

Epilogue

On tour with Sri Swamiji, I met a lady who told me her experiences during her search for a guru. She was a seeker like anyone else. She had been practising yoga for a few years and it had triggered off a process of inner development. She then began to realize a growing need to relate to a guru, someone who could guide her to the deep mysteries within her soul. She had so many questions that were unanswered. She needed to know so many things. And the question she pondered over a great deal was "How can I know my guru?" She was often apprehensive that perhaps she would never find one. One day she heard that a guru from India had come to her town and was meeting people who wanted spiritual guidance. So she went along, wondering if her search was over. In her mind she assembled all the questions that had been tormenting her. She was impatient to clarify many things.

She arrived at the appointed place and was asked to wait until the guru was free to see her. She thought about what she would say to him, and tried to create an image of him in her mind. Every new thought brought on a new image. Her conception of a guru was obviously tainted by the confusions of her mind. After exhausting her mind with pent-up thoughts and emotions, she began to notice a sense of tranquillity which crept into her. She looked around, and for the first time noticed the room she was sitting in. Just as she was pondering on the bright cheerfulness of the room, someone called her and led her to the guru.

He was seated cross-legged on a cushion. He smiled, and the warmth of his smile crept into his eyes. "What have you come for?" he asked.

"To meet you," she replied.

He was silent for a while, with his eyes closed. Her gaze was totally fixed on him. Then suddenly he opened his eyes and, looking out of the window, said, "Nice day, isn't it?" She simply nodded as if she had lost her tongue.

"Do you have any questions?" he asked.

"No," she answered, "I simply want to be in your presence."

He nodded his head slowly and for what seemed like ages sat motionless.

She got up to leave. At the door she turned around and almost in a whisper said, "Can I be your disciple?" He simply nodded and smiled.

When she left the room she felt euphoric, as if walking on air. There was joy bursting in her. The sun was once again shining through the clouds. It was not until much later that she realized that when before the guru, her mind had ceased to question. She felt a great joy just to be there. There were no questions and no answers to be sought. Her search was over.

I felt a deep respect for this lady. Perhaps unknowingly she had realized the true essence of a guru-disciple relationship. When a disciple meets the guru, there are no questions, no intellectual bantering. Something is kindled and the link between them is established. After that, the disciple's adventure is over. The disciple donates himself to the guru and then it is the duty of the guru to do what he chooses. The guru now begins his adventure. He decides whether the disciple is to practise karma yoga, bhakti yoga, jnana yoga, raja yoga or kundalini yoga, or no yoga at all. The tensions and neuroses of the disciple simply disappear. When the ego in all its forms is resolved and when the guru has been realized, then and then alone does every mental state become samadhi and full-fledged realization. Disciples have erred again and again. They have been neurotic about sadhana, god-realization, moksha, siddhis, samadhi, and have therefore failed to fully realize their relationship with their guru. They simply transfer their neuroses to guru.

For a disciple, the first and last adventure is to realize a guru and establish an unbreakable relationship with him. Leave everything else to guru, then in time you will be able to experience the glory that is truly yours.

Part II

Selection of talks given by
Swami Satyananda Saraswati

Awakening

When the distinction between mine and thine is no more,
I am you.
Then what is there to give, to whom, from whom?
I looked behind and saw the river going dry.
The sun was high,
And you were standing by my side.
As the light grew brighter,
I lost myself and there remained only you.
As the boundless waves of the incoming tide
Break on the shore,
I feel you coming close to me.
But when they flow back out again, I wonder,
Were you really by my side?
What would the course of my life be,
If I had not accepted you?
As the ups and downs carry me far from shore,
You become my rudder and I swim across fearlessly.
With you at my helm, I do not fear the waves.
I find your bosom limitless,
Your embrace without an end.
When I am merged in you,
The beauty of the universe is before me,
Though I cannot name or express it.
Do I love you or do you love me?
You love me? Yes, it is sure.
You offered me a gift of love
You are my love, you are my gift of love.
Every day you come,
But in the dark I cannot see you or any other.
Many times I was frightened when you came,

And I tried to light the lamp, but in vain.
When I asked your name, you remained silent.
As you approached, I heard you whisper in my ear,
But that soon was lost in uproarious clamour.
Though surrounded by people
Again I hear you whisper.
My heart is intoxicated
And my eyes sink down.
The door is opening
But I am unable to see you.
You come and you go, for what?
Why do you come, and since you have come
Why do you disappear in a moment?
I never called or invoked you.
I did not don this geru cloth to attract you.
I renounced the desire for all that is beautiful.
And now you, the supreme beauty, have come.
I was in a deep and blissful sleep.
Who awakened me and why?
Now I am awake day and night,
Hankering for light.

Swami Satyananda Saraswati

25

Yoga Begins with Discipleship

The moment you have a yearning in your heart to follow the path of yoga, either for the welfare of your body or mind or for spiritual illumination, you must accept the fact that you are going to become a disciple first. Only then should you take up yoga.

A disciple is like an open pot; the rain showers fall and by and by this pot is filled up. To be a good vessel, however, this pot must be clean and if there are any leaks they must be repaired. It is not enough to think that you are going to become a disciple now without taking care to clean the pot that you are and without repairing the great leaks in your personality. All this does not happen in one day or in a few weeks; it takes many long years to perfect the role of disciple.

To desire to become a disciple is one thing; to become a perfect disciple, however, is an entirely different process. It must be remembered right from the beginning that you are not only to expect the nectarine showers to fill up the vessel. But at every moment of your life, all your effort must go into two things, cleaning the vessel and repairing the leaks.

There is an old story which will clarify this point. Once a swami went to the door of a devout businessman and asked for alms. The man was very glad and gave him nice food, in return asking the swami to initiate him into mantra and make him a disciple. "Prepare yourself through service," said the swami, "and I will initiate you the next time I come."

A year passed before the swami came again to the same house and asked for alms. The man was happy to see him and after putting nice food in the swami's begging bowl, he again requested a mantra. "Next time," replied the swami.

So another year went by and the swami came to the same house once more, received the alms and the request, and again gave the same reply. Thus twelve years rolled by; twelve times he came and twelve times he was asked for a mantra. Finally the householder lost patience. "When are you going to give me a mantra?" he demanded. "I have given you alms for the last twelve years and you are so unreasonable and discourteous that you won't even give me one mantra?"

Immediately the swami urinated all over the delicious cream and other special preparations which the householder had placed in his alms bowl. The man was shocked. "Why are you doing this?" he cried. "I have served you for twelve years with my food and you have urinated all over it."

"Isn't this exactly what you want to do?" asked the swami. "Your heart is not clean and ready and you want me to initiate you and put a mantra over it. What is mantra going to do for you? First purify your heart through service, and when your heart is rendered pure, I will give you a mantra as you give me alms."

Therefore, in every religion of the world, the emphasis is laid on service first, because by service you are able to dispel the ego which is a great barrier between guru and disciple, between God and man, between man and man. This ego has to be dispelled first.

Discipline and service

In 1947, when I was living with my guru Swami Sivananda, I decided to leave the ashram and lead an independent life. As soon as Swamiji heard about my plan, he called me. "Why are you going?" he asked. "I know everything now," I told him, "hatha yoga, raja yoga, kundalini yoga, and I can practise it all on my own." "No," he replied firmly, "you have to dispel your ego, the ignorance in your personality,

130

the dross in your mind, and reduce yourself to a tiny speck. Only then will the light emanate from you."

What followed is a long story. I lived in the ashram for twelve years and worked very hard, day in and day out, in order to overcome the deep-rooted passions, complexes and personality barriers. In the course of my training, I was reduced to a skeleton and everybody who came to the ashram used to count my ribs and asked me what kind of a brahmachari I was. My mind and body were so totally occupied with service that there was not a moment when I was not celibate in thought, action and in dream. In order to dispel the ego, I passed so many years like this with my guru – in absolute discipline, in suffering that brought happiness, in austerity that brought effulgence and light to the soul.

There are two types of disciples in the world – the renunciates or monks and swamis, and the lay disciples or householders. For the swamis or monks who have renounced all ties with their family and society, total surrender and dedication to the service of guru is the only way to become a disciple. Only when the discipline and understanding are perfect does one get bliss. It is not psychic power, scriptural learning, an act of devotion, yoga or intense sadhana that makes one a disciple, it is bliss. That is why swamis are known as *anandam* (blissful).

Stepping stones to discipleship

The other type of disciples are the householders who must always remember that the life which has been ordained for them, the path which they are destined to follow, the family in which they live, the children they have and the responsibilities they face are stepping stones to discipleship. This life which has been ordained to them by their karma is not for enjoyment, accomplishment or acquisition of worldly things – these are only by-products. The primary purpose of the life which has been ordained for them and the circumstances and events that come their way is to develop the qualities and personality of a disciple.

131

The purpose, aim and destination of all householders should be to purify, train, prove and modify themselves from moment to moment, in whatever circumstances they have been placed. Whether it is education, marriage, a particular duty in connection with the family, the birth of a child or the death of the nearest and dearest, poverty, prosperity, love, hatred, profit, loss, jealousy, greed or compassion – all the things that come in this life are to make one a disciple. At every moment, whatever is happening, one must try to discipline and adjust. Therefore, the life of a householder is as important as the life of a monk.

When the disciple is ready, the guru comes into the picture. Guru is not only a teacher; guru means light, illumination, effulgence. Therefore, when you become a disciple, the guru is already within you but you can't see it, so you project the guru on somebody who becomes your external guru – this is the secret. The unconscious, which at this moment is in total darkness, has to be awakened and illumined. The one who can awaken this state is the guru and none other.

Guru mantra
The guru awakens this unconscious potential, the deepest part of our spiritual personality, by the help of mantra. The mind is the illuminator of all that is existent in the material world, but this is not the only world. There is another plane of existence – the universe within the universe – which you cannot see because it is enveloped in total darkness and you are unable to illumine it. This total darkness, known as ignorance, avidya, maya, which is enveloping your potential awareness, has to be dispelled. When the unconscious is illumined, you see great things, beautiful things, and that is the road of mantra which the guru gives you.

In order to awaken and illumine the deeper plane of consciousness, one spiritual practice is enough. I teach other practices and I'm not discouraging them, but the truth is that one mantra is enough. By this practice the whole of your mind and consciousness are converted into the mantra; they become a part of the mantra. Your whole personality, your total being, are permeated by the mantra which you have so fortunately received from your guru. Then this spiritual practice opens up a whole new fantastic view of life.

When a disciple receives a mantra from the guru, he understands it mentally. Then he practises it with his breath and in every part of his being until the mantra overpowers his existence, and gradually the consciousness of the disciple is transformed. The previous consciousness, which was dissipated, broken and disintegrated, is consolidated into the form of the mantra. That crystallized essence gradually goes deep into the subconscious and deeper into the unconscious where it opens the doors to the superconscious.

Mantras are not simply syllables or words. Mantras are sounds which enlightened rishis and yogis heard when they transcended the mundane planes and penetrated the unconscious where this material world was no more. At first they heard certain sounds which became the ordinary mantras. However, when they went still deeper, these sounds where no longer there and they also lost awareness of themselves. Then they entered into the unconscious, Shivaratri or the 'dark night of the soul'. When they entered the unconscious, they heard other powerful sounds known as *bija* or seed mantras. In this way, mantras were revealed to those who where able to go beyond this material existence. This is the source of the mantras which have been handed down from guru to disciple for thousands of years. Such a mantra can completely explode the whole personality and open the gates to higher awareness.

How to use the mantra

Spiritual life begins with becoming a disciple, then guru imparts the mantra. Now we must discuss the practical side – how to use the mantra. You can repeat it audibly or mentally, using a mala of tulsi or rudraksha beads, rolling one bead with each repetition. Usually, beginners repeat the mantra with the help of a mala and later on they integrate the mantra with the heart beat. Finally, the awareness of mantra is in the spinal cord.

No matter what is happening to your mind, the awareness of mantra should not vanish before your eyes. The most important thing is awareness of mantra even if you are sleeping or your mind is vacillating. All the time, the awareness of mantra should remain constant. Only then is spiritual progress certain and definite, otherwise not. When you are repeating your mantra, usually the mind wanders and thinks about the ways of life. Don't become panicky about this; it is not dangerous or anti-spiritual. However, when you are practising your mantra for half an hour or so, there may be moments, sometimes minutes together, when you become unconscious. At such times you are not aware of yourself, the practice or the mantra. Your mind is not vacillating, but you are in *shoonya*, a void state which is dangerous and anti-spiritual. It is for one second in the beginning; it could be one hour later on.

Right from the beginning of your practice, you must take care that your mind does not become void even for a split second. This is very important. Knowledge is awareness and not void; God is awareness and not shoonya. Awareness is totality, completeness; it is not zero. Therefore, do not try to forget yourself or dispel your own existence. During your practice, the awareness of *Om* or whatever mantra you may have should be there constantly and you must not miss it for a split second. While practising, you can concentrate on the sound, the vibration, or the form of the mantra.

There is a beautiful and wonderful thing in this body and that is the spinal cord. You can elongate your breath, making a soft hissing sound *(ujjayi pranayama)*. Then hold your tongue back against the upper palate *(khechari mudra)* and practise that breathing in your spinal column. Synchronize the breath with the mantra and rotate them up and down the spine from the perineum to the eyebrow

134

centre, from mooladhara to ajna. Go up and down with the rhythm of the breath, practising your mantra. The spinal column is your spiritual ladder. Go on ascending and descending a number of times. By and by, you will find that the different centres in the spinal column become vivid. These centres control both hemispheres of the brain and are the master keys to spiritual awareness. Finally, this mantra takes you directly to the awakening of kundalini and makes you a master of yourself.

QUESTIONS AND ANSWERS

I am looking for a sadhana and a means to transform my life. Can I become your disciple?

It is you that has to decide that, not me. In spiritual life, discipleship is the most important thing. There should be innocence, one-pointedness and stability in the disciple. Guru is only the symbol. Guru is necessary, no doubt, but the disciple is more important. It is not the guru who makes the disciple but the disciple who makes the guru.

I don't have to make you a disciple; you have to make me or someone else a guru. If you don't make me your guru, I'm not your guru. Once you have made me your guru, you can divorce me if you like, but in spiritual life this should not be done. If your guru is not living up to your expectations, you can fight with him if you like, but don't leave him. The same thing applies if you are not getting along with your husband or wife. You can fight, it doesn't matter, but what is the use of leaving? It is like jumping from the frying pan straight into the fire.

What is involved in the actual initiation, and what qualifies the disciple to receive it?

The Sanskrit word for initiation is *diksha*, meaning 'the desire to give'. Mantra diksha is the giving of a mantra. There are also some higher initiations. However, these are not given unless the disciple is absolutely steady physically, emotionally and mentally. For instance, before the guru leaves his earthly role or body, he may want to transfer certain spiritual powers to different people. This is done with great care. The first thing the guru makes certain of is that the disciple's mind will not waver or lose control at any time. You can cut off his nose, shoot him, pierce his ears or throw him into the Ganga, but he will always remain steady and unaffected.

When the mind has lost all worldly and lower sensitivity, it is completely receptive to higher vibrations and unreceptive to lower ones. The lower sphere of the mind is paralyzed, but the higher sphere has become active and sensitive. Only then are the higher initiations given – the transfer of psychic and spiritual power or traditional knowledge. This is what everybody seeks.

Initiation may be given anywhere: on the banks of a river, in a chapel, underneath a tree, in a lonely forest, in an ashram or in a small room. Great yogis like Swami Sivananda could even impart initiation by letter. But to receive initiation, everything should be quiet. The body must be still, it should not shake or move around. The mind must be relaxed and receptive.

Should one receive a mantra from a person he does not consider to be his guru?

Mantra should always be taken from one's guru, only then will it be effective. This is the first form of contact or initiation between the guru and the disciple. Neither mantra nor guru should be changed.

Before the guru can pass on the powers of a mantra, he must feel that the aspirant is strong enough and ready to receive it. Many gurus can transmit certain magnetic powers to their disciples, but if the disciple is not ready, it can disturb the mental and nervous balance. Initiation is something like an electric shock entering the person's mental atmosphere. In same cases, with emotional people it can even result in imbalance.

136

After accepting the mantra, you then become the disciple. When you practise that mantra, you strengthen the guru-disciple relationship and once this is established, then you can become the channel through which the guru's thoughts are conducted. The disciple must be regular in his meditation. If there is regular contact with the guru, one can draw upon his unconscious help and guidance. In this way, maximum benefits are derived from the sadhana.

It is the unconscious mind of the guru which interacts, not the conscious mind. At this level we are all interconnected and related to each other, permitting communion of thought and feeling. Because of this interrelation, the guru knows when a disciple has become unsteady in his mind or when a calamity is going to befall him. If the guru is truly capable, he can even alter the disciple's destiny.

The guru is concerned with only one thing, removing the duality and distance that exist between the two minds of the guru and disciple. The disciple may have certain worldly aspects: heart, mind and intellectual power of reasoning, but the guru is not so concerned with these. He knows that his disciple has to leave him at some stage. Therefore, he must be sure that the disciple is detached from ego and there is complete unity and oneness in their relationship.

Do all disciples have the same type of relationship with the guru?

Well, as I see it, the relation between guru and disciple should mostly depend on the guru, as he has to determine the evolution of the disciple. Whereas some disciples see a guru as their guide, others see him as their friend and inspirer, or even as God. Some of my disciples will not consider me as their guide, but as a symbol for their devotion, concentration and one-pointedness and nothing more that that. They do not accept my guidance, but they definitely love me. So it all depends on their evolution.

26

How to Choose a Guru

Sometimes gurus are in search of disciples. Then the disciples do not have to worry because guru will find them. This is a fact. But disciples are very impatient; they want the best guru, without understanding and knowing that they have to be the best disciple. A disciple can only get a guru according to his or her own development.

Where does the disciple stand? What is his spiritual attainment? What is the level of his detachment? Whether he is a beginner or advanced, accordingly, guru will pick him up. Gurus keep wandering throughout the world in search of disciples. They do not search for disciples in order to increase their tribe. They are selfless souls inspired by higher inspiration, who want to help all those souls groping in avidya and darkness.

Please do not worry and waste your time searching for gurus. Maybe you will get the wrong material. It is better that you prepare yourself. Develop your detachment; improve your sincerity to the purpose; correct the order of your thinking and living; improve the quality of your concentration, and go to satsang, kirtan, bhajan, puja, swadhyaya, lectures, Gita discourses.

It is said that a guru has to be a brahmanishta, but what I have found is that a brahmanishta guru is Veda in himself. Kabir was not learned in the Vedas, nor were Mirabai, Ramakrishna, Ramana Maharshi and many more. It is important that a guru must be a sadhaka. Even if he cannot sing or deliver lectures; even if he cannot interpret the *Brahma Sutras* and the *Bhagavad Gita*, he should be in a position of experience. If he has no experience, if he is just a logician, a person with intellect who can explain the scriptures, he is an acharya, not a guru.

People like Ramakrishna Paramahamsa, Ramana Maharshi or Anandamai Ma, Kabir, Mirabai, Tukaram and Gyandev could tell you the nature of every type of reality because they had experienced it by removing avidya. When Kabir died, his material body turned into flowers. When Mirabai left the body, she just transformed her physical form into light; she became jyoti. Chaitanya Mahaprabhu also transformed his body into light; he entered a temple and remained there.

One who has control over the tattwas, who has control over the samskaras, who can travel within himself and outside, who has been endowed with the vision of light, who can lose his consciousness with no fear of death – such a person is the guru.

Guru is a word composed of two letters, *gu* meaning darkness and *ru* meaning dispeller. *Guru* means dispeller of darkness. What is darkness? Avidya is darkness. We are all in darkness because we cannot see the light. What is the light? *Atmajyoti*, the self, is light.

So do not worry about how to find a guru. Let us become good disciples and then we shall find a guru. Gurus are born as gurus, disciples are born as disciples. If guru is great, disciples are also great. Don't think that when disciples are promoted they become the guru. Disciples are never promoted to guru. My disciples may call me guru, but I am a disciple for all time because I was born a disciple and I shall remain a disciple. Disciples are those who evolve and come to a point of perfection. Gurus are those who descend with the particle of divinity, from the higher realm of awareness to our plane consciousness. Therefore, we remain disciples and they remain gurus.

Unless you have a guru, you cannot become a disciple. It is very clear as far as I am concerned. I am always a disciple to my guru and I cannot and will not become a guru because I think if a disciple is full of glory, he is greater than guru. If I become a guru, my ego will become as fat as a buffalo. And I think you will agree with me; ego is the greatest enemy of a spiritual aspirant. "I am a great man", this is a time bomb. "I am a guru", this is a poison, a virus. "I am a disciple", this is humility; this is simplicity, because if you consider yourself humbler than a blade of grass, you are nearer to yourself and to God, and much nearer to his creation. So I have always been living with the consciousness of a disciple, because I am working as a medium, or as an instrument, for my guru.

A Joyful Penance

Renouncing everything, free from all doubts
Today I walk the divine path
An image of illumination on land and in the sky.
And now you come with your brilliant lamp to brighten my hut.
With your flowing stream of compassion
To lighten and soften the austere life of this sannyasin.
Now my life will be joyful with many festivals.
In the womb of Penance, knowledge awakes.
With scores of cherished dreams, today my bed is decorated.
Penance has come this time to awaken me and make me laugh.
Today I am content, come let us celebrate
This festival of life by working for mankind.

Swami Satyananda Saraswati

27

Establishing the Relationship

When you decide to accept a mantra from a guru, you have accepted a relationship with him. First, the guru-disciple relationship is within the spirit, then that spiritual relationship comes down to the emotional plane and then the mental plane. After that, you are able to understand it and you approach the guru, ask him for a mantra and he ordains it. Thereafter, the guru becomes immaterial and there is only one thing to be done. You have to practise the mantra day in and day out, so much so that in the course of time the mantra permeates your whole personality.

Devotion is a very spontaneous process. Just as you can't be taught how to love and hate, you also cannot learn devotion and it cannot be forced. If you don't have devotion for your guru, nothing can be done; there are no vitamin pills to make our devotion strong. It has to be congenial, natural and spontaneous. Of course, the guru-disciple relationship has to become very, very intimate in the spiritual realm, but it is not possible all the time. There are degrees of devotion and everybody's devotion cannot be exactly the same. Some disciples have lukewarm devotion while others have very feverish devotion.

Many guru-disciple relationships are merely customary, and of course the relationship will depend on how deep and how evolved the disciple is. I became a disciple three times. When I was with my parents, I came in contact with a lady

141

saint. I was barely ten and she was in the prime of her youth – twenty-five years old. She gave me some spiritual instructions, so she became my guru. I appreciated her because she was so radiant and glowing.

Then, many years later, I left my home and wandered all over the country in search of the person who would be my guru. The first place I went to was an ashram in the western part of India. I went there because my sister had been studying kriya yoga there and she thought her guru could become my guru as well. The guru was a good man, aged about seventy. He did not speak very much, he was calm and very peaceful and he liked me. I also liked him, but I knew he was not my final destination.

After a few weeks, I left the ashram and again wandered in the wilderness. I had the name of a swami in Rishikesh so I went to meet him. He was a great Sanskrit master and he lived very close to Swami Sivananda's ashram. I told him I wanted to become a disciple and he pointed to Swami Sivananda's ashram and said, "Go to that ashram". So I went there in the early morning and met Swami Sivananda. He must have been fifty at that time, and when I looked at him, I knew I had arrived at the final point of my journey. And my assumption was correct.

I was with him for a very long time, but never felt emotional; I never became hysterical and feverish. However, the influence of his love and my devotion to him were so great that I worked around the clock without allowing time for sleep and often missing meals. I was working to build the ashram like one possessed, but he never wanted it. Every time I finished a room and called him to bless it, he said, "You have created one more maya, one more subtle bondage." And like this, for years and years, I worked for Swami Sivananda with a different type of devotion. It was not emotional devotion, nor was it intellectual or mental devotion. It was actual devotion; devotion in action.

What is the use of having devotion for your guru and constantly repeating his name while you are seated in the dirt? If his ashram is desolate and his garden has no flowers, is that devotion? A disciple's devotion should become actual. When my guru's birthday was being celebrated, all the disciples used to go to worship him, but I never did, I went to kitchen and worked there instead. The other disciples used to ask me, "Hey, why don't you show any devotion for Swamiji?" I used to say, "Your devotion is emotional, my devotion is actual."

Now, you must remember that there are different types of guru-disciple relationships. In tantra, the guru-disciple relationship is complete. All kinds of relationships can be practised with one guru and one disciple in the tantric frame. However, if you are a householder, this is not possible. Someone who is a husband, a wife, a son or a daughter has social commitments and emotional obligations. Therefore, they must maintain a balance between their obligations to their family and their obligations to the guru.

So, everyone's relationship with the guru must be practical and customary. If you are a householder, go to your guru, ask for a mantra, accept it and wish him 'Hari Om'. Then go back to your home and practise your mantra. Each time you sit down to practise, remember your guru, and at the end of your practice, remember him again. That should be the extent of your relationship with the guru.

28

Linking with the Spirit of Guru

We all have some understanding of physical, mental and emotional contact because we have been experiencing this for so many years. But it is more difficult to grasp the implications of the spiritual link between two individuals unless it is clearly defined.

The spiritual link is not a religious link, it is not even welded closer by faith. The spiritual awareness or the spiritual being within us is still in dormancy. It is not yet born. I don't think it is even in the embryo stage. We can unite physically and, of course, we can unite mentally at any time by developing our extrasensory perception. Emotionally, we can also be one by having love and devotion for each other. But it is oneness on the spiritual plane that is the real purpose of communion, union or linking with the guru.

The first prerequisite

Spiritual union will never occur unless we have awakened our atman. Atman is a word which is not properly understood. Some call it self or spirit, but I understand it to be a type of awareness which knows no limitations. It has no barriers and is beyond the confines of time, space and matter. Physical awareness has many barriers. Mental awareness has fewer barriers while emotional awareness has still less and is the most efficient. A mother can feel her little child and commune with it at any moment, no matter how far apart they are. But spiritual or atmic awareness surpasses even emotional awareness.

When atmic awareness, or *atman anubhuti* as it is called in Vedanta, is awakened, then not only do we feel unity with the guru, we feel it with all beings, even with those belonging to the animal and vegetable kingdom. Atman anubhuti is a difficult thing to explain, but if we want to establish some sort of link with our guru, this is the first thing we have to develop.

A life of dedication and service

The relationship between a guru and disciple is very difficult to practise and even harder to understand because it is non-intellectual and non-emotional. Therefore, we frequently fail to establish this particular relationship, not because we do not fulfil the religious or ethical conditions, but because we do not know exactly what attitude we should have towards our guru. Should we have the attitude of a servant, a son or a daughter, a sister or a brother, a husband or a wife, a friend or a devotee? As far as I understand, it is none of these, although the relationship between guru and disciple is definitely a complete relationship.

When I was living in the ashram of my guru, doing *seva*, selfless service, and working very hard physically and mentally, I never thought about the physical form of my guru's spiritual grace. It was not my nature to think about the person I loved. I found it far better to work for him and to dedicate all my physical, mental and emotional energy to him. Even now, in dedicating every action to him I feel I have done much more than just meditating on him. I feel I have almost accomplished the act of union with him. This has always been my practical approach to guru and to spiritual life.

During those years in the ashram when I worked for my guru in various capacities, it was not important for me to be with him either. Of course, I saw him when I needed guidance concerning the work. And when I typed his manuscripts, I used to go every day to get them from him. But when I was administrator of the ashram, it was not even necessary for me to meet him once in a month because I had my own area of operation which did not really concern him. That was how I lived in the ashram for all those years, hardly ever thinking about my guru, but constantly working for him.

Now I think I must have been working much more for my own inner peace and awakening than for seva. Because at the time I was very young, highly energetic and extremely turbulent, and it was necessary for me to channel my energies in the right direction. Otherwise my mind would have gone astray. Even with all the work that I did, I still found enough time to get into all types of mischief. In fact, even though I was totally engrossed in service, I was still one of the chief terrorists of the ashram.

I had so much energy that I used to swim across the Ganga four times every morning before starting work. When I finished work at night, I used to read for a while, then sit on the bank of the Ganga for my *purascharana* or mantra sadhana. For this I used a mantra which I had formulated myself; it was not given by my guru. The mantra was as long as Gayatri, and I had resolved to repeat it 2.4 million times. So it took me many, many years to complete the sadhana. After I finished my purascharana, every night I assumed my duties as night watchman and checked the whole ashram, which was spread over a vast area. First thing in the morning, I was ready to start work again in the kitchen.

The result of all this hard work and sadhana was that gradually I came to meet with the atman anubhuti; the spiritual awareness took birth in me. Then, quite naturally, I was able to forge a greater, deeper and more truthful link with my guru.

A living experience

In 1963, when I was staying at Ananda Bhawan in Munger, I had a living experience of my guru, as real as this experience of me talking to you and you listening to me. I think I only had that experience because the atman anubhuti in me had already matured and was able to forge a link on the spiritual

146

plane with my guru. So, on the 13th July in the middle of the night, I got the first order, the unspoken command as you call it. And when the experience came to an end, it was very difficult for me to determine which was the reality, the internal space or the external place. After an hour or so, I came to know that I was in Ananda Bhawan and that I had just had an inner experience.

Mastering the tool of experience

In order to forge the link, you must develop that higher personality or dimension which can remain aware of the guru all the time. It is possible and it is not so difficult. We already have the raw material for the development of that higher awareness in us. We are evolved human beings and we can transmit between the three realms of awareness – *jagriti* (waking), *swapna* (dreaming) and *nidra* (sleep).

In fact, the state of dream is much more powerful and efficacious than the waking state, but because we have no control over the tool of experience, we are unable to manipulate our dreams. However, if we can extend the dream experience and voluntarily dissolve or create the dream, we can come closer to the awareness of atman.

In the jagriti state we can only experience the interaction of the senses, mind and objects. If there is no rose, you can never experience a rose. Jagriti is a very limited state because everything depends on the *indriyas* or sensory organs. If you have no eyes, you cannot see; if you are deaf, you cannot hear, and so on. However, the dream state has no limitation, provided you are able to control or master the tool of experience.

What is that tool? It is the awareness of the whole dimension of consciousness. What is a dream? It is an expression of your untrained mind. Just as a baby falters and falls when he tries to walk because he has not trained his body or limbs, in the same way the untrained and undisciplined mind expresses itself during the dream in relation to the samskaras it has stored within. When you are visualizing the samskaras with a defective vision, that is a dream.

147

By means of asanas, pranayama, mantra and other techniques, you can perfect the dream and visualize anything you want. You can even see objects which are beyond the mind and senses. You can create a flower, an animal, a human being or any object. You can create a sensation, an experience, an act or even an entire story. By gaining control of the whole dream process, you can develop your atman.

Establishing the inner link

Many people draw their guru to them through mastery of the dream process. They can feel his presence by calming their mind in this state. And by bringing the mind closer to the self, they can visualize him as if he were real. Then they are able to communicate with him as they would on the physical plane.

So, if you are able to sharpen the inner tool of consciousness, then you can raise your awareness to the level of the atman or the self. After that, the communication or the link between guru and disciple is established. Then the duty of a disciple is to carry out the behests of his guru. I received one direction from my guru and that was, "Yoga is the light, and you should help spread it to everyone." That is all. That is the link between myself and my guru.

Now, those of you who wish to be linked with the guru must bear one thing in mind. Just by devotion or emotion you will not come close, as it is very difficult for the guru to respond emotionally to anyone. I don't understand that language at all. But there is one way for us to be linked. If you work for yoga amongst your family and friends, and if you are able to pass on this science to at least half a dozen people and give them a direction in life, you can come very close to me. Conveying the message of yoga is the one thing I have in my mind all the time.

Sharing the load

As a servant of my guru, carrying out his behests, I only wish for many people to share my enormous load. In the coming years it will be necessary for everybody to play a vital role in the awakening of spiritual life. One prophet will never be able to do the job. Everyone will have to join hands in the event of the spiritual renaissance. Only if·millions of people join hands, will the work ever be accomplished. I am the last to believe that a prophet will come to perform miracles and accomplish the work single-handed. Mankind could not be led by one man today. The contribution of everybody is required.

So, when you go back to your homes and you see that your family members, friends, relatives and fellow workers need peace of mind, relaxation and sound sleep, good health, a philosophy to sustain them and the correct frame of mind to work in the world, remember that you can help by offering yoga. By sharing with them some of the lessons you have received in the ashram in the form of asanas, pranayama, shatkriyas, dhyana, yoga nidra and yoga therapy, you may not be able to awaken thousands (that is not important), but you will be able to give a direction to at least half a dozen people.

You will find that when you are offering the light of yoga to others, you feel very close to me, because I am not a guru, I am a disciple. And as a disciple I need co-disciples to help me fulfil the command of my guru.

Letter to a Disciple

To evaluate the guru after taking diksha is a waste of time. This should have been done first. It is difficult for a disciple to know the guru until he has perfected his faith in adwaita (oneness). Even if you have an iota of doubt, you may change your path without any hesitation. In matters which are not of this world, both guru and disciple live beyond the planes of body and mind and reside in the state of oneness (adwaita). I desire that you should perfectly understand the implications of your decision. Your discipleship is of a very high order. You have to secure my confidence; therefore, think well.

QUESTIONS AND ANSWERS

What is the link between guru and disciple?

I have lived a very independent life always, and have had no personal or intimate connections with anything, neither individuals nor objects. I never surrendered my loyalty to anything, but there is one person in my life who has permeated my consciousness through and through, and this is my guru. Not that I wanted it, no, but somehow this happened. Love is intense awareness, total awareness, non-dual awareness of one person, but in my case this did not happen. I never thought much about my guru, but in my final analysis I realized that he loved me and always thought about me. Even when he entered maha samadhi and freed himself from his mortal frame, he became so much aware of me that, wantingly or unwantingly, I had to work.

When a guru loves his disciple, he is always aware of him, always thinking about him, and he suffers from a 'disciple neurosis'. When the disciple loves the guru so much that he can think of nothing else, he has a 'guru neurosis'. This is a strong form of shakti. In the *Ramayana* there is a story about a ten-headed monster, Ravana, who was Sri Rama's rank enemy. Later on, he became his greatest devotee because he thought about him day and night. There are positive and negative aspects of love. Awareness is love. If you are aware of guru all the time, you love him and this is a powerful link.

In order to know love for the guru, you must practise it. This is not the same type of love that exists between family members, but something much greater and longer lasting. The relationship is neither rational nor emotional, but of a psychic nature. The spiritual interaction between a guru and disciple takes place without any disturbance to the mind, and the guru's presence is always felt. The moment disciple thinks of guru, his mind quietens and communion takes place.

When relationships are of an emotional nature, there is no peace, only disturbance. But the relationship between

150

guru and disciple is complete without any emotional or negative reaction. This is because on higher levels of psychic interaction, the emotions are more subdued and do not play a great part. After a few years of developing this relationship, you will experience how the mind can think and function in a different way and then you will experience this love.

How can we develop the inner link with guru?

We should not concern ourselves with anything transitory. Body, mind and emotions are temporary; the spirit is eternal and our relationship with the guru should be based on spirit. If there is anything between you and him, it is between your spirit and his spirit, not between your body and his body, or between your mind and his mind. It is not a physical, mental or emotional relationship. Of course, sometimes you do take the help of this emotional relationship, but you have to step out of it. Otherwise, the sobriety, tranquillity, stability and homogeneity of the mind are lost.

In order to understand the deeper link with guru, you must read about the attitude the gopis had towards Krishna. Although many people consider the gopis as mere girls who played with Krishna, this was not so. The gopis' relationship with Krishna was transcendental. It wasn't his physical frame that they loved, but his cosmic body. Whenever the gopis were with Krishna, they did not feel they were with a human being. They always felt that they were in the company of divinity. When you feel you are in the company of divinity, you are very much in touch with your guru.

To make the link with guru stronger should the disciple practise concentration on the guru?

When you try to really concentrate on the guru, you get very tired because there is no dynamism and the mind is restricted. But if you practise a dynamic form of meditation, there is no restriction on the mind. You can abuse your guru, you can sing to him, talk to him in Spanish or English, or you can leave him if you wish. You can love him and you

151

can hate him, you can worship him and give him a mala of flowers, or you can beat him. You can travel everywhere with him and you can learn many things from him.

I think everyone has fantasies. So, wherever you go in fantasy, we will go together. If you want to go and buy samosa and lassi, we will go to the market together and I will buy them for you. If you want to visit Tibet, China or the Antarctic, we will go together. And if you go to the bank or office to collect the money, we do it together.

By nature most people are very imaginative, and this is a very easy and systematic way for them to practise meditation and to develop constant awareness of guru. You know, according to tradition and booklore, Radha and Krishna only met once in life. When she went to the river to fetch water, they met each other. That's all; that was the first and the last time, yet they are together eternally. You can never say Krishna without thinking of Radha. This is union of the inner spirit. And this is what happens in the true guru-disciple relationship.

Is the disciple attached to his guru?
Well, it is up to him. I was never attached to my guru, and even now I'm not, but he is a part of my mind and a part of my life. I don't know how to explain this, but detachment and union can go together, although it is very difficult.

29

Guru Tradition

Just as people around the world observe All Saints Day or All Souls Day, here in India on Guru Poornima we celebrate All Gurus Day. *Poornima* is the full moon which represents the highest point of realization, when the light shines in absolute and utter darkness. So, guru is the one who shines like the full moon on a dark night. Therefore, once a year, on the full moon of July, we get together and celebrate Guru Poornima and rededicate everything to guru.

We observe Guru Poornima each year in order to remind ourselves of our spiritual heritage and to re-establish our link with the higher forces that guide our evolution. Guru is the one who has completely transformed his consciousness. He lives in this world, but his spirit is always soaring in the highest dimension beyond space and time. Having completed his evolutionary cycle, there is nothing left for him to do but help raise the consciousness level of humanity.

The guru tradition is not a modern one; it is most ancient. Even before the advent of man, guru existed in the form of nature, which guided the seasons, the plants and the animals. Prehistoric and stone age people had gurus; the animists, naturists and idolaters had gurus. Those who practised animal sacrifice, who believed in abstract gods, who wanted to learn magic, siddhis and witchcraft, had gurus.

The tradition of guru is not only confined to India. The Atlantis civilization had more gurus than any other civilization

153

up to date. South America, Europe, Egypt, Mesopotamia, Tibet, China and Japan had gurus. The guru tradition is universal, but with so many wars and the ravages of time, it was gradually destroyed all over the world. No country was able to preserve it except India. Therefore, we are celebrating Guru Poornima only in India, but if you study the ancient South American traditions, you will see that they also had Guru Poornima. Thousands of years ago, there must have been Guru Poornima all over the world.

The guru-disciple relationship is surely one of the most significant aspects of human development. This relationship forms the basis of all cults, organizations and institutions, whether spiritual or otherwise. When we think about the great cultures that have flourished in the past, as well as those in existence today, we realize that they too are based on this same vital relationship. All the traditions, arts and sciences have been handed down generation after generation from guru to disciple, master to apprentice, father to son, mother to daughter.

The guru-disciple relationship is our link with the higher faculties, the greater dimensions of our being. Without it, we would be hopelessly lost in the external world of diversities. It is only the saving grace of the gurus and masters which guides us back to the inner source from which all our higher potentials emanate. This is why the great teachers have always been regarded as the cornerstones of higher culture. Without their knowledge and inspiration, the traditions would not be enduring, the culture would not last.

In India, we consider the gurus and rishis from ancient times right up to the present day as the light and strength of our cultural heritage. What they taught and wrote in the Vedas, Upanishads and tantras was not an empty philosophy, but a complete science of living. They encouraged the people to strive to fulfil their lives with abstinence, self-control, inner vision and self-knowledge. These qualities have a powerful influence on the whole society. Should all people cultivate them, you can well imagine the heights to which

154

such a culture would rise. Indeed, it would become a virtual utopia.

Our gurus and rishis had in their minds the creation of exactly such a culture. After thousands of years of experimentation, they came up with a system by which every individual could re-orientate himself and push open the doors of his perception. This is the science of yoga. Just as the potter fires his clay pots to make them strong, so yoga provides heat treatment for the vulnerable mind. It tempers and makes it strong enough to bear the upheavals of life.

Although the gurus envisioned an evolved human race, and knew that such a culture had once flourished throughout the world, they were unable to effectively introduce yoga into the society of their times due to the adverse political situations. So they remained in isolation and preserved the knowledge of this system for the time when mankind would again be ready for it.

This was the situation that prevailed right up to the twentieth century when the Age of Aquarius finally dawned. In this period, the rulership of the kings and monarchs passed into the hands of the individual. As people were given more freedom to participate in the affairs of community and state, they also began to assume more responsibility for their personal lives. At first, with the distribution of wealth and the coming of industrialization, people developed a more materialistic approach to life. But today this trend is rapidly reversing as more and more people become tired of materialism and look to yoga for a solution to their problems and a better way of life.

Now the people are ready for yoga and the time is ripe for restoring the yogic culture. Many realized souls are now moving amongst the people and helping to make yoga more accessible by establishing yogashrams and centres around the world.

So today we are witnessing the beginning of a great yogic renaissance. We are preparing for a gigantic leap forward in the evolution of mankind. Soon people everywhere will be practising yoga, and those who are not practising will at least know something about it. This year we are celebrating Guru Poornima in India, but before long it will become an international festivity as men, women and children everywhere gather to dedicate themselves to the guru and to the coming of the yogic culture.

Letter to a Disciple

The secret practices which are indicated in the guru-disciple tradition can neither be given out nor written in books. You know this; still I have to repeat it. Secret practices are not usually given out before kriya and dhyana are perfected. Sadhakas eager for these should carefully observe rules.

In the guru-disciple relationship, mutual trust, cooperation, self-denial and tolerance are necessary. For this tradition is sacred and beneficial as well. My tradition is the tradition of the first Sri Shankaracharya. We are therefore bound by such ties that we are blessed with truth, bliss and beauty.

30

The Indispensable Ingredient

For most people the guru is absolutely indispensable. Of course, there have been quite a few people in history who did not have a guru. Ramana Maharshi never had a guru, but we are not Ramana Maharshis. We are incomplete. Our minds, bodies and senses are confused. There are so many ways in front of us and we don't know which one to follow. We need a traffic policeman to say, "Go this way. Slow down. Now stop, now proceed."

Without a guru, what often happens is that people follow books which describe the siddhis and benefits to be achieved through the different types of yoga. Accordingly, they decide what path they want to follow and then practise until they get some experience. As long as the experience is pleasant, they continue the practice. But as soon as there is something terrifying or even something pleasant which they don't understand, the yoga stops.

Many people who claim to have immense knowledge of themselves think they do not need a guru, but this is not so. When you were a child at school you used books, but still you needed a teacher to tell you the meaning of things. In the same way, you can learn yoga from books. You may even be able to choose a suitable sadhana for yourself. But after wandering in spiritual life for some time, you will find that you are not able to get ahead. At this point you are advised to seek initiation and instruction from a guru, to practise a

157

suitable form of sadhana and progress accordingly. Then the guru becomes the light.

In order to find the guru, you need to search or else to wait for the right moment. Some people make a mountain, photograph or a statue of their guru, but generally it is easier to relate to a guru in human form. Yet a true guru is not to be defined in the physiological sense. Actually, when you realize the need for a guru, you seek the person who can show you the inner guide, who can communicate with your inner self. Guru is not concerned with the superficial level.

It is difficult to find a guru and difficult to remain with the same guru. Just as there are so many divorces in modern life due to a failure of communication, similarly, disciples have been divorcing their gurus because of this same failure. So before seeking a guru, it is essential to prepare yourself by spiritual practices for a considerable time and widen the dimension of your knowledge. Become spiritually mature, then your selection of guru will be without fault and the relationship will definitely be successful.

Don't hunt for a very great guru. A disciple has to judge himself and he should know where he stands. According to his status, he must select a guru. If a little boy in primary school seeks tuition from a big professor at the university, the professor will not be able to teach him anything, nor will the child be able to assimilate any knowledge.

When you take initiation, the guru will give you some small practice which must be done regularly. This regularity is the basis for higher yoga. The guru may ask you to practise mantra for only five or ten minutes daily. At first, this may seem very little to you, but the test is in maintaining the practice. Many disciples spend hours in useless talk and useless work, yet they find it very difficult to spare only five minutes either in the morning or in the evening to practise mantra, pranayama or a few simple asanas. In the life of a disciple, regularity is sadhana, regularity is spiritual training itself.

The initiation which we take is a voluntary acceptance of the life of discipleship. Disciples, whether householder or

158

sannyasin, must have complete dedication to the guru's mission and the attainment of wholeness. In order to develop this the disciple is advised to spend as much time as possible near the guru. By visiting the guru or living in the ashram, the guru is able to test you and show you how he expects you to conduct yourself. The guru may ask you to do hard work outside in the hot sun, but this is only to test your sincerity. It shows that the guru is making an effort to bring you to that infinity.

Disciples are sometimes disturbed because they think that the guru is punishing or ignoring them or that he does not care for them. This is not so. As soon as you accept the guru, he begins to know you. But how deeply and seriously do you want to follow the spiritual path and his guidance? How sincerely do you want to go ahead with your spiritual life? In order to push you forward the guru may use any method, even though it may seem very hard and rigorous to you.

That disciplined life comes to the disciple who is sincere, who thinks correctly and is ready to go deep into the way of light. He does not mind any method that the guru teaches, even if it is strict and hard. But the disciple who misunderstands all these things thinks, "Oh, I picked the wrong person for my guru. This man doesn't like me at all; he wants to punish me." Please understand that the guru can never be wrong because, in fact, everything is within you. Your relationship with the guru is based on your own faith and conviction. As you deepen your faith in the guru, so it is that you grow.

Many people don't want a guru because they are afraid of surrender. But in surrendering, you lose nothing and gain everything. At first when you surrender to the guru, you may feel you are bound to him, but this is just a small control or restraint in your life which brings great benefits. Once you have surrendered to the guru completely, you become as free as a bird, able to fly anywhere and do anything. So do not be afraid of surrender; commit yourself and discover infinity.

If you make yourself humble and open, like a river, you will have no choice but to flow on to the ocean. You will flow by whichever way is meant for you, whether it is through the jungle, mountain or rocks. The river's course may seem narrow at the beginning, but eventually it will take you to the clear, open sea.

The guru-disciple relationship is not for today and tomorrow, or for this life only. It goes on and on, because you do not evolve in one day alone. Regardless of how badly you may behave during the years of your training, it matters not because you are always a disciple to your guru. You may become a guru to thousands or even millions, yet your guru has to guide you. This you should never forget. From time to time, owing to ignorance, clouds come over the sunny season of life. You can never be stable or correct when your mind is clouded by ignorance, weakness or some foolish thought. One mistake can pull you down completely and it may be hard to raise your head. Then, the guru's help is necessary. Don't ask for it too early in the relationship. It is the greatest treasure in your life.

Everyone needs a guru. The guru may be disreputable or he may be a saint, but the disciple always loves him and believes in him. His guru is his life. He may be handsome or ugly; he may be kind or abuse you all the time, yet he is your guru. Without a guru, there is no way. It is not necessary that the guru teaches you how to practise kriya yoga or tantra. If he has accepted you as a disciple, that alone is the light. Through that you grow and obtain the final goal.

It is not to be doubted, you can try, but without the guru life is incomplete. In order to experience fulfilment in life, the heart or the spirit has to have another base, and that is the base of guru and disciple. This relationship completely transcends the physical, emotional and mental planes. It is nothing like the love you have felt for anyone else. Guru and disciple do not consider the physical or emotional factors; they only consider that which is deep and transcendental.

Guru and disciple are like one soul living in two bodies. One is always aware of the other on the spiritual plane. External communication is no longer necessary here, because the disciple does not function on the level where he needs the guru's physical presence. He has the guru's spirit within him which illumines the dark corners of his being. What need is there to talk to him or see his face?

As Kabir said, "If your beloved lives abroad, do write him a letter. But if your beloved dwells within, there is no movement, no emotion, no question of even being together. Wherever you are, you are always close."

The Last Journey

You have gone on a journey in your youthful days
Of seeking and wondering who you are,
And what is the meaning and purpose of all.
Journey on bravely, have no fear,
For now you are no longer alone.
You are protected by a mantle of love,
And unseen hands guide and direct you.

Though your footsteps may falter, your strength seem weak,
Be assured you will reach that goal which you seek.
Journey on bravely and if you feel tired,
Give yourself time to pause and reflect
On the glory of the sublime heights before you.
For if you get too fatigued, you may fall prey
To temptations and thoughts of return.

What have you left that demands your return?
Your days of worldly ambition are over,
Though you may not yet have fully grasped this fact.
You still feel you belong neither here nor there,

But in truth you are already with me.
You have realized the emptiness of worldly life,
Yet have not attained to other planes of existence.

You are not certain of where you belong,
But I know who you are and where your home is,
And where you will find all the things that you seek.
What is past is over and cannot be restored.
It was all a part of the journey of your soul,
And your search to find your real self.
You have begun to realize what you really are
And what the purpose of your life really is.
If you return to the world now, you will be lost
And your life will have been spent in vain.
O child, keep your eyes fixed always on the goal!
You are my child who has returned to me.
Let me see who can keep you from me now.
You are surrounded by love and by light.

Swami Satyananda Saraswati

31

Role of Guru

A guru lies within all of us. That guru is known as the inner guru, or *satguru*. And, ultimately, there is no guru other than the one who lives within each and every one of us. This is the truth of the matter, but unfortunately there is always a gap between truth and reality. It is not enough just to believe that the guru is always within us. This belief is nothing more than an intellectual concept – that is, it is a concept which exists simply as a pattern of the mind. Even though our minds can accept and believe that the guru is within us, this does not give us the guidance that we need, as we are not yet capable of tapping that inner guru.

There is energy present within all matter, but in its natural state you cannot tap it and use it. First, you have to submit this matter to a scientific process which will release the energy. Then it can be harnessed and used. So how can we unlock and give expression to our inner guru? It is to this end that we practise sadhana; with these practices we are trying to create a situation in which the inner guru can emerge. So the guru we can see and understand and whose language is within our intellectual grasp is only our first guru. And he shows us the way to our own satguru.

Selecting the right practices

Part of this process involves helping us find the right yoga practices. We learn about so many different practices that

163

we become confused and do not know how to put them to use in our own spiritual life. If you go to a shop, how do you know what to buy? You see everything in the shop and you want to buy it all. There are hundreds of techniques which can open the door to the inner life. And when you read about them, they all seem very tempting and impressive. Hence it is necessary for a sincere aspirant to seek the help of a guru. The guru alone has a thorough knowledge of each practice and can select those which the aspirant is capable of accepting and assimilating.

The guru's knowledge also allows him to adapt the classical age-old techniques to meet the needs of the present time. The structure of the mind, intellect and emotions is not constant; it differs according to the characteristics of the particular period in which one lives. It alters with each century and with each major political, social, geographic and economic change. What we taught one hundred years ago may not be wrong, but it still might not be suitable for today. The techniques that have been taught in the past were suitable for the culture, society and human mind of those times. In every generation then, the guru plays a vital role in selecting and adapting yoga practices for his disciples.

Emotional needs

However, the role of the guru extends far beyond the level of techniques, into the subtle areas of the emotions. Human beings need many things for their emotional fulfilment, and the extent and nature of these emotional needs are different at different times. Satisfaction of these needs is necessary for the development of our inner awareness, otherwise we will develop what is called an emotional blockage. For instance, many people need to have children or to establish other forms of emotional and social relationships. These relationships have a deep impact on our emotional patterns and emotional growth and, in time, they remove obstacles which block the development of spiritual awareness.

A relationship with a guru is one of man's emotional requirements. But this need makes itself felt only at a certain level of evolution. A child of five does not need sexual fulfilment because of the limitations of his physical and emotional age. But when he is eighteen and has outgrown the previous limitations that had been set by his biology, then he will become aware of that sexual need. In the same way, there are many people in the world who feel they do not need a guru and who do not care if they ever have one or not, because this is the level of evolution they have reached. When they have evolved further, they will begin to understand that need. When a person has grown spiritually or psychically and has felt the need for a guru, then that relationship will become a necessity for him, just as a man is necessary for a woman and a woman for a man at a particular age or at a particular level of emotional development.

Guru as guide

But as well as satisfying these emotional needs, the guru has yet another role to perform. In the uncharted space of the inner life, he functions as a guide. The inner life is a life in the wilderness. It is an infinite space in which there are no directions and no signposts. There is no right or left, no east or west and no up or down. Trying to find one's way in this endless space is like trying to fly a plane at night without instructions from the airport control tower. Wherever the pilot goes looks the same to him. And that is true for everyone who has entered this inner space. It is infinite and many people get lost there.

No doubt you find it very pleasant to think about spiritual life and you find the idea of it very encouraging and inspiring. But I must tell you that it is not what you think. People talk about the awakening of kundalini very casually as if it were a dose of marijuana. It is very easy, too, to talk about samadhi, but in our state of awareness we cannot know what it is. It is only when we have achieved this state that we can know what it is like. People who do not know the way have great difficulty trying to find it.

165

However, if there is a light in front of you at all times, then you know which way to go. That is what the guru provides. At a particular level of awareness, every aspirant feels a strong desire to have a guru. At that stage the guru becomes a guide for him or her. He provides a point of light, a direction to follow. Without this, everything becomes shoonya or void, and there is no knowledge, no experience and no growth.

The guru provides guidance by operating through ajna chakra. To understand this, we must understand the nature of perception. Perception is an internal matter. If you perceive me here now, the perception is not taking place outside of you; it is taking place within. The perceiver and the knower are inside. It is not the eyes which see, or the ears which hear. Every perception, every cognition and every experience that we have takes place within us. In fact, all knowledge and all perception are derived from an inner point, and that point is also the centre of guru, known as guru chakra or ajna chakra. *Ajna* means 'command, direction or control'. Whether it comes from our bodies or our minds, or from inside or outside ourselves, all of the control, monitoring, instructions and guidance that we receive pass through ajna chakra. So, utilizing this control mechanism of ajna chakra, it is possible for a guru to give direct guidance to a disciple.

Transforming the means of perception

Usually a disciple is not aware of this process because normally the only means of perception open are the five physical senses. But these senses of ours have their limitations and there is knowledge that they cannot give us. We cannot see the whole guru. As long as our means of perception are confined to our senses, all we can grasp of our guru is his physical body. But a guru has much more to him than that; he also exists in higher, non-physical bodies. And it is through these that he gives us guidance. But to be able to perceive these, we will have to change our means of perception. And, ultimately, it is not the physical side of guru that we have to grasp, but rather his spiritual side.

If you give a foolish man an uncut diamond, what will he do with it? If he needs money, he will sell it in the market as some sort of precious stone. Well, he is certainly not wrong, because the diamond is definitely a stone. But because of his limited knowledge, he understands only one aspect of what the diamond is. However, if you give the stone to a diamond cutter, he will not see it just as a stone because he is capable of seeing the quality in it.

Now, where does this difference in perception come from? It arises because our instruments of knowledge have different degrees of refinement, and you can only see what your instruments of perception allow you to see. If these instruments are crude, then the knowledge derived from them will also be crude. If the instruments are refined, then the knowledge they transmit will also be refined. This applies to knowledge about guru as well. So the most important thing we have to learn is how to refine the instruments of perception. When we do this, we will open up centres of perception that go far beyond the range of the physical senses and we will see for ourselves that the guru exists in different ways at different levels of awareness. And when, through yoga techniques that the guru teaches us, our total being has been refined and purified, our own satguru will emerge.

Two kinds of relationships

Before the guru can give us guidance, we have to establish a relationship with him, and in time that relationship has to become very deep. It should be established as early as possible in the disciple's life, because everybody has a spiritual mind and personality. These are truly god-like, and it is very difficult to involve those parts of oneself with other people or to express them in any other way.

The relationship between a guru and a disciple is a complete relationship. All other relationships are partial or lopsided, but the relationship with guru is total. Once it has been established, the awareness of guru will permeate your

167

entire personality. When you close your eyes he will be there with you, and when you open them he will be with you too.

There are two kinds of relationships that can be developed with a guru. One is devotional and the other is inimical. A devotional relationship is one where you have positive feelings for your guru. An inimical relationship is one where you are constantly finding fault with him. I have disciples whose relationship with me is inimical and they actually get on better in spiritual life because their consciousness is stable, constant and unperturbed. The flow of feeling for the guru, although negative, is strong all the time. There are many people who have been with me for five, ten and twenty years, who still do not like me, but their dedication to me is internal and not external. This inimical type of relationship is an unusual one and very difficult to practise. The more usual situation is where one has positive feelings for the guru. These feelings are sometimes very strong, sometimes lukewarm and sometimes quite cold. But whether it is devotional or inimical, this relationship must develop if the guru is to become the fixed, stable centre of one's existence.

The trimming of ego

Once it has been established, this relationship must be made to work. And this brings us to the question of ego. If there is an iron curtain between you and me, then no amount of yoga practice will make any difference; the relationship simply will not work. You cannot have a guru if you have an ego. But the problem is that everybody has an ego; sometimes it exists in a gross form and sometimes it is subtle.

Why do we have ego? Because we do not want to lose ourselves. We want to maintain our identities. We want to be ourselves and not other people. Every human being has these feelings; they are a symptom of his insecurity and fears for survival. If you are travelling by plane or train, you do not give your fare to somebody unless you are sure of who they are, because you do not want to lose it. And man does not want to lose his ego because he is very insecure.

But, paradoxically, the moment you let go of that insecurity, it drops away and you become fearless. And when you are fearless, egolessness becomes automatic. There are two ways of getting to this point. One way is first to surrender your ego and then to become fearless and secure. The other way is first to practise fearlessness, to practise feeling secure all the time. Then within a relative short time you will find that your ego has automatically declined.

In India, when a disciple comes to visit a guru, he brings a coconut, a flower, a sweet and a currency note. These things symbolize the ego and its many ways of surviving. Ego lives on your thoughts and emotions; it lives on your activities and achievement in life, and on the amount of money you possess. Therefore, the coconut symbolizes your head, the flower symbolizes your heart and the sweet, your desires. The currency note symbolizes attachment to wealth and money. So, when you take a guru, surrender your ego. If you don't, then you will clash with him all the time, just as you clash now with your wife or husband. Two egos cannot live together; therefore, let there be only one. There is a very special event which can then take place in your spiritual life: when a disciple loses his ego, he becomes a conductor for his guru's energy, message and mission.

To summarize, the first and most important role of a guru in the life of a disciple is to render him helpless. The next is to give him a point to follow in his inner life and from time to time to guide him in his yoga practices. Finally, the role of guru is to give a disciple an immense sense of security and fearlessness, because for centuries and centuries man has been fighting for survival. Personality is for survival; religion is for survival; government is for survival; armies are for survival and weapons are for survival. All throughout history man has been very insecure. But if a few people can become completely fearless, then they will be able to grasp the real meaning of life. And that is what gurus and disciples are seeking to achieve in spiritual life.

QUESTIONS AND ANSWERS

What are the deeper aspects of the guru-disciple relationship?

Mother and daughter, father and son, brother and sister, husband and wife – these are the social relationships through which individuals are bound to each other. By virtue of a relationship, you cherish someone or something in your life – a husband cherishes his wife, a mother her child, you cherish money and so many other things. The relationship between guru and disciple, however, is the closest of all relationships, with one great difference – it has no carnality. It is not based on physical or emotional attachment. It is not a blood relationship or one of worldly love. Between guru and disciple there is a spiritual relationship only.

When guru and disciple are connected with each other on the spiritual plane, much of the disciple's karma can be assimilated by the guru. If the guru is highly evolved, he takes the karma of the disciple, but he does not suffer it; he just throws it away. This is only possible, however, when there is perfect communion between guru and disciple on the spiritual plane, not on the physical or emotional plane. This means that, while sitting for meditation with the eyes closed, you forget the whole world and everything, except for the guru who is always there in front of you – that is communion on the spiritual plane. When I close my eyes, I see my guru. If this is the depth of the relationship between you and your guru, then you can get anything from him – nothing is impossible. Maybe you can even become greater than your guru, but this is not easy.

There are so many barriers between 'me' and my guru, between 'me' and God, and these barriers are so high, so strong, that a disciple can't break them. That is why the guru and disciple behave as two and not as one – there is duality. You have your own personality, limitations, passions, pride and ignorance. You are also not sure of your guru and your relationship with him. Maybe he is not so highly evolved

170

after all. You understand the purpose and meaning of the relationship, but still you have so many doubts; you are not convinced about him. So what happens? Even though intellectually you understand everything, on a practical level, the union, the communion, does not take place.

Where do guru and disciple unite? Not on a physical, emotional or mental plane; they unite in total darkness, when everything is finished, in the innermost chamber where everything is dead. There you do not hear a sound or see any form of vision. You are aware of nothing but the guru, shining like a lofty light. That is how guru and disciple must commune with each other. If I am your guru, it is not necessary for you to say, "He is my guru; he is so fantastic." We are one; praises are for worldly people, not for us. The guru-disciple relationship is also very secret and absolutely personal. Without a guru, the disciple can go astray and without a disciple, the guru can go astray.

How does the guru manage the disciple's mind?

It is the duty of the guru to guide the mind and spirit of his disciple in the right direction. Before illumination can take place, a lot of work has to be done with the personality of the disciple. The greatest problem is that the disciple is very much influenced by what is happening in his mind. If the disciple is not well developed, he is not so aware of his own mental activity. But when the disciple is intelligent and sharp, he becomes very much aware of all that is going on in his mind, and in time this influences him greatly. Therefore, many disciples live a life of mental panic.

This is a very delicate problem. If you try to silence the mind, you lose the mental capacities. Therefore, you must deal with the mind very carefully. This is the role of the guru in the life of a disciple. If a disciple's mind is completely one with the guru, he has to face his mind very little. So, the relationship with the guru is like a diversion until the vagaries of the mind are exhausted.

171

Does the guru look for the disciple or does the disciple search for the guru?

There are certain cases when a guru may have a mission to fulfil and receives a mandate or message from the spiritual plane in which the disciples are revealed to him. Then he will search in order to find them. The visions are not always clear; sometimes only the image is seen and the name is not given or vice versa. It can also happen that a disciple may see his guru in a dream, even before seeing him in the physical form. Then the disciple searches for the vision revealed in his dream. When spiritual life becomes the aim of a person, he will begin to look for a guru. When the time is right, the guru will come to him or he will find the guru.

How does guru's guidance help us?

When the guru's guidance is of a pure nature, the disciple will never fail. He may get discouraged and leave, not understanding the true nature of the guru's help. This sometimes happens if the disciple doesn't feel results quickly enough, or when sickness arises.

The guru watches, instructs and warns his followers in many different ways and on different levels of consciousness. With pure love and constant awareness, he is always guiding them. A mother continues caring for her child even if she is on the other side of the world. In the same way, the guru's guidance is both present and necessary at all times.

32

No Greater Power than Faith

I am often asked what role the guru plays in relation to the disciple's karma, and it is difficult to give a clear-cut answer because the whole thing depends on the depth of their relationship. If a disciple has thrown the entire burden on to the guru, then the guru takes full control of his destiny. However, if the relationship with guru is based on certain motives and fluctuating self-interests, then guru does help the disciple, but he does not accept the burden of his destiny.

Why only talk about guru, we can even bring God into this discussion. God can remove all your obstacles and difficulties in an instant, like magic. If you pray, if you have strong conviction and go deep by stopping your mind and other sensations, all your problems, regardless of their nature, can just be rent asunder. It's quite a simple thing, but still people cannot do it.

Once a disciple had a great problem and he sought his guru's advice. The guru said, "My boy, go and pray to God, he will definitely help you. However, you may find there are many obstacles between you and the divine being. You will have to clear them first to make contact with him." The disciple went to his room and prayed. He prayed and prayed deep into the night. Then, right at midnight, he heard a terrible, frightening sound in the room and he felt that there was an ominous black shadow standing behind him.

He was so terrified that he ran from the room and soon after he collapsed.

Now, tell me, what can poor God do? If your telephone call does not reach him at all and your telegram also doesn't get through, what can he do? You see, what applies to God also applies to guru. If you dedicate, consecrate and surrender yourself to guru and God with total supplication and humility, then your destiny becomes his destiny.

How devotion is practised

I'll tell you a joke we have in India. There is a prayer in Sanskrit which says, "You are my father and you are my mother. You are my wealth and you are my friend. You are everything for me." Now, in India, when you go to a temple, the custom is that you must leave your shoes outside. Some rich people, when visiting the temple, leave their shoes at the door, and while they are inside praying, "You are my father", they have one eye on the shoes. Still watching the shoes, they mechanically repeat, "You are my prosperity and you are my friend." Not even for a moment can they give themselves to God. The whole time that they are praying, their thoughts are on their shoes. So this is how devotion to guru and God is practised.

There is another joke. Actually, these are not really jokes because all of us are like this. In a temple in India some people were praying and, as is the custom, they were waving lights before the deity. Now the prayer was, "I do not want pleasures, I do not want comfort, I do not want money, I do not want fulfilment of passion. All I want is your grace." While praying, the devotees offer coins to the deity. Now, there was a group of people praying and offering coins to the deity. A one rupee coin fell on the floor beside one of the men. Immediately he put his foot on the coin and covered it. And do you know what he was praying at that moment? "I don't want money, I don't want prosperity" – ("but I do want that one rupee coin").

174

Intellect and faith

We have to analyze the faith and dedication that we have placed before God. If there is torrential rain and you have kept a plate outside along with a corked bottle, the plate will soon be full, but the bottle will remain empty. It doesn't matter how much it rains, the bottle will never fill because it is corked. God's grace and guru's grace are showered on everybody, but you must be open and receptive to receive it. You have to be like the plate and not like the corked bottle.

There is no greater power than faith. With faith, anything is possible. And you know what the greatest enemy of faith is? Intellect. These two can never coexist. Just as a man cannot keep two women by his side and keep them loving each other, we can say the same about intellect and faith; they are like co-wives.

For most of us, faith is a very illusive subject. What does it mean? Usually, it only means that you are intellectually convinced. But faith is more than this. Faith is a higher energy in a concentrated form. What most of us have is belief, and we always mistake this belief for faith. Belief can fail and it does sometimes; intellect fails, but faith is infallible, it will never fail. One is so sure because faith is not an expression of the mind. You understand it through the mind, but you don't express it through the mind. It has a different source and a different channel.

Faith is much deeper than thought; it is an expression of the inner spirit. As you progress along the path of your evolution and leave behind you a trail of things, emotions, sentiment, memories, sense objects and so on, there is a peak of experience where things that come within a certain range of the mind appear to be a reality. That experience is the basis of faith.

Protect your faith

You may have read many stories about saints, sometimes stories of miracle men, and also lives of great devotees. Things have happened that cannot be explained in terms of human knowledge. This is due to faith. Therefore, you have to guard your faith. You have to protect it, because intellect and logic kill faith. But if the difference between faith and intellect is properly understood, then both can develop simultaneously in their own directions.

In order to protect faith, to increase and experience it more fully and intimately, the relationship between God and devotee, or guru and disciple, comes first. But this relationship is a matter of total faith. It has to be a living faith. You have to believe even as you believe in your mother. How do you know that she is your mother? That is faith. In the same way, you have to have faith in God and guru.

Most of us believe in God. We love, respect and worship him, but nothing happens. Why? That is belief. That is what we have learned from our parents. They have taught us nice things, but these have not become a living experience in our life. There are many people who even kill that little belief in God by which they have survived on the psycho-emotional level. People say there is no God and they have arguments about it, thus further damaging their only link with the divine forces.

It is necessary to protect one's faith and belief. Therefore, the most important thing in life is the relationship between guru and disciple. We need it to fulfil the sublime aspect of our life, and yet it is difficult to maintain. How can a man have faith in another man? When you are born on the human plane, no matter who you are, you are limited, imperfect. The body itself is a replica of imperfection. You are born and you die. You should be immortal, but the body is not.

When a guru is born in the physical body, he lives on the gross plane where he is subjected to imperfect laws. There are many imperfections – he eats, sleeps, talks in the same way as others do. Once you enter a human body, no matter who you are, you are conditioned. When the disciple sees that the guru is conditioned, his faith wanes, for he sees little difference between himself and the guru. He wants

176

guru to exhibit some miracles so that he can have faith in him, but guru never does. Any magician can perform miracles, so that is not a basis for developing faith.

Mending the split

Faith is the greatest asset of the disciple. If you have faith, you have everything; without faith, you have nothing. Faith is not a result of external observances; it comes by constant inner awareness, not of the senses or the turbulence and disturbances of the mind, but of the soul, the atma. As you go deeper within and face the inner light, you become faithful. Where there is faith, there is power and enlightenment.

A disciple lives by faith. If the behaviour of his guru has broken his faith, then the disciple has lost everything. Once the faith is destroyed, it is very difficult to mend it. Perhaps, as a man, guru is imperfect in some respects, but at the same time a disciple cannot completely relinquish his responsibilities. When he chose his guru, was he right or was he wrong? Now, under certain circumstances which are not pleasing to the disciple, he sees some fault which may or may not be in his guru.

At this point he should immediately approach his guru and tell him what is going on in his mind. He should compel his guru to understand his point. There is no use running away from the guru convinced that he is bad and spreading vicious stories about him. If a frank and open dialogue takes place between the guru and disciple, many complications can be thrashed out.

Search for a new guru

Sometimes the disagreement can be smoothed out and the relationship mended. However, if it cannot be settled, then the disciple should ask his guru what to do? If the guru has realized his mistake, he should also realize his responsibility. He must know that he is no longer in the position to handle his disciple. If he is sincere, he will be frank and tell the

177

disciple that he can no longer be responsible for his spiritual welfare and that he should now seek another guru.

If the guru has not made any mistake and the whole incident has arisen because of a misunderstanding, then the guru must have the capacity to convince his disciple that he has misunderstood him. However, if the guru is arrogant and insists that he is right, although he is wrong, then the disciple must again start his journey afresh and search for a new guru. At this juncture, it is important that the disciple does not react. Most do, and they cultivate the belief that a guru is not necessary. Then they express this opinion to as many people as they can. But the disciple who is a true seeker will think calmly and quietly and accept that the guru with whom he has lived was not able to convince him and therefore it is his duty to look for one who can.

Quality of the disciple

There is also another point of view regarding this subject. Sometimes the disciple is related to the guru by faith and not by the high qualification of the guru. In this type of relationship, it is the disciple who has something special in him, and not the guru. The quality of a disciple is his absolute faith, unflinching devotion and total absence of a critical mind. It does not matter how wretched and bogus the guru is. If the disciple has absolute faith, it will bring him face to face with the inner guru. Such a disciple is greater than his guru.

If the guru lacks faith and the disciple has faith, then the whole work is accomplished completely. If the guru has faith and the disciple has none, even then the task can be accomplished. If the guru has no faith and the disciple also has no power of faith, then both are doomed to destruction and despair. However, I don't believe such situations ever occur.

About a year ago a lady came to me complaining bitterly about her guru. She had a lot of written complaints and she was passing them around amongst the people. I tried my

178

level best to resurrect her faith because I knew what could happen. If the guru had faith, even though she had none, everything would be all right. But if the guru had no faith and she had no faith, then she would be spiritually destroyed.

Actually, her point of view was absurd. She did not say that her guru could not guide her and she did not say he was bad or criminal by character. She only said that she had been in touch with some hierarchies, including Lord Buddha, and they told her that she did not have the right guru. I said, "If you are such a great person that you can communicate with Lord Buddha, forget your guru completely. Actually, you should be his guru." One more thing she mentioned was that her guru makes a lot of money. I told her, "This is your view. You were born in the West, and money is the ultimate there. So you see these negative things in him." I am not sure if I was able to convince that respected lady.

Father of miracles

If you have faith, you have hope and if you can strengthen your faith, you can do great things in life. The purpose of all the different rituals we have in life is to strengthen, revive and resurrect the faith. When you lose faith, you lose hope, and then everything in life is lost. Those people who have broken hearts have lost their vision of faith.

When you practise yoga or mantra, or when you approach your guru, you are strengthening your faith. But to keep your faith strong all the time, you must remain intimately connected with your guru. If you begin to doubt him and if your mind is filled with negativity towards him, you are assassinating your faith.

In all the scriptural books, it says very clearly that a sadhaka must take care that his faith is not subject to confusion. It is also said, "Don't worry if your wealth is lost, don't worry if your body fails or if you are reduced to poverty and become a pauper, but protect your faith. Even if you have lost everything else in life, faith will bring it all

179

back, because faith is the mother and father of miracles. Anything can happen, anything can be accomplished if you have that faith."

Remember, faith is not belief; it is a stronger force than that. With powerful faith you can control nature and even material substances. And in order to strengthen faith, first comes guru. Lay your head and heart and body before him. You belong to him and he belongs to you. And when negative thoughts come into your mind, please remember that maya is playing a game and it could bring disaster. It is very difficult to be a faithful disciple.

QUESTIONS AND ANSWERS

How does one find out if the guru he has selected is a true master, a realized soul?

If you have such doubts in your mind, it is better to wait. Even as love is blind, so is faith. Love and faith are free from any intellectual interference and this question is a direct intellectual interference with your faith.

When you see the *murti* (form) of your ishta devata, you fall in love with him. It is not the *buddhi* (intellect) which decides. It is with your heart and your *bhavana* (inner feeling) that you begin to love that murti and always remember it. In the same way, when you meet your guru, if you analyze him intellectually as a spiritual, moral or academic individual, then you are not going to get anywhere.

If you judge your guru with your bhavana instead of with your buddhi, you will not recognize the loopholes which every guru has, no matter who he is. Once a guru or even an avatar is born into a physical body, undoubtedly he has some flaws because his physical body is governed by its own dharma. And if you begin to search for the loopholes in your guru, you will not find one; you will find thousands.

Please understand one thing. If you look for a guru with your intellect, you are not going to find one, because there is no one who can fulfil your intellectual needs. Guru is not an intellectual need, just as love or marital life is not an intellectual need.

How is the guru-disciple relationship formed?

In deciding one's spiritual relationship with guru, one's eternal relationship with the supreme being, absolute sincerity and devotion are required. When you enter into a relationship with the guru, it is very important that he should be able to handle you without any difficulty. So the disciple could be compared with a pet dog. Of course, the necessity of the guru in teaching yoga or meditation is always there, but in forming the guru-disciple relationship on a practical level, it is the guru's knowledge, experience and ability to direct the awareness of the disciple that is important.

For that purpose, gurus give different sorts of exercises to check whether the disciple's awareness is responding. If the disciple does not respond to the guru's hints, instructions, suggestions or inspiration on this ordinary intellectual level, then how can the guru direct him in that higher realm? If the guru is not able to direct his disciple's conscious thinking, how can he direct his dreams? Guru should be able to influence and direct his disciple's mind in any direction – right, left, up, down, into the ditch, into the river, into the fire. And the disciple says, "Take my life and let it be." That is the concept of guru-disciple relationship.

Why does the disciple lose faith in the guru?

Faith is spontaneous, you can't force it. In order to have faith in your guru, you need some deep, inner basis. If that faith is wavering, it could be that your mind is vacillating or that the guru is creating a drama. The faith that the disciple has in his guru is seldom constant because the disciple is in the human body and so is the guru. As guru and disciple live intimately, the intimacy often brings contempt and dissatisfaction.

Sometimes the guru is also testing the disciple. Whenever a cyclone takes place in the mind of a disciple, he must clearly know that it is either a trick of the mind or a trick of the guru. In any case, it is a trick. So wait for a minute, please, the tempest will calm down and the sun of faith will shine again.

I don't believe that faith can be intensified because I know that everybody has absolute faith. If you do not have absolute faith in your guru, it does not mean that it isn't there. It only means that the dust storms are hiding the faith. Wait with patience and the dust will clear. Then the faith which is inherent in you will shine like the sun.

I have little faith in the ideals of spiritual life or in the concept of guru. How can I change this?
Go to an ashram, live with the guru for some time and involve yourself in selfless service. If you change the order of mental activity and live in a completely new situation, your mind will undergo a great change.

What is the difference between faith and religious belief?
Faith is not just religious belief, it is an inner conviction which comes after the total surrender of ego. Faith is an effulgence which is in every person. When you surrender your ego in totality, then faith unfolds by itself; you don't have to import it from the scriptures. Faith is the inherent quality of every being, but it is hidden behind clouds and wrapped in ignorance. So, the first and foremost duty of one who is a candidate for discipleship is to unfold this faith.

The nature of faith is almost identical to the innocence of a child. Innocence is an expression of total purity. When you are in absolute association with inner purity, only then can you be innocent. People may look and act innocent; that is called diplomacy, the political character of man. But faith is his real being. A child has faith in its mother. In the same way, this quality of faith when it unfolds makes you perfectly innocent, removing intellectual logic, fears, insecurities and doubts.

182

33

Qualifications of Guru

The guru should be chosen with a background of faith; the one who has faith will find a guru. People who are sincerely seeking the spiritual way of life will become disillusioned with the miracle performers and the gurus who exhibit siddhis for selfish reasons. The self-realized guru is high on the spiritual plane, beyond the psychic plane from which these powers arise. He has no need to perform these siddhis for his disciples. If you seek a guru, then you must approach with an unselfish heart and pure faith. Then you will find your true guru. Pure faith will never fail you. But the search also depends on your state of consciousness. If you seek money, you will find money; if you search for a guru with a selfish purpose and an ignorant background, then those who display powers will appear.

It is important that the guru or teacher from whom we learn the science of yoga is qualified. One of the most important qualifications is that he has established himself in peace and unity. This concerns his own mind and personality. If he is restless, unstable and caught within the storms of life, at the most he can be a tutor.

Yoga is not just a science to be learned like biology, botany or chemistry. Yoga is a science which we learn, not only for the sake of knowledge, but in order to cast its positive influence on our mind, body and emotions. Therefore, the guru or teacher is also supposed to lend a part of his personal vibrations, magnetism and qualities along with the teaching. This is precisely the reason why many times when you go to learn yoga from a teacher, although you know many things already and you can discuss them, when you really think about it, you feel that in your spiritual life or in the realm of your internal personality, you have gained nothing.

What can a teacher of yoga give to you? He can give you knowledge or an experience. Knowledge is confined to the intellectual domain. That is your intellectual knowledge. Experience is something which you imbibe, which you have. What is the experience in yoga? Facing life with peace, courage and understanding. Life is not a flat plane, or just a simple path. It is a series of experiences of ups and downs, some on the economic plane, some on the emotional plane and some on the spiritual plane. And the teaching and inspiration that a real guru can give you cannot be given by instructions. They can only be given by an emanation of his personality, which is completely independent of the intellect.

I may have studied Latin or Sanskrit. I may have mastered the Bible, the Vedas and the Koran – that is different. I may have learned nothing, intellectually speaking, neither Latin nor Greek nor Sanskrit. However, I might have attained equilibrium, harmony, understanding and the totality of my personality. That I can give you, and that is called spiritual emanation.

When you go to a guru or teacher, do not look for certificates or the amount of knowledge he possesses. True, sometimes certificates are necessary for opening an institution, but for a disciple or student they are not important. Instead see if there is complete agreement between the two lobes of your teacher's brain.

The right and left side of the brain are generally in conflict. What the right brain thinks, the left side is discharging and what the left brain is trying to think about, the right brain is criticizing all the time. That is the source of conflict in our behaviour. A harmony between these two

hemispheres in our head is very necessary. In fact, in India they often ask the question, "Who is guru?" The ultimate answer is, "One who has experienced peace within himself." And when you know that the teacher of yoga is well disciplined and has united in silence within himself, and that he can give you an experience of peace, then he is a person who has stabilized his consciousness.

In the *Bhagavad Gita* the question is answered properly. Arjuna is the name of the great hero, the commander-in-chief. Krishna, whose name you sing, was his charioteer. Krishna was a very important personality in our history, who played very important roles, including the role of a yoga teacher and guru.

In the second chapter, verse 56, Arjuna puts the question, "What is the definition of one who has united the mundane consciousness with the divine or higher consciousness? And when a person has stabilized this consciousness, how does he speak, how does he move and how does he think?"

Krishna replies to Arjuna's question up to verse 73, and in one of the verses he says, "The teacher or the guru should be able to express himself or to withdraw himself like a tortoise." The turtle is able to expand the limbs of his body whenever he wants, and withdraw all his limbs whenever he is in danger. In the same way, you should be able to involve yourself in the life of the senses, that is the day to day life, but when you find that it is getting dangerous, immediately withdraw yourself. Well, you know that the interaction between the senses and the sense objects is going to lead you to accidents, but still you are not able to withdraw. The teacher or the guru must have such command over the behaviour of his senses and the mind. The verses of the *Bhagavad Gita* should be the guideline for all disciples and students to understand their gurus or teachers. When the guru has a right to screen his disciple, the disciples should also have something by which to screen the guru.

34

Surrendering the Ego

The real guru is within everybody. The external guru is not the real guru. Therefore, we use two terms – guru and satguru. *Guru* means 'the one who teaches outside', and *satguru* means 'inner guru'. Now, everybody has within them an inner guru which they have to find. In order to find this inner guru, you have to develop your inner vision, your inner consciousness. In order to develop these, you need a support in the beginning. The support has to be a very enlightened and experienced person, not just anybody.

Significance of guru

A teacher is not a guru and a guru is not a teacher. The literal meaning of guru is the dispeller of darkness. In this room there are many things. If you come to this room in the night when it is very dark and you want to find your key, you will not find it. So, what do you do? You shine a torch. Then you can see everything and you will find what you want. The outer guru is the torchlight. He dispels the darkness. He helps you that much.

This inner darkness is a very important point in spiritual life. What is that darkness? I am not talking about ethics and morality, please remember. No, when you can only see this world, you cannot see beyond this, and that is darkness. This world which you see with your eyes and the senses and the mind is not the only world. There are many things existing beyond this, but you don't see them. There are many people existing around you, there are beautiful worlds nearby, but you cannot see them. There is beautiful music going on, but you cannot hear it. There are many fragrances other than the fragrance of these flowers, but you cannot smell them. Why? Because there is darkness. And because of this darkness you are unable to experience these objects and your own self.

I am not talking about everybody, I am talking about a few people. We think the whole day practically, but can you see your thoughts? No, you cannot see your thoughts, your emotions, your fears. That is your incapacity, your disqualification. When you cannot see your thoughts, how can you see your self?

So the external guru comes to you as a torchlight and then your inner mind is enlightened or illumined. In that illumined state of mind, you realize your inner guru. This is the significance of guru.

Guru explodes the consciousness

When you choose a guru for yourself, what you are doing exactly is fixing a detonator. The bomb is there, but it is not detonated. Every bomb has to have a detonator in order to explode. There are different types of detonators. The inner guru is like the bombshell, let us say. And the external guru is the detonator. Now you may say, "Well, if the guru is inside me, I don't need an external guru." But that is wrong because although the guru is within you, do you hear him? Do you see him? Do you receive his guidance from time to time? If so, you don't need an external guru. If not, then you do need an external guru just because the inner guru is beyond comprehension. He is beyond the reach of your knowledge and understanding. You just believe that he exists, but you don't know him. There is an object a hundred miles away, but you cannot see it. There is no use telling you it is there. You must have binoculars to see the object.

187

To realize the inner guru, you need an external guru first. And this external guru becomes an important influence in your mind by exploding your inner consciousness like a volcano. In this volcano each and every thought, emotion, memory and past experience becomes a vision. You can see in the form of visions, experiences, dreams, feelings. And that is the capacity which you develop through guru.

Behind the iron curtain

It is true that the inner guru is in you, but there is a barrier between your inner guru and yourself, and that is the ego. Ego is the substratum of our human existence. Without ego, your intellect cannot function. Without ego, there is no duality, no distinction, no survival of self-consciousness. Therefore, ego is an essential factor behind everybody's existence.

In animals and other incarnations, the ego is subdued. It is undeveloped, unmanifest. But in us the ego is exposed. I know I am. I know that I know that I know. That individuality through which we relate with the entire creation, with our lovers and enemies, with the objects of attachment, with the sun, moon, stars and clouds, with flowers, with children, with government, religion, church and temple, that is ego. It is through ego that you are related with everything around you.

This ego is very strong in human beings. It is like an iron curtain between yourself and the guru, between yourself and spiritual vision. To remove this ego is a very difficult task because before you can remove it, you must know it is there. As far as you know about yourself, you are perfectly all right. And everybody thinks the same way as you think: "I am all right, I don't have much ego, maybe I have a little bit." Everybody has a very noble and grand idea about themselves. Even people who are suffering from an inferiority complex have a very grand idea about themselves. In order to cover that inferiority complex, they pose as grandiose: "I am okay. I know gardening, I know swimming, I know how to talk, I know how to tackle the people." You see, these things are there.

Guru points out the ego

This ego has to be pruned, but who is going to do it for you? Your wife can never do it. If she tells you anything, she gets a kick from you. Your husband can never do it. If he does, he gets half a dozen abuses. Your son can never do it. If he does, you will say, "Keep quiet. You are a kid, sit down." Your father cannot do it. If he says you have ego, you will say, "Your times are gone; our times are different." Nobody can point out your ego to you; even I cannot point it out. If I say anything at all, you are going to throw me out. Many times I tell my disciples, "Look here, you should not do this." They say, "Swamiji, you are sixty and we are twenty. We know how to tackle our matters."

Even the guru finds it difficult to point out the ego. Only a guru who has so much endurance, understanding and patience can do it. And he tries and tries and tries to awaken the ego of the disciple, first by loving him, then by inspiring him, then by teaching him sadhana. By so many ways, the ego is brought out. And when the ego is brought out, guru gives a kick, because when the ego comes out, you never know it. You know only when you get a kick. "Oh, I had ego."

This ego is not merely pride; there are thousands of forms of ego. There is a very simple story. Once a disciple was practising sadhana in his hermitage. It was about ten p.m. and it was raining. A young lady knocked at his door and he opened it. She said that she needed shelter because it was raining. He said, "Okay come in." It was very difficult for the disciple to get a sound sleep that night. He was turning to the right and the left and asking the girl, "Are you asleep?" The girl was snoring, but the poor disciple was not able to sleep. So he started putting on the light and going to the bathroom, and doing so many things.

Eventually, she got up and he asked, "Are you all right?" She said, "Yes, I am all right." He said, "But I

189

heard you crying." Actually, she was not crying, but he wanted to peep at her. She said, "Maybe I was crying." He said, "I think you have a fever, can I shampoo your feet?" She said, "Okay, do it." When he shampooed her feet, the guru changed his disguise. Suddenly the guru appeared and it was such a surprise. The girl was none other than his guru.

Guru is a mirror

You see, this is how the ego is exploded and crushed. And crushing of the ego in relation to every manifestation of mind is necessary, because in one realm of samadhi, when you are transcending this mind, and when you are taking off, you have to see that there is no pull of gravity that keeps you to this lower plane. The speed has to be very high in order to take off. The consciousness leaves the empirical base and at one point you have to stop.

So, in my opinion, it is always good to have a guru, live with him for some time and get a few kicks, a few blows and let him criticize you. Yes, that is an important point. I don't know if people like to be criticized. I also don't like to be criticized because this is my personality and this is my ego. But you must see that there is someone who can criticize you, and you will have to accept it.

If there is anything in spiritual life that can purify your consciousness, that is criticism. But the problem is you don't criticize yourself. You don't allow anybody to criticize you, so let there be a guru who should criticize you. You have a mirror in your bathroom. Why do you have it? It makes no change. If you are fair, you are fair; if you are black, you are black; if you are brown, you are brown. The mirror does not make any change, but still there is a mirror. In the same way, there should be a mirror in which you can peep and see your tendencies reflected. Your instincts are reflected, your ego is reflected, your emotions are reflected, all your idiosyncrasies are reflected. Every shade of thought is reflected. And that mirror is a guru.

Real gurus do not try to please their disciples. They tell things point blank. And the gurus who are not really gurus and benefactors, I don't know what you call them, they always say very soft and tender things to their disciples so they can get the best out of them. If I talk nicely about you, you will do a lot of work for me, you will give me a lot of donations. It is nice, it is practical, but the gurus need not be practical along these lines. They have to tell the truth, but then the disciple must also be ready to face the truth.

There is an old story and it is true. I can tell you so many stories but perhaps this one will already be known to you. A hundred miles south from where I stay in India is a place called Nalanda, which was one of the oldest universities of India. It flourished about two thousand years ago and had a residential capacity of about ten thousand students, with sixty-four subjects being taught. It is the same university in which Christ spent thirteen years of his life. From there a tradition of gurus started and went to Tibet: Tilopa, Naropa, Maropa.

Marpa took Buddhism to Tibet. After some time, one morning a young boy of ten or twelve came to his house and asked the guru to teach him the science of spiritual illumination. The guru looked at the boy and said, "You dirty rascal, you want illumination. I will give you a kick. Get out of here." Well, the boy went, but he sat just outside the guru's door. Guru took his food inside and did his work there. At midday when he went out, he found the fellow was sitting at his door. "What, you are still here!" he exclaimed and gave him a kick. "Get out of here," he shouted, "I don't want to see you again." The boy said, "But I have come for initiation." The guru said, "No, no, you are fit for nothing, you are wretched, you are a pig, a swine."

He gave him all kinds of abuse, but the boy did not leave the place because he was prepared. He had prepared his ego to be attacked, pruned and disintegrated. His name was Milarepa. He later became a great yogi of Tibet.

Every time the guru went out, he gave the boy abuse. He gave him very bad and stale meat. It stank and was hard to bite, like leather. One day the guru went out and the guru's wife brought the boy fresh, hot meat. She said, "Hey, my boy, take it." While he was eating the meat, the guru returned and shouted angrily, "Oh, I know what is conspiring between you and my wife. No, I cannot go on. I will kill you both." He gave a kick to his wife and she fell down. Then he turned to the boy and said, "You rascal, get out of here. You cannot stay near my door; you make your cottage on that hillock."

That poor boy had to carry large boulders up the steep mountain every day, boulder by boulder. And when he had collected the boulders, he built himself a small house. When the house was competed, Milarepa.wanted to stay there. The guru said, "I am going to inspect it." He went and looked at the house and said, "This is a beautiful house, but it is not good. If you stay here, you are going to become lazy. You are going to sleep and nobody is going to tell you what to do. It is better you come down."

So, the whole house had to be dismantled, block by block, and the boy carried the boulders back down the mountain. Now, tell me, who was crazy, the guru or the disciple? If I were to judge him, I would not stay with him, because I would want a guru who had a little common sense and logic. This man was beyond all logic. I don't know exactly what he was thinking.

Boulder by boulder, everything was brought down. One day he was bringing a boulder on his shoulders. He was covered in wounds and his feet were blistered and bleeding. He was so tired that he dropped the boulder and it rolled down. So Milarepa thought, "Okay, it does not matter." He went back to pick up another boulder. In the meantime, the guru came and asked, "Hey, where are you going?" Milarepa said, "I am going to bring another boulder." The guru said, "But you were coming down, weren't you?" Milarepa said, "Yes." "What happened?" the guru asked. Milarepa said, "The boulder rolled." The guru asked, "But why can't you roll?" He gave him a kick and the boy fell down the mountainside.

The story goes further. When Milarepa was given initiation later, he sat in meditation, keeping an earthen lamp alight on his head. He sat in the lotus posture for hours together without the slightest movement. The lamp did not flicker and it did not fall. Milarepa stayed in caves, far away from human habitation, just living on water from the river and green nettles until his whole body became green like grass. And when people passed by they saw him sitting calm and serene for one day, two days, three days, four days at a stretch; the body did not move. The earthen lamp was still on his head; it did not fall down. He did not even scratch. This is just a very extreme example of the relationship between the guru and chela.

Gurus are very few in this world, because disciples are also very few. Where there is demand, there will be supply. If your demands are genuine, the genuine gurus will come. If you want the pleasant gurus, sweet speaking gurus and those who can praise and butter you up, then naturally such gurus will be supplied. What is necessary is that one becomes a disciple and accepts that he needs inner cleaning. You need inner cleaning, you cannot say that you don't need it. If you don't need inner cleaning, then you will be a guru and I will be a chela.

For this inner cleaning, either you become your own guru, if you are capable, or if you are not capable of becoming your own guru, then have one guru. No matter what he does, no matter what he says, no matter how he ill treats you, you have to accept it.

QUESTIONS AND ANSWERS

How do we surrender to guru?

Surrender to guru does not mean that your life is paralyzed. It only means that there is no difference between you and the guru. Your body and mind, your day to day life goes on unobstructed, but what is important is that you begin to think that the guru is not different from you. There is a feeling of total oneness.

193

There are three different types of disciples. There are the lay disciples or householders; sannyasin disciples or the monastic order; and the interior disciples who are always very few. For each of these three types, surrender takes place in a different dimension. The lay disciple has to surrender through devotion. The monastic disciple has to surrender his desires and worldly ambitions, and the intimate, interior disciple has to surrender everything.

A guru ordains his disciples for different purposes. He teaches his lay disciples in order to give them peace of mind and right understanding in life. Therefore, it is sufficient if they offer their devotion to him. They do not have to surrender their business, family and children to their guru, but they must offer their true devotion so the guru can help them. This is the first type of disciple.

Then there are the monastic disciples. They remain in the institution of the guru or live in other branches of the guru's ashram. Here, every activity of the monastic disciple has to be controlled by the guru for at least twelve years. Because the guru has to transform the whole person, he has to change not only the way of thinking, but even the way of sleeping, eating, walking and talking. He even controls the number of times the disciple visits the toilet. Like this, for twelve years, monastic disciples are completely under the control of the guru, so that when they come out of monastic life, their whole personality is transformed. Then they can be very good messengers of their guru's teachings. This is the second type of disciple.

The third category of disciple is very rare. They are the interior disciples, and the guru selects those for himself. First they are tested, and only those who prove worthy are taken in. Then every aspect of their life is controlled – their thinking, eating, sleeping and their emotions and passions. In the same way that you control the switch, you control their whole world. These interior disciples are never very many; you can count them on your fingers. They become the main distribution poles of the guru's energy. The

194

monastic disciples are the transmitters of the guru's knowledge, his gospel, but it is the interior disciples who transmit the energy. That is why there are so few of them. There will always be more monastic disciples, and the lay disciples may even number in the hundreds of thousands.

So, the third type of disciple transmits the energy, the second type preaches the gospel and the first type practises the gospel. The type of surrender which has to be practised depends on the type of disciple. The first type of disciple offers his devotion, the second offers his life and the third offers his soul. So, it is the choice of the disciple, and if a disciple wants to offer everything, nobody should object.

What happens if a disciple cannot surrender to his guru?
It may take time for a disciple to surrender completely. On account of ego, it is a very difficult process. However, in the course of time and with the help of sadhana, the ego is gradually curbed and surrender occurs spontaneously.

Even though my guru, Swami Sivananda, had his own character, composed of kindness, charity and compassion, and I had my own personality consisting mainly of self-discipline, punctuality and perfection, still in the course of time surrender came about.

My guru was a great and extraordinary person and because I had a certain capacity to think, our ideas often clashed. I just couldn't agree with some of the things my guru did. For example, he would send fruit and biscuits to a thief while I would be chastising him. I would think, "What level is my guru at?" He would say, "Don't talk harshly or dismiss him." But this was beyond my administrative and institutional understanding. Therefore, how could I surrender? He said, "Sit down and be quiet," and of course my mind reacted. It was many years later that I came to the conclusion that he was right and I was wrong.

You know, I never believed in ashrams, but later I was involved in many. I used to criticize yoga and say it was only for animals. This is because Vedanta was my pet subject and

195

Vedanta says that nobody is bound and there is no need for sadhana or to control the mind. But Swami Sivananda's commands were felt strongly within and his voice compelled me. Eventually, I understood and my surrender became complete. Even though Swamiji is no longer in this world, I feel no separation.

How does the disciple make himself empty?

When the disciple links with the guru, he must work very hard to eliminate his ego. If he is able to surrender, there is not much problem with the ego. But if he is not capable of doing this, then the guru has to perform egodectomy on him. Just as you operate on different parts of the body, in the same way there is an operation in yoga called 'ego-dectomy'. Elimination of the ego is the most difficult task in the life of a disciple. In fact, very few are able to bypass the ego, perhaps only one in a million.

What does it mean to surrender to a guru?

The purpose of surrender is to become an efficient instrument of the guru on all levels. If the disciple's surrender is complete, when the guru tells him, "This will happen through you," it happens. The guru can work wonders through the disciple who has surrendered.

The attitude of the disciple should be, "I am nothing. I am the medium. I am the channel." This is bhakti yoga or total self-surrender. When you practise yoga and spiritual life, that is an act of ego. It may be a positive act, but in relation to the surrender required for transmission, it is egoistic.

What are the dangers in spiritual life?

Throughout my life as a disciple I have observed many important points which are very dangerous in the life of a disciple. When I was living with my guru, Swami Sivananda, myself and many other swamis often thought we knew more than he did. In fact, we believed that the growth and development of the institution was only taking place because of our efforts.

There was a lot of intellectualism in us and because of it, we could not approach our guru like children. Once we brought this problem to our guru. We said, "Often we feel that we know more than you do, and there are times when we feel that you make mistakes." Swamiji replied, "You are right." That was his greatness and that was our mean-mindedness.

When you become a disciple, either a lay disciple or a sannyasin disciple, and you have accepted a mantra from your guru, then it becomes very important that he lives in your heart like a constant light. By maintaining constant awareness of the guru, you will be able to develop the satguru, that guru who dwells within.

Letter to a Disciple

One indispensable qualification of a great disciple is that he should carry out immediately and spontaneously the commands of the guru. If in this sphere he acquires that good quality, then in the next sphere also the same happens. When the entire individuality of the disciple becomes obedient to the commands of the guru, only then unforeseen success comes in the sadhana performed according to the guru's instruction.

35

Learning through Transmission

Nowadays people from all walks of life have a better knowledge of yoga than ever before because they have been attending yoga classes for many years. This method of learning in a class situation is called tuition, and it is the most prevalent way of imparting knowledge to students. History, geography, mathematics, philosophy, science and yoga are all taught in formal classes where a teacher stands up in front and speaks, while the students remain seated and listen. The teacher speaks from an intellectual point of view, repeating what he has learned from books and tutors. He does not speak from his spirit or his personal experience.

In ancient India, there was another concept of learning, known as transmission, whereby the student did not depend on the external aid of the senses. This process was completely internal. In tantra, transmission was the traditional method used to pass down the teachings from guru to disciple. In this way, a direct link was maintained between the original preceptor and the disciple receiving his knowledge perhaps hundreds or even thousands of years later.

The main difference between these two systems is that one is intellectual while the other is intuitive. One is based on the concepts gained outside from study, logic and experience. The other is a form of inner attunement, resulting from a highly charged energy spark entering one of the psychic centres of the brain.

Today, in spite of years and years of yoga training, many people have hardly grown spiritually. Their greed, pride, prejudice, fears and complexes remain the same. This is because they have been only learning yoga through an intellectual process and have not been able to imbibe it spiritually. Consequently, they have not yet transcended the weaknesses of life or managed to stabilize the state of happiness.

When a disciple or aspirant learns yoga through transmission, he comes to live in his guru's ashram. He does not attend any classes, but just by living in a yogic atmosphere, he learns yoga in spirit. Through the process of living with the guru, a state of communion develops and the disciple's consciousness expands inwardly, enabling him to imbibe the knowledge of his guru.

Living with the guru does not mean living in his room. If you live with a guru, it means you live with him spiritually. When I lived in Rishikesh with my guru, I seldom met him, but still every moment I was living for him and with him. Rishikesh ashram covers a wide area and the room where I stayed was so far away from where my guru dwelt that if I had to walk there twice a day, I would be exhausted. But from dawn to dusk, in every action I performed, I felt my guru was there. You know how if you love someone, he lives in you and you live in him, well, this is the situation between guru and disciple.

So, you see, there are two ways of imparting knowledge. You have experienced learning yoga by means of tuition. Now, however, you should stop trying to learn yoga intellectually and start imbibing it spiritually. To explain this process, I will give you an example. From an electrical powerhouse the electricity travels to a transforming station. From the transforming station it travels to different electrical poles and into your homes. Now your homes are connected with electricity, and it is entirely up to you whether you switch on the power or not.

Similarly, in spiritual life the power line is connected, the switch is there, but it is up to the disciple whether he

199

makes use of it or not. When people come to the Munger ashram to learn yoga, I generally meet them occasionally, either once a day or once a week. But mostly they feel that as a guru I am neglecting them. Just because I do not see them and speak with them every ten minutes, they think I'm not teaching them. But after many years of teaching yoga through formal classes, I now feel that physical contact is not the final means of communication. The guru and disciple must talk to each other in different realms through the method of transmission.

When the mind becomes quiet, the sensory channels are plugged and the ego is dissolved for some time, then the power of the soul or spirit becomes very, very strong. It knows no geographical barriers, no psycho-emotional barriers, and man can meet with man and hearts can talk to hearts.

In one of the Upanishads, it is said that the atman or spirit is homogenous silence. How do you experience this? Not by the sensory or psycho-emotional communications, but by tuning yourself into silence. This is what you must all do to experience the process of transmission. You don't have to become rigid at all, and you don't have to put on that serious 'Sunday face'. Be as bright and as natural as you are. The barrier is not in the spirit, because spirit is one. The barrier is in man's mind because he has individualized it. Just as you have attained a personal home, husband, wife, child, name and religion, in the same way you have developed the concept of personal mind. Once you surrender this personal mind, then the mind becomes homogeneous and is called the cosmic mind.

So, try to put aside your personal mind and be as relaxed as possible. This can be done through satsang, kirtan and spiritual discourses and by trying to simplify your mind, habits and lifestyle. I will try to be with you all the time, not physically of course, but spiritually.

36

Secret of Transmission

There are two ways in which knowledge can be imparted from teacher to student. One is known as tuition and the other is known as transmission. When knowledge is imparted through word of mouth and is received and grasped, analyzed and registered by the intellect, that is called tuition. But when the knowledge is transmitted through the astral plane, and the vehicle of transmission is the subconscious mind, and the receiver is also the subconscious mind, that is called transmission.

Positive proof

From time to time there have been such gurus and disciples by whom the knowledge was transmitted without any physical contact. Such transmissions know no geographical barriers. Even in modern science, investigations into these transmissions have been made. One of the most astounding recorded documents is the report of two Russians. The transmission was investigated in order to find positive evidence about the possibility of extrasensory perception (ESP). It was a part of parapsychological experiments conducted in Russia.

The experiment involved two individuals who were communicating with one another telepathically. At first the transmission was conducted at the distance of two metres, and gradually the distance was extended until finally they succeeded in transmitting and receiving from a distance of one thousand six hundred miles. After that, both of them were enclosed in a specially insulated room called a Faraday's cage, in which electromagnetic waves, radioactive waves cannot penetrate. If you turn on a transistor inside a Faraday's cage, it will just remain silent. This room is completely insulated from all kinds of subtle vibrations. But even in a Faraday's cage, the transmission succeeded. That was a positive proof of the existence of powerful mental waves working at a high frequency in what we call the psychic plane or psychic field. There are various fields for the transmission of different forms of energy, electromagnetic fields, radioactive fields, and so on. In the same way, there is a subtle energy field called the psychic field through which the transmission of guru travels. In Vedantic terminology, it is known as vijnanamaya kosha.

There are five koshas (the word *kosha* meaning body or sheath). The grossest of them is *annamaya kosha*, the food body; then comes *pranamaya kosha*, the energy body; the third is *manomaya kosha*, the mental body; the fourth is *vijnanamaya kosha*, the psychic body; and the fifth is *anandamaya kosha*, the bliss body. All of these bodies, from gross to subtle, have a particular energy field. Those of you who have studied a little bit of Kirlian photography can very well understand that even this material body has an energy field. Now these fields relate to the channel of transmission.

As you know, prana can be transmitted in many ways. In pranic healing, the science of prana vidya, if a person has surplus pranic energy, he can pass that energy on to others. Previously, such healers were considered to be quacks, because medical science had no understanding of how pranic energies were transmitted. Recently, however, pranic healing was exposed to scientific investigation. And these investigations revealed that from the palms of pranic healers, energy flows. It is a sort of magnetic energy. And now in European countries, spiritual healers by profession must be certified. Only then can they practise. Mòdern instruments

202

can provide the evidence that this person has an extra amount of magnetic impulses or radiations coming from his palm. These experiments are done in many ways, one of which is Kirlian photography, where the hands are exposed to a very high voltage of electricity and then the aura is taken.

A personal experience

So, pranayama kosha is made up of the pranic energy which can be transmitted from one person to another. It has, of course, its limitations, they say, but as far as I know, for a powerful person even the pranas do not have any limitations. I had a personal experience with a person living in Maharashtra. He had a temple dedicated to Lord Dattatreya. Whenever there was a case of snake bite, a telegram would be sent to him. As soon as he received the telegram, he would go inside the temple and place his palms on it, and there would be instantaneous revival of the person who was suffering from snake bite.

When I heard about this, I wanted to see the healer myself. I stayed in his village for about six months during my parivrajaka days. I visited his ashram and he accorded me a warm welcome and wanted me to speak to his disciples. I spoke to them about sadhana, and while I was sitting with my eyes closed doing some practice, they put a garland around my neck. After some time I felt the garland was moving. When I opened my eyes, I saw it was a Russell's viper, which is one of the most poisonous snakes. My heart started palpitating. At that moment the healer looked at me and said, "Don't worry. He is not going to do any harm to you because he is my chela." I knew that it was so. That night a telegram arrived and the healer took me inside the temple with him and he showed me how he cured snake bite from any distance. He raised his palms and said, "The prana is being transmitted, my life prana." Later I found out that person who had sent the telegram had been bitten by a deadly snake, and he was alive. So I have seen for myself that prana can be transmitted and that there is a pranic field.

The mental field

The mind also has a field which ranges from gross to subtle, and you can transmit your thoughts, emotions, passions, jealousies, compassion, mercy. All kinds of mental qualities that we have can be transmitted. For that you have the mental field. Now, the transmission that takes place between guru and disciple usually occurs on the mental level or manomaya kosha and the psychic level or vijnanamaya kosha. Usually, an initiate, a new disciple, is able to communicate with the guru on the mental level. That is where he becomes linked with his thoughts, emotions, etc., even blessings.

When the communication gets stronger and the link becomes steady, and the level of consciousness rises high, then there is a communication between guru and disciple on the psychic plane. For the last two years, we have been working on the possibility of transmission. It is an age-old science. And this is precisely the reason why sadhus, yogis and mahatmas do not meet people often. It is the general custom, the general tradition. If you go to any ashram, you will find the guru is always absent. It is hard to meet with him because the more you isolate yourself, the better is the chance of transmission. But when you live with him intimately and meet a number of times every day, and can tell him your problems, then you do not exert your psychic body. But when guru is not there to attend to your problems and when you cannot express them, then you evolve your mind, and you keep on thinking and thinking and thinking, until suddenly you raise your consciousness.

When you are able to raise your consciousness, then a link takes place between guru and disciple. The mantra is the sutra. It is through the mantra that the transmission can be manifested. Therefore, the mantra is known as guru mantra. Whichever mantra you get from your guru, it is a sort of link between you and the self. And through the practice of this mantra, you are able to raise the level of your consciousness.

Once I conducted a special seminar outside Paris at the site where they have made a yogic university. I did not see the students for seven days. I was there for all seven days. I inaugurated the meeting and closed it. In between, I did nothing. During this period, they were practising their mantra, mouna, fasting, and other practices of yoga as they were instructed. At night, between ten or twelve, they used to forge the link. And I found from their diaries that everybody succeeded on the fifth, sixth and seventh days. Whatever was in my mind between ten and twelve in the night, on those days they could receive it.

Mandala – medium for transmission

This knowledge, which is transmitted by guru and received by the disciple in his inner brain, is completely free from intellectual contamination. I am using the word intellectual contamination because it is like that. The intellect is a very inefficient instrument. Spiritual matters can never be decided by analysis, mathematics or even by modern science.

In tantra they have what you call *mandala*, which can be understood as a pictorial concept. There are various types of mandalas in our tradition, Kali, Durga and many forms of devi and devata. So these mandalas also form the medium for transmission. Many people offer their worship, for instance, to a shaligram or a shivalingam. These are also mandalas. And when they offer their worship to a shivalingam, it is not merely a religious practice or tradition, it is not merely dharma. It is something very important by which you can elevate the mind.

Now you have to remember one thing. If you are not able to tune your mind to the wavelength, you can never receive the transmission. If your transistor has only medium waves and not short waves, you cannot receive any transmission, any broadcast which comes through the short waves. In the same way, if you are not able to elevate your mind to that particular frequency, then the transmission is not possible. In order to elevate the mind to a higher frequency, a particular kind of mandala has to be introduced. You should not get into the unnecessary controversy of form or formless worship. We do not know and we do not even care whether God is sakara or nirakara, whether God is saguna or nirguna, whether God has a form or no form. That is none of our business. We are only concerned with a science through which the mind responds immediately.

The cosmic mind

Mind is matter composed of many elements. Mind is not homogeneous. Homogeneous means made up of one element. Mind is a composition of twenty-four or some say twenty-six elements. These elements form the objects through which you hear music, through which you experience touch. This is called the *sthula manas*, the gross mind.

Now this gross mind has to be pulverized, the gross mind has to be purified, or rarefied, so that it becomes *sukshma* or subtle. The energy can be manifest at different levels, the mind can attain a very high frequency because it is a part of the cosmic mind. In the scriptures this is known as *hiranyagarbha*. There seems to be one total mind of which we are part. There is one electricity flowing throughout the city, but you see the various circuits working differently. The electricity is just one, whether you switch on the tube light or the exhaust fan or you put on the fans. In the same way there may be millions or billions or trillions of different minds. But all those are circuits of the one mind, known as the cosmic mind or hiranyagarbha.

As you go on breaking the barriers of your mind, you realize that you are part of the cosmic mind. Kabir sang in one of his songs, "The pitcher is broken. The water becomes one with the source. There is total identity. What is the difference then?" How can the water in a pitcher and the water of a pond retain their separate identities with the loss of the pitcher? In the same way, the mind has many attributes; it has its own formations, like raga, dwesha, vritti. These formations will have to be disintegrated. And this is the first and foremost sadhana of a disciple.

As long as the chela has his own identity and his own personal ego, he is existing on a different wavelength. And you should know one thing, That all of us are tuned to some wavelength. And what is that? That is the wavelength of maya.

However, if you change the wavelength of your mind, then you can be in tune, in connection with the wavelength of the higher frequency. Sometimes when you are perturbed due to the death of somebody in your family, you are tuned to a different wavelength. In the night many people hear peculiar sounds, they see frightening faces, because they are tuned to a particular wavelength. Therefore, in the yogic science, in the relationship between guru and disciple, the first and foremost thing is that the disciple will have to elevate the mind. And the basis, therefore, is called guru bhakti.

Guru bhakti is not the type of devotion which you practise in your temples and churches, where you go and pray and do some sort of rituals. It is not like that. The communion has to take place, then what happens? There is another song by Kabir which comes to my mind, "If your darling is away, you long to be together. But my darling is within myself, and I don't have to make the slightest movement." That is the secret of transmission.

QUESTIONS AND ANSWERS

What brings us closer to guru?

A disciple is always close to his guru. A sannyasin is always very close to his guru. Of course, householders are also very close to their guru, but from time to time there are distractions and diversions in their life. There are many chances for dissipation. As far as a sannyasin is concerned, he is very close to his guru because he tries and has been trying to remove the veil of distractions and dissipation which hang between himself and his guru. Unless one has great faith and understanding and a sort of enlightenment within himself, he will not be able to choose a particular guru.

The choice that one makes for a particular guru is a result of the deep understanding, the conviction and the faith that is in him. And these are the things that really bring both of them closer to each other. You see, guru is like the main transforming station. The inner guru or atman is the generating station. We can never see the inner guru. We have only heard that he is the generating station. The visible guru, the guru in the physical body, is the transforming station; what we call the substation. Energy comes from the generating station and is transformed according to the need of the town or city. The disciples act as channels for that energy to different centres. So the important thing is that the disciple has to be a good conductor.

Even the good conductor can fail. They are like zinc wire. Zinc wire is a good conductor, but what happens when it rains? The zinc wire accumulates carbon and that brings a distortion or some sort of block in the energy flow. Although the zinc wire is connected with the mains, still the electricity does not pass because the nature of zinc is to accumulate carbon when it rains. However, copper doesn't; copper is the best, most reliable and efficient conductor.

Therefore, disciples are of different categories; some are copper wires and some are zinc which accumulates carbon from time to time. Aluminium is a good conductor and is also very flexible, but it produces a lot of dirt. So the disciple should not only be a good conductor for the flow of energy from his guru, he should also see that he is not too flexible and doesn't accumulate too much carbon. For that purpose, a process of understanding himself in relation to the situation has to take place. Then the disciple and the guru come closer to each other.

When we say that the disciple comes closer to the guru, we don't really mean this in an emotional sense. In spiritual life, there is a different sense. Coming closer to each other in the case of a disciple means that he is a good conductor or channel through which the energy of guru and the energy coming through the guru, the energy from the supreme guru, can pass on to him. He can carry that energy as a good conductor and as a good carrier to different places wherever the light, the illumination or the energy is required. That is the meaning, that is the idea of the closeness between guru and the disciple.

If a disciple thinks that he is very close to me, or if I also think that he is very close to me, it shouldn't be understood in the emotional sense, just because I love him or he loves me. It is because, whatever I have, whatever I'm passing through, or whatever I'm loving through, that energy should be carried on by him to different places. Many of my disciples are all over the world in different countries. They are passing on to the people the theoretical knowledge, the practical knowledge, the spiritual peace and inner understanding about themselves and a life in harmony and concord. This means they are passing on spiritual energy to different people and they are the transmitting poles. Disciples, when they become transmitting poles, should be considered close to their guru.

Is transmission a necessary part of spiritual life?

Spiritual life does not consist of teaching alone. Spiritual life consists of transmission and contact. A guru may or may not give lectures and teach, but it is very important that the guru and disciple are transmitter and receiver. This is the real relationship between guru and disciple. There is an emotional relationship because we belong to the emotional plane. This emotional relationship between the guru and disciple becomes the vehicle for transmission of spiritual energy.

Guru and disciple may live anywhere, but there is an unseen connection between them. When one becomes a disciple, definitely this connection has to be established.

Then the transmission is possible. This is a much more powerful way to be together, and this is how I live with all the disciples in my ashrams. I tell them, "Let us live and work together and in the course of time our spiritual relationship will definitely develop and deepen."

When the spiritual awareness unfolds and the mind is rendered clear, all the scriptures are revealed, all the practices understood and the whole philosophy is at your beck and call. You know about Ramakrishna Paramahamsa. He was an illiterate saint, but he could speak on any subject. People came to him and he taught the Upanishads, or talked to them in the language of the Bible. When the spirit unfolds, knowledge becomes natural to you. This is what we all have to understand and to aim towards.

I read that sometimes disciples get fused and burned by the transmission of energy. So now I am a bit afraid.

All disciples do not belong to the same category, and according to their category, they react to the transmission. There is a constant transmission and communication that takes place between two individuals who are connected to each other. In fact, everybody is connected to each other on the cosmic plane. Just as all the beads of a mala are connected by an interpenetrating thread, in the same way all the bodies in the world, all the bodies in creation, are interconnected by a thread. That is called 'cosmic consciousness', and all matter in creation is known as the cosmic body.

The same thing happens with guru and disciple. The transmission takes place from different levels. It can take place from the emotional level to the emotional level, from mental level to mental level, from spiritual level to spiritual level and psychic level to psychic level. They are different wavelengths. Transmissions taking place between mother and child, guru and disciple, or between two people loving each other, have different wavelengths.

Now, it sometimes happens that guru is transmitting on one plane and the receiver, that is the disciple, is not getting

210

it accurately. This is because his personality is existing on two different planes – the mental and emotional, or emotional and psychic, or psychic and spiritual. So both personalities are influenced simultaneously. Besides this there are other important factors that have to be considered. When we sing kirtan, different people react differently. Some sing and talk; some are just quiet and something happens within them, and some do not react at all. Now the transmission was the same, but the receivers were on different planes of consciousness, and therefore their reactions are different.

Many times when a guru transmits energy to the disciple, the disciple reacts very favourably, but sometimes he acts in a diametrically opposed way. You know, sometimes I have seen disciples talking only against the guru after transmission. They criticize and abuse the guru; that is one type of reaction. Another type of reaction is they love the guru, they surrender, and they are always thinking of him and him alone. And it can also happen that when the guru has transmitted his energy to the disciple, the disciple may react in a very negative way. He may even try to kill his guru.

So, there are different types of bhakti, that is, devotional emotions, which the disciple expresses after he is able to receive the transmission from his guru. Therefore, the disciple should first of all clean himself and, after a certain amount of purification, then he should connect himself with his guru. There will then be no short circuit.

What is the correct relationship between the guru and disciple?
The disciple is the fulfilment of the guru's wisdom. The guru is like a beautiful rose plant and the disciple is the blooming rose. The right relationship between guru and disciple should be the relationship of knowledge and expression. On the physical plane the disciple and guru are inhabiting different bodies, and for a very long time the sadhana of the disciple is to use his physical body. But if the disciple can make himself competent in the right place for

211

fulfilling the aspirations of the guru, then he can be the best expression for knowledge of the guru. This is because knowledge is expressed from the guru through the disciple. The blooming of the flower, the transcendental experience, also takes place in the disciple.

Letter to a Disciple

Give up living on the plane of intellect. How long will you cling to this obsession? Let thoughts go; let intellect go. If this continues, I may not give you the key. Not only will you have to follow my instructions, but my unseen commands too. Even if I speak from above the sky, you will have to listen through ajna chakra. Nothing can be achieved if you ignore my commands. I tell you that my path is the path of the brave ones, of heroes, of proud men. It is the path of those who are prepared to die for it.

Those who have intellect will remain unenlightened; those who are doubters will wander in darkness. It is the duty of the disciple to think according to the spoken, written or inspired thoughts of the guru. Let me take into my hands the reins of each one of your thoughts and actions. Do not fear, this is the word of God! I say it because I know it to be so. Do not treat me as if I am a book, or else you will grope in darkness.

37

Where to Find a Guru?

A few decades ago we did not have any engineers in India, so we sent our boys to be trained in America, Germany and England. We have plenty of well-qualified engineers now, so we don't need to send anyone abroad for training. Of course, a few still go on account of their own personal ambitions. When the Spanish people wanted gold, they went to Latin America to obtain it. They could have dug for gold in their own country, but it was more readily available in Latin America. When oil and petrol are required, you have to bring them from other countries because they are not available here. Every culture has a distinct capacity for producing vital materials and also particular types of geniuses. Right from the beginning, India has had the capacity to produce spiritual personalities and geniuses.

Therefore, all those who want to learn yoga can learn it in their own country, but if they want to pursue a deeper spiritual life, they should make contact with the gurus who live in India. Some gurus remain in India and never visit other countries, whereas others who live there do travel abroad from time to time, because the West is now ready to receive them. Wherever there is demand, there will be supply.

Decades ago the West had a closed mind. It could not think beyond the frontiers of its own religion and science. But now the people of the West are wanting to look beyond the frontiers. Therefore, many enlightened and highly evolved teachers and gurus do come to the West and at the same time they have their own dedicated and benevolent disciples working in European countries. They have also been writing many very sincere and informative books on yoga, Eastern philosophy and spiritual life.

Amongst those gurus who have penetrated the West there was Swami Vivekananda first, then Paramahamsa Yogananda, then Swami Ramatirtha, Swami Ramdas and so on. Swami Sivananda did not go to the West, but his disciples have been going there. There are also many highly evolved gurus in India who prefer to remain unknown. And to find them, you have to make a sincere search.

It is important to note that everybody finds a guru according to their own personal evolution. Many people might have travelled far to meet Sri Aurobindo of Pondicherry or Ramana Maharshi of Tiruvannamalai, but upon meeting them they were not impressed. In such circumstances, the key point is that if you have endeavoured to search for a guru in the course of your travels, you will surely come across a great personality who is to be your guru.

Having considered this point, I came to a conclusion. Those sincere spiritual aspirants of the West must go to India for a higher education in spiritual life. They should not only learn yoga, they must also live ashram life, because yoga and ashram are inseparable elements, just like science and the laboratory. Surely, in every nation and in every community there must be a very small handful of people who are ready to renounce. Of course, renunciation and sannyasa are not for everybody. This path is only for a small minority of aspirants, but if the West has produced so many sisters and clergymen, it can produce sannyasins as well.

Those who are suited to the path of sannyasa should live in India for a long period and imbibe spiritual life into every fibre of their being. Then they should return to the West to spread spiritual light and to function as gurus. Just as twenty years ago in India we sent people abroad for higher

214

technical education, the West must follow the same procedure. We have incorporated technical science, and now the West must do the same and accept spiritual science.

Europeans are not materialistic by nature. They were compelled to become like this. Up until one hundred and fifty years ago, when the technological revolution took everyone by surprise, if we were to compare the Indian and the Western spiritual traditions, we would find that they were very similar. But then, with the development of such stark, naked and obnoxious commercialism and materialism, we who represented spiritual life found it very difficult to penetrate into the Western fibre because people did not understand what we were talking about.

When people have a lot of money in their bank accounts and pockets, they become arrogant – "I can purchase three cars, I can build five houses, I can start a factory. I don't care for you." This was the blind arrogance that existed in the West for one hundred and fifty years, and now for the last fifteen to twenty years, it has been creeping into certain parts of India also. However, the heart of the West is intrinsically and basically spiritual. In spite of the tempest of materialism, the Westerners are trying to stand on their own feet spiritually.

In some Western countries, yoga universities have been established and the governments are encouraging people to practise yoga. If Westerners were not spiritual, how could these things happen? Behind this external Western civilization, there is an internal spirituality. There are thousands of registered yoga teachers in Europe and hundreds in the eastern European countries. There are many different yoga magazines published in Europe and each magazine is far superior to any you find in your bookshops. Most yoga federations have their own fully automated, computerized printing presses, just as I have in Colombia, Spain, Greece, Australia and Denmark. This proves that people in the West are sincerely searching for a higher value in life.

As I told you, the external structure of the European society is not its atma, its soul. When Indians come to the West, they only see that external view of Western life. They do not see the atma of life in the Occident. I have so many thousands of young boy and girl disciples in the West and hundreds who have renounced and become sannyasins. When Indians see the Western women in nightclubs, they think that is the Western mind, but it is not.

The East has misunderstood the West and the West has misunderstood the East. The West thinks that the East is only poor, uneducated, illiterate, backward, primitive and superstitious. And the East thinks the West is all nightclubs, drink and women being kicked about like footballs. This is the impact of materialism, but it is not only Occidental, it has also gone to many places in India. You see it a lot in Bombay nowadays. It's time for the East and the West to jointly fight this onslaught of materialism.

In materialism, we think that matter is ultimate and the soul is insignificant. This is why when many Indians go to the West, they are deluded and misled, and they lose the trial of their own culture.

So let us hope that more people from the West come to India. If they can take sannyasa, they should. Then they should stay in India for quite a number of years. When they develop and understand the spirit, mind and consciousness, they should go back to the West and teach the young boys and girls there who are thirsty for this spiritual knowledge.

Many people have come to India for this purpose. One man came to India from France, and he remained for at least twelve years, spending his time in the ashram of his guru. Then he went back to France and started a movement called 'The Great Fraternity'. He speaks about the same things as I do – supremacy of soul over matter, supremacy of light over darkness, and so on. This man brought the vegetarian movement to the West like a storm. And like him, there are hundreds of Western people who are now living with gurus in India and furthering their spiritual knowledge.

In my ashram in India, there are many people from Australia, America, South America, England, Denmark, Ireland, France and Germany. They will stay for six to twelve years, and when they perfect themselves, they will go back to the West and become gurus.

Letter to a Disciple

Make sadhana the objective to be achieved; the only object of bliss. Let your family life be your ladder, your life the wall, and the sadhana the effort to reach the terrace. Life, body, house and family – all these are means to the end but not the end in themselves. Learn to understand all things and to offer worship to the altar of peace.

38

Every Guru is a Light

I believe everyone is a seeker and should be free to find his own path and his own guru. I don't believe that there are good and bad gurus, and in the same way there are no good and bad husbands or good and bad wives. When two individuals are not able to compromise with each other, how can you say which one is bad and which one is good?

There is so much talk about certain gurus being frauds, destroying people's minds, ruining their lives. If you cannot manage with your guru, it is your problem. There are no good gurus, no bad gurus, no saints and no charlatans. Even those people who wear the robe of guru in order to make a profit become responsible in due course. I have seen this happen many times.

The thing that all spiritually minded people should strictly and adamantly avoid is creating confusion in the minds of the people: "This guru is great, that guru is nothing at all." Differences and gradations are always there in the systems of teachings and also in the case of gurus. At the same time, lapses can also occur in the lives of gurus, but that does not mean I should idolize my guru and condemn yours, either directly or indirectly. We have only to notice one thing: the positive contribution of a person in the life of a seeker. Even if you guide one or two hundred people, that is enough.

There is a small candle and there is a big light. You cannot compare them. The candle is not useless and the light does not illuminate everything. The candle works well in places where there is no light. So, gurus like us are the little candles on the dark footpath of human evolution, and we try to shed some light on a certain destination in the distance. Beyond that there is another candle, and beyond that another. So, in the name of our own guru or our own fame, it is not good to blow out the lights of others. That is what we must all remember at this particular point of the century.

This is what I have been telling every swami and each and every disciple lately, "Don't condemn anyone. If you cannot speak well of him, just keep quiet." I am saying this in the interest of humanity. Otherwise there will be so many little fishes, so many sects and so much strife, with everyone bellowing, beating, kicking and wailing. No, we must have a non-violent method by which we can collect the positive contributions of everybody for humanity. One person is teaching mantra, another is teaching meditation, a third is teaching pranayama, a fourth kriya, a fifth tantra. One day we will all come together with our different practices to a church of a different face.

Satyam's Door

Knock knock knocking on Satyam's door.
Knock knock knocking on Satyam's door.
Take this self away from me.
I can't use it any more.
It's getting dark, too dark to see.
Take me to the light of Satyam's door.

(An English kirtan)

219

QUESTIONS AND ANSWERS

How does one become a guru?

Guru dispels your darkness and then you begin to have experiences – living experiences, you can see without eyes! Gurus are born; they come with a higher awareness in order to guide sincere seekers and aspirants. But at the same time I must tell you that a guru and disciple are not senior and junior cadres. A disciple remains a disciple for himself all the time. But his disciples whom he teaches consider him a guru.

The best way one should think is how to become a disciple. If people begin to think about how to become a guru, it is a very dangerous idea. Then some people start thinking about how to become a prophet, a more dangerous idea; how to become a multimillionaire; how to become the Secretary of the United Nations.

I know how to become a disciple, and to become a disciple is to become a guru. If you are a true disciple, then you are your own guru because a disciple surrenders everything – his emotions, brain, intellectuality, good and bad deeds, ego, vanity, past, present and future, security, fears and passions. Nothing belongs to him, he just gives it to his guru – he is empty, like bamboo. And when he empties himself, then he is filled with melody. In the same way, a disciple's dedication has to be so thorough, so complete, that he is no more a disciple. Then what is he? He is a guru, he is the dispeller of darkness.

Guru is not a superior social position, it should not be a superior social, religious, spiritual position. Anyone can dispel my darkness, and the one who dispels my darkness and gives me the capacity to experience within myself the inner light, the inner peace, the harmony, the bliss, is the guru. So, then ask the question – how to become a real disciple?

With so many false gurus in the world, how can we tell when we have found our true guru?

A disciple has the eyes to decipher the guru. If you want a good guru, then you should be ready to become a good disciple. Often people meet up with false gurus, and later on they tell everybody, "Keep away from gurus, they are very bad people. I met one and he cheated me." Whenever people tell me this, I say to them, "No, you cheated him."

According to the quality of the disciple, a guru is obtained. When the disciple is sincere, he will find a sincere guru. If the disciple wants to attain psychic powers, he will run after those gurus who display psychic powers. If a disciple wants affluence, he will run after gurus who have affluence. If the disciple wants to be enlightened, he will find an enlightened guru, there is no doubt about it. So, a disciple should know himself rather than trying to know the guru. And if he wants a highly qualified and saintly guru, he should try to be a highly qualified and saintly disciple.

Why aren't there more female gurus in the world today?

In tantra, women are regarded as the first guru, and for initiation a female guru is definitely considered to be more powerful than a male guru. In many religions women are not allowed to become priests or spiritual leaders, but in India there is a tradition of female gurus, and any woman who has followed the path of spiritual life and qualified herself can be accepted as guru.

In my opinion, if more women became gurus, there would be greater beauty, compassion, love and understanding in life. But we must always remember that, whether male or female, guru should not be judged by sexual specifications. Guru is guru; there is actually no difference.

I have lost all affection for my guru and want to become your disciple.

All gurus are one, although in form they may appear to be different. If you surrender to me, I will accept you, but if you consider your guru to be different from me, then I think you do not understand the universality of guru. Guru can love everyone because he sees one in all. In the same way, whoever your guru is, you have to see all gurus in him.

221

When choosing our guru, should we make our selection according to our heart and feelings or according to our head, logic and thinking?

In choosing anything in life you need heart and emotion. When you go to a flower shop, how do you choose a flower, through the intellect or emotions? You like it, therefore you take it. That's true with everything, particularly with gurus. If you choose by intellect and logic, you will have many gurus.

How should we react to criticism of our guru?

Let your path be easy, full of faith and hope. You may feel hurt at the slander of the guru. But just as one has to overcome being sensitive to one's own criticism, similarly, this sensitivity has to be overcome. The disciple who is filled with vanity at the guru's praise is exploited.

On the other hand, the disciple who becomes egoistic through the guru's appreciation becomes blind with conceit and fanaticism. The disciple who is aware of his own limitations, in spite of the appreciation of the guru, makes good use of the ego in propagating dharma. If anyone praises the guru, I would wish him to follow this practical religion. If he praises my guru and fails to fulfil his duties, he does nothing.

39

Importance of Constancy

Many disciples are interested in the works of different saints, authors and teachers. They are often inspired by other great teachers, and there is no harm in this, but according to tradition, guru must be one. You can derive maximum possible spiritual energy from other sources, but don't be misled by those teachers who happen to convince your lower mind. When a teacher allows you to live in any way you want, of course you will like him. You will listen to what he has to say, not because it is the truth, but because it is convenient for you.

Do not be guided by superficial philosophies. You must plumb the depth of the teaching. In certain systems you are instructed not to oppose the mind, but this does not mean that you have to be undisciplined. During meditation or japa, when the thoughts are swirling through the mind, that is the time not to oppose the mind. But when you are tackling the daily problems of life and the mind compels you to make wrong decisions, then the instructions, "Do not oppose the mind," no longer apply. At such times, if you go along with your mind, you may drive your car into the ditch.

Life anywhere, whether in the East or West, has to be very disciplined. Whether you are working in a factory, hospital or telephone exchange, there must be total control over the mental impulses. If you allow the mind to start jumping in the telephone exchange, it will be catastrophic.

It is only during moments of introspection, when you are alone with yourself, that you can safely allow the more volatile thoughts of greed, passion, violence and aggression to come into the mind. This does not mean that you should do these things; that would be total anarchy. However, many people interpret the teachings like this and so they live a very undisciplined life.

There have been many great teachers in the past such as Buddha, Christ, Krishna, Mohammed, who have left footprints in the sands of time. We should have total respect and reverence for them because they represent the divinity in human form. Their teachings and good works still inspire us today.

All these great men who have passed through the experience of divinity have continually taught one and the same thing. There is no conflict between their teachings. If you read the *Bhagavad Gita*, *Ramayana*, *Bible* or *Koran*, you will find that they have not drifted. However, those professors, psychologists and intellectuals who teach without having passed through the experience of divinity have drifted from the main teachings year after year. Sometimes they say one thing and then later they say something completely different. There is no uniformity, continuity or permanence in their message.

Continuity is a very important aspect of spiritual life. Although you may have respect for the different masters and spiritual paths, when it comes to your personal sadhana, you must follow one guru and one set of teachings. This is necessary so that the mind, which is dissipated and full of rajas, does not find an excuse to escape the practice. If your guru tells you to practise japa, continue the practice without changing it. This is the only way to progress in spiritual life.

I will give you a gross example. Once a girl marries, she has a special relationship with her husband which she doesn't have with any other man, and it is much better that she doesn't. But this does not mean that she should not talk to other men. One man may work in her office, another may be her brother-in-law. There's no harm in her talking to them.

Even as a girl has a special relationship with her husband, but a normal, workable relationship with everyone else, in the same way, the disciple must have a special relationship with the guru, but normal relationships with everyone else. We should respect all saints; we should not criticize anyone. But at the same time, we should not lose faith in our guru just because another one seems more attractive.

There is no end to attractive men in the world. There is no end to attractive faiths. From time immemorial, hundreds of thousands of saints have been born on this earthly plane to guide human beings to the spiritual path. That is why today we are still surviving in a comparatively less spiritual society.

40

Should the Guru be Praised?

It is always good to talk about your guru to your guru bhais or to people in satsang, but to beat the drum and announce his name is not a good practice, nor is it right according to tradition. There's nothing wrong with talking about your guru and this guru and that guru if the person you are speaking to is responsive and interested, but you should never try to influence people into accepting your guru with the intention of adding more followers to your guru's sect.

Sometimes people will criticize your guru. All prophets and gurus have been abused and criticized, and in this world it is a perfectly natural event. If ever you hear criticism of your guru, you should not get emotional about it and try to defend him. If you are intelligent, you will deal with the person calmly and rationally. You can talk to him in such a nice way that your personality reflects the philosophy of your guru.

Once I was in Guatemala and a man came to me and asked, "Do you know that man?" He was referring to his guru. I said, "Yes, I heard that he is in gaol." The man became angry and said, "What are you talking about?" I remained quiet for a moment and then answered, "Well, that is what I heard, but I may be wrong." He said, "It's all false. He's not in gaol." Very casually I said, "Yes, you may be right; I may be wrong." There was nothing to argue about so the man calmed down.

You see, if you represent the philosophy of your guru, there is no diplomacy in it. I represent the philosophy of Swami Sivananda. How can you say it's diplomacy? That's the way of life. If someone says to me, "My guru is a very good man," I just say, "He may be good, I don't know him," and that's all.

My guru, Swami Sivananda, was a non-controversial figure. Nobody has ever said a single word to me against him so I have never really had to tackle this problem. But about me people say many sound things. It's better if you ask one of my disciples this question, as they have been confronted with this situation. Swami Sivanandaji used to sing a song –"Bear insult, bear injury, that is the highest sadhana", but it is very difficult.

Once when I was travelling, I met someone who was talking about Lord Krishna, and everything he said was very negative and critical. I didn't make any comment and we started to eat our dinner. Then, because I had not responded to the subject at all, the whole conversation changed. We started talking about yoga and philosophy, and about good and bad. I then had a chance to say whatever I wanted, so firstly I started to talk about the removal of ego. It just came about spontaneously. When I was discussing ways to remove the ego, I gave him exactly the same illustration of *cheerharan* (the incident of Sri Krishna snatching the gopis' garments when they were bathing) which he had previously criticized.

I also spoke to him about Krishna's sixteen thousand and eight ranis. I was talking about one *purusha* (consciousness) and eight *prakriti* (matter). Eight prakriti permeated and combined becomes sixteen thousand and eight wives. Even if Lord Krishna married a wife per week, how many years would it take to marry sixteen thousand and eight wives? I mean, you must understand that these things really should not be taken literally. They mean something more and something deeper.

Similarly, in reference to the *Mahabharata*, this man had condemned Krishna, saying that he was nothing but a preacher of war and violence. I referred to what Krishna had said in the *Bhagavad Gita*: "Therefore, you must fight." But before that, what did he say? He recommended karma yoga, bhakti yoga and jnana yoga. "Therefore, Arjuna, you must fight Therefore, Arjuna, you must be a yogi." In yoga, there is nothing else but fighting. In yoga there is trouble; there is conflict between the internal and external forces. These external forces are the Kauravas, born of the blind father, and these internal forces are the Pandavas, born of the *tejas* or the light. Gradually, everything he was criticizing, I carefully put back on him.

You see, it's not necessary to defend your guru, and you are not going to gain anything from it. In actual fact, you are only trying to defend yourself, not your guru. If someone says your guru is a mahatma, you are very happy and proud, but if he puts your guru down, you take it as a personal insult and, feeling injured, you tend to fight back. Then have you reflected anything good about your guru? No, you have reinforced the other person's negative belief. So, when people talk against your guru, mahatma or teacher, I think it is best to remain quiet. That is my philosophy.

41

A Free Mind

When the relationship between guru and disciple is established, the only thing that is expected of the disciple is that he free his mind. Making the mind free is very difficult to explain. The mind is always engaged on either the sensory, mental, emotional or deeper planes, and often we don't even know what holds our mind. Every thought of the past, present or future, every association with pleasant and unpleasant, with a person or an object, should be separated from the mind. None of these things should hold our awareness. When the mind becomes free from these involvements, then it expresses itself as a very powerful force in the form of an experience, vision, light or revelation. This is precisely what I expect from my disciples.

Two thousand years ago, when the disciples of Christ carried his teachings from continent to continent, who were they? They were the people with free minds, and that is why they could illumine the minds of others and distribute healing energy to the sick. And this is what I expect from you.

You may be able to work in the ashram or outside as a good yoga teacher, but this is a very gross and simple quality of a disciple. There will always be better teachers than you, just as many people have become better teachers than me. They have better power of expression, and they can speak and sing better than I can.

If you are not learned, I don't care. If you have not read spiritual books, I don't mind. Even if you do not have a good power of expression, it doesn't matter. You have a mind, and you have a body and senses, and you have knowledge of the objects of pleasure and pain. And from time to time you will be drawn to pleasant things and you will withdraw from unpleasant things. This does not matter, it is the natural and habitual behaviour of the mind, body and senses. However, it should not arrest the free expression of the mind.

The mind remains free whether you live amidst pleasure or pain, wealth or poverty, young people or old. The mind must not identify itself with the external circumstances and think, "I am poor", "I am rich", "I am in pain" or "I am very unfortunate." As sannyasins, we live a life of poverty by choice. Why? Because our minds must be free. Wealth, name, fame, passion, all these things hold down this great energy of man.

The disciples, particularly the younger sannyasins, should understand that they have not undertaken this particular way of life just to represent a particular sect or order. We are trying to simplify our lives on the physical, mental and emotional planes so the mind will remain free. If we can keep the mind free, awakening will take place automatically, even without any sadhana. This is a simple and scientific principle.

You know what happens in physics? You take matter and you disintegrate it. In the beginning it is a composition of many elements, but when you separate those elements from matter, what remains is energy. Nowadays, they call this nuclear energy. Energy is always present in matter, but it is dormant and invisible. If you take a handful of uranium or plutonium, you can't see anything but a handful of sand. You cannot see or perceive it, but there is energy hidden in the gross matter. Just as a scientist removes those elements, one by one and finally liberates energy, in the same way, when you free the mind from the tattwas or elements, then it becomes a power. Every disciple must awaken this energy, and then move amongst the people, giving them whatever help they need, whether it is healing, peace of mind or spiritual illumination.

Now this energy is untapped in man. It is in everybody and at any time it can come out. In sannyasa, the discipleship in which you are ordained is to facilitate this process. When this energy is at your disposal, you must be very careful not to misuse it, either consciously or unconsciously. If you have a revolver, it can kill a friend or a villain both. It depends on what is in the mind. Therefore, it is of utmost importance that the mind is purified. That is the second thing that I expect from my disciples.

With an impure mind which is withdrawn or filled with anger, prejudices, passions, hatred, jealousy, greed and likes and dislikes, if this energy wakes up, then one will do more harm than good. Whatever the situation may be, the disciple should be very calm and quiet within himself. Even if he is being choked or punished, he should still have peace of mind, equal vision, total humility, no hatred and no sense of revenge or defence. A calm, quiet and serene disciple, filled with understanding, and compassion for all, is ready to use his awakened power for the good of humanity.

Now of course you are few, because we only started our work a few years ago, but I am certain that in a short time, my disciples are going to be the guiding stars of the whole of humanity. The signs are very clear. Therefore, I expect two things from my disciples: a free mind and a mind that is purified.

QUESTIONS AND ANSWERS

How does one become a good disciple?
A great disciple is not a good disciple. There has to be total humility, egolessness, total submission, as if you don't exist; as if you are a flute. You know a hollow bamboo can be made into a flute, but there must be no knots at all. Only then can

231

you produce a sweet melody. It is a sort of self-denial. As long as you exist, the guru cannot be in you. In order to allow him to function through you, you will have to empty yourself. And this process of emptying oneself is the only practice or sadhana that a disciple has to do. He need not practise hatha yoga, raja yoga, karma yoga, bhakti yoga; he has just to empty himself.

My Lord, before you, I do not exist. I cannot think. You think through me. I leave the choice of my life in your hands. This is the type of self-surrender, *atma samarpan* we call it. Self-surrender is the key to what we call higher knowledge. How long can you hold your head high if it is full of arrogance and ignorance, if it is full of conflict and duality? In order to rend this duality, it will take lives after lives.

Maybe your guru is not great. He may be an ordinary man. Maybe my guru was much more ordinary than I was, I don't know. But when I emptied myself and surrendered myself completely in total humility and obeisance to him, things happened.

Guru represents two realities – the teacher and the permeating reality. Guru is a teacher and the indweller of your heart. As a teacher, he can teach you and as an indweller of your heart, he guides the steps and the passages of your evolution and fulfilment. Let things happen. Guru is the shepherd, if you let him, he will take care of you.

How can disciples who are not living in an ashram serve their guru?

The purpose of service is self-purification. Householders can serve the guru by serving their fellowmen with an attitude of detachment and by following the rules of initiation which the guru has laid down for them. In India, according to tradition, the guru gives spiritual instructions; he is totally dedicated to spiritual life and is not committed to earning his livelihood. The guru devotes his life to contemplation and realization of the greater truth, to deep meditation and

232

cultivation of the divine power. He is surrounded by his monastic disciples, and householder disciples who support his entire establishment. Either monthly or annually, they contribute something towards its maintenance. On the birthday of the guru, householder disciples conduct a poor feeding, for which they prepare a sumptuous meal and then invite all the lepers, blind, orphaned and helpless people of their locality to partake of the feast. Householder disciples also serve the guru by transmitting his message to their nearest family members, friends and associates.

In the guru-disciple relationship, isn't there a danger that the guru's personality will cover the personality of the disciple?

The disciple is passing through the stage of ignorance; he is a seeker, searching for light. Therefore, he looks to his guru, and the guru in turn transforms the entire personality of his disciple. This transformation is gradual. It is not the surrender of one's personality but rather the handing over of one's limited self to one who will change it into infinite self. He will add the raw materials to the big furnace, and finally steel, copper or gold will be produced. In the same way, the disciple is the raw material and the guru makes him pass through this furnace of spiritual evolution until he becomes pure material.

We must remember that when we surrender to the guru, it's not because we want to become a slave, but because we want to become a master. A disciple should never feel that he is working for his guru. When the disciple begins to think that he is doing a great service to his guru, then his ego is becoming great. When a disciple is serving his guru, he should be aware that he is serving the guru for his own spiritual evolution.

What happens to the disciple after initiation?

On receiving the divine spark from the guru, the disciple begins to have experiences according to his disposition. If

233

he is intellectual, his intellect will be sharpened so that he understands subtle subjects and finds satisfactory answers to his questions. If devotional, he will experience intense love. Craving may get stronger for a while but will gradually disappear. Chronic and dormant diseases may erupt but will eventually be expelled from the system forever. Thus the awakened shakti firmly sets the disciple on the road to spiritual perfection.

Devotion to the guru is essential. The divine power is all-pervasive, yet it is the guru who removes the veil of ignorance. As a seeker progresses, he has to become his own guru, remaining a witness to his inner processes while surrendering to the inner shakti. The true guru does not make his disciple renounce the world, but his limited self; he takes away, not limited wealth and riches, but sins and anxieties. The greater the disciple thinks his guru to be, the greater he himself will become. The guru is Brahma because he creates for his disciple a new and wondrous world; he is Vishnu because he sustains and protects him; he is Shiva because he annihilates his world of individuality.

42

The Story of a Disciple

When an aspirant meets his guru for the first time, he may experience some sort of devotional explosion. However, this is not always the case. This sort of experience is not necessary for every disciple. If the guru is not able to excite your emotions at first sight, it does not mean that you have failed to experience his presence. Some disciples are made of a higher quality stuff. They are like the diamond. How hard it is to cut a diamond. How easy it is to cut a piece of paper; you don't even need a knife. How easy it is to saw a piece of wood; you just need one small tool.

When a devotee approaches the realm of the divine, he is influenced by his own background of faith and belief. He has created for himself a hypothesis, he has created conditions for self-hypnotism. Whenever you go into the realm of the divine, whether before your guru or in a church or temple, you unconsciously create within yourself an atmosphere of faith, and that is why you are at once affected. You become emotional, and you affect yourself. It is not the guru or the divine atmosphere which is affecting you, it is something within.

If you are not excited by the guru at first sight, it is a very good indication that you can be a wonderful disciple, but you will have to work hard at it. You should not lose heart or hope. This is a very positive sign, but you must understand it. You may think that, when you see the guru, you will burst into tears, your body will tremble and you will say, "Oh Guru!" . . . then you will start quivering and this and that. No!

There is a story about Swami Vivekananda, the famous disciple of Ramakrishna Paramahamsa, the mad saint of India. Ramakrishna was mad after him. Every evening, he used to wait for his arrival at the door of the temple and he would ask everybody, "Has Narendra come?" (Narendra was Vivekananda's first name), because Narendra used to go to his home right from the university, and then he would come to Ramakrishna. He was least affected by Ramakrishna's love and attention. In fact, he was very hesitant about submitting his will, his personality and his ego before this uneducated madman.

This graduate of India's most eminent university, Calcutta University, a replica of intellectualism, who had studied about all the great scientists, how could he be influenced by this illiterate saint, who did not even know how to sign his own name? Gradually, however, the butter began to melt, the hard substance which he had accumulated for many lives, began to break into pieces. Eventually, there came a time when Swami Vivekananda became a part of his guru. Those who know the story of Swami Vivekananda during his experiments on mendicancy; those who have read about his life, can understand this very well.

After the death of Ramakrishna, Swami Vivekananda set out on an all-India tour on foot with only two dhotis – no money, not even a penny. And during those days he underwent great hardships, but whenever he lost heart, he saw the image of Ramakrishna illumined before him and this gave him comfort and inspired him. When he was asked by a rich man in South India to travel to America, he did not know what to do. Someone had told him that there was a Parliament of Religions in Chicago and he must try to go because he was a very good speaker. So, he was put on the ship. He landed in America with absolutely no money, no friends, in a country where he had never been, and he faced

236

many difficulties – you know what Americans are like. When you knock on the door, they open it and then slam it in your face!

When he went to address the Parliament of Religions, with the recommendation of some influential person, he got ten minutes to speak. Swami Vivekananda said, "I did not know what to tell them because they knew everything." So he got up on the platform and he just began to address them. Before he started to speak, he saw the face of Ramakrishna, his guru, illumined before him like flesh and blood. He had an experience of his living presence and he lost himself – I don't mean the prana, I mean the ego! He lost his ego and he addressed the Parliament of Religions for ten minutes amidst cheers and cheers, people began to throw their hats, they were so happy.

Swami Vivekananda did not know exactly what he spoke about. It was as if he was transported into a land of slumber and somebody spoke from within him. After that, he conquered the hearts of the Americans. This has to be the relationship between guru and disciple. So please wait until the guru is able to excite you.

43

How to Kindle Devotion

The guru-disciple relationship has to be unselfish. Sometimes it is, but most times it is not. When it is unselfish, it can endure. If it is selfish, it cannot. Suppose you go to guru for something and he gives it to you, then you have faith in him. Later he is not able to give it to you and so you say, "Oh, now he is no longer my guru, he has lost his powers. Formerly, he had spiritual powers, now he is caught by maya and so he has lost his spiritual power." What kind of faith and devotion is that? Once you have accepted him as your guru, there ends the matter. But it does not happen like this because our analysis is intellectual.

The relationship between guru and disciple must become more and more intense day by day. You can develop the relationship to an extent where you and he are experienced as one – I am in my guru and he is in me. And whenever you close your eyes, he is there. It is not necessary that you should be with him all the time, but it is necessary that he live with you much closer than your own breath. You breathe twenty-one thousand six hundred times in twenty-four hours, and if the breath stops for three minutes you are gone, finished. Such an essential process of life and so very close to you, still you seldom know that you are breathing.

In the same way, the guru lives in us, but we do not know he is there. How do you develop that awareness? First, you must have an external guru. As he is a man, you can love

238

him, you can think about him, you can understand his love, his benediction, his compassion, his nature. You can understand his frivolities too. You see, he is like us and we can identify ourselves with him because he lives more or less on the same plane. Thereby the awareness is made more and more intense. You can go on thinking about him during meditation, then during lunch and dinner, when you are unhappy, tired, fighting with your husband or wife, when your child is sick or something is wrong. On hundreds and thousands of occasions you can practise awareness of him, thereby developing the faculty of constant awareness. Then you project the same on to God.

So, the relationship between disciple and guru must be developed on any dimension. You may consider him worshipful, an honourable man, a man whom you can love, it's okay. If you do not like an object, you cannot concentrate on it. Buddha once said in one sutra, that in order to develop one-pointedness of mind, first comes liking and pleasantness, next love and affection and thirdly concentration. If you want concentration, total absorption in guru or anything, you must follow this order. First liking for him, and this liking must develop pleasantness in you – you like to think about him. After that, affection or love and devotion must develop, and automatically concentration will occur. If you do not like the object, you cannot be comfortable with it and so it will not develop love within you and you will not be able to get concentration of mind.

44

Instructions to the Disciple

There is a state or experience, a little beyond the mind, in which you can see a person or an object that you love very much. Then you can materialize it on your inner plane of awareness as clearly as reality. Of course, this only happens when your consciousness is raised. Then the image appears and becomes clear. In this elevated state, you can see the guru just as if you are sitting in front of him and he is talking to you. So, try to develop this by practising a little every day, for half an hour to an hour.

There are two states of consciousness. In one state you know that you are witnessing everything, but in the other state you do not know. Afterwards, when you come out, there is a little imbalance, but it passes shortly if you are under the guru's direction. However, if you are not under the guidance of the guru, and the imbalance continues, it is possible to go crazy. That is why sadhana should never be done without the instruction of the guru, never; not even kunjal and neti should be done. The disciple must completely resign himself to the guru. Then at the proper time, the guru will give him sadhana. I could not tell you these things before, because a certain maturity had to be reached.

If your relationship with guru is very simple, you can have any relationship with him. You not only have a guru, but a parent, child, friend, lover. Of course, he is a man and you are a woman, but the guru's relationship with all disciples

240

is very clear. Whatever he does is only to impress their consciousness. Guru does not have disciples for any other purpose, but most disciples do not understand. So what happens is that emotional imbalance often develops. Sometimes you think, "Swamiji loves me too much," and at other times, "Oh, now he does not love me at all." But that is a mistake. The guru never loves anyone. Whatever he does is solely to change the quality of the mind.

You have seen how adding sugar changes the quality of milk. If you mix tea with boiling water you change the quality of the water. In the same way, once the guru gets into your mind, he changes the whole quality and structure. It is a very simple process; there are so many ways in which he can do it: by mantra, sadhana, lectures, singing, thinking. When the guru comes in your mind, then the sadhana has to begin. But never think that the guru is attached or loves anyone in any personal way.

At a certain point, the disciple should be able to develop his own awareness. Then he does not need the guru physically at all. There is no difference between that state of awareness and physical contact. It is exactly the same. Maybe even that state of awareness is more tangible than this one. If you can visualize or feel me in the moments of solitude, that is far more fulfilling and satisfying than communicating with this physical form. You can try.

However, first of all you must know that I am your guru and you are to be controlled by me at every moment. That is what guru means. Sometimes I may get angry and abuse you, kick you, or put you out the gate. All these things must be accepted too. The disciple is one who is always controlled by his guru.

Otherwise, even though many disciples work very hard in spiritual life and develop some experience, afterwards they still go back to normal. Because they have no guru, they go on doing what they like, always sitting and talking about useless things. If I ask you not to sleep, to keep quiet, not to argue with me, you must obey me without any thinking

241

or hesitation. With guru, the sadhaka disciple should have no personality; then only can he be helped.

So, you have all the elements with you. Work hard. Once in a month, once in a week, once in a day, practise this. Develop the inner awareness. Have communion with your guru, inner communion. That is more tangible, satisfying, potential and real than the outer one. You will know it after practising a few times. It is not unreal. Perhaps this seems real and that unreal, but it is only because that is a higher awareness.

You know how the awareness is projected. You can see it in moments of extreme fear, passion or bluff; this manifestation of consciousness. But when you practise it, there is one thing which you must be aware of. You should not do it unless you know that whatever I say to you is final, no argument. Only after this can you practise it. Otherwise, if manifestation of consciousness takes place even momentarily, it becomes very difficult to control. You might say, "I am going to Australia." And if I say, "No, don't go," you will not listen.

Therefore, first of all, you must establish a relationship in such a way that whatever I say is final. There is no second word on it, no argument, analysis, judgement or after-thought. When I say no, it is finished. Otherwise, what will happen when the consciousness manifests? All sorts of thoughts come to the mind and people get uprooted. So, if you say, "I am going to Australia," and I say, "Wait, not now," then you should say, "Okay, Swamiji said no, so I will not go." What the guru says, the disciple has to follow quietly, right or wrong. Until this relationship is established, the disciple should not attempt higher sadhana, otherwise he may be misguided after that experience.

In the normal affairs of life, you have your experience and I have mine, but the relationship between guru and disciple is always spiritual, even if you are involved with accounts or money. Therefore, everywhere you go, this awareness has to be there. It does not matter if you make certain mistakes in your department because of what I have

242

told you to do. After all, I have told you to do it. If you are working in the kitchen and I say, "Keep the wheat outside," and then ten bags of wheat are destroyed, it does not matter. It may be a material loss, but it is a spiritual gain because you obeyed the guru.

A guru does not exploit the disciple. If the disciple has great devotion, the guru can never exploit him. Only if the disciple is selfish, can the guru exploit him. In many books it is written that the guru exploits the disciple, but it is my experience that the guru can never exploit the unselfish disciple. A guru can only exploit a selfish disciple. An unselfish disciple, a sadhaka, never loses anything, no matter what the guru asks him, because he goes on developing his higher consciousness.

QUESTIONS AND ANSWERS

How does the guru communicate with us on the non-physical plane?

When gurus have developed the universal mind, they can operate anywhere, because the universal mind is able to unite with every mind at any time and in any place. It is not a matter of transmission, but of communication and interunion. The individual mind is only a concept; it is nothing. There is no individual mind, only the universal mind. Since you are a part of the universal mind, the guru can communicate with you from any point and at any point. Two individuals can always communicate with each other because they have the same mind.

This has to be understood properly. Due to mis-understanding, the gurus sometimes have difficulties with the disciples. If a man is singing songs and a deaf man is sitting in front of him, the deaf man will say, "This fellow is not singing at all." In the same way, the universal mind of the guru is capable of communication, but the disciple is not able to receive, so he says that the guru is useless. The disciple is living in the quagmire of the individual mind.

243

The guru is sending messages every now and then, but they fall on deaf ears. In order to communicate with the guru on an inner level, the disciple must develop his universal mind.

If a swami wishes to contact the guru, is there a particular hour of the day or night which would be the best to do it?
A disciple can contact his guru at any time because the barrier is not geographical. The contact can be made by the deeper and higher mind – just by thinking the contact can be made. However, the mind has to be rendered very subtle.

There is a moment when the individual mind identifies itself with the universal mind. When the individual mind identifies itself with the universal mind, then personal ego is lost for the time being.

How can a guru know and personally direct the individual evolution of so many hundreds of disciples?
In the atmosphere there is a satellite and all the radio communications pass through that one satellite. When they pass through the satellite, they are undifferentiated and unclassified. And if you could tune your radio to that satellite transmission, you would only hear undifferentiated humming sounds.

Thousands of messages pass through that satellite every second and are received by different radio centres in the world. There they are differentiated, classified and interpreted, and then you can talk to your friend on your telephone. It happens in the same way between the guru and his disciples.

The transmission, or the thought waves transmitted by the disciple, reach a guru and they pass through his universal consciousness. And when they pass through his universal consciousness, they are undifferentiated. It is not a language there, it is not an idea there, it is only the vibration. Then that vibration passes from his universal consciousness to his individual consciousness. When it passes through his individual consciousness, he becomes aware of his disciple. It is not only the case with guru, it is so with everybody. You

244

remember so many people throughout the day; you remember so many things throughout the day; it is nothing but the transmissions from universal consciousness to individual consciousness.

Physically, a guru has a body, but the physical body is not the guru. The guru is something other than the physical body. The physical body is only the residence, the guru is beyond that body. The guru represents elevated awareness, or you may say he represents higher consciousness. Therefore, the inner persona I am talking about receives the messages, classifies them, differentiates them and disposes of them. And all this happens just because he is an elevated being.

How should we understand the concept of universal consciousness?

In creation, billions of human beings, animals and things, all appear to be different, but in fact there is only one body. You see, in the body you have millions of cells, each representing one complete life. If one of the cells begins to think, it will consider itself as different from the others. But is it different?

Because we are able to analyze, we see the cell as a part of the whole body. In the same way, a person who has advanced in spiritual life looks at the whole world as one composition. Therefore, are we different at all? Is guru different from disciple or disciple different from guru? Are they not integrated by one universal consciousness? All of us have one universal brain; all of us have one universal body. Then where is the difficulty of communication between guru and disciple, because guru and disciple are two cells in the whole universal body?

Therefore, don't worry. Sit down in the morning, practise a little bit of yoga, calm down your mind and senses, get rid of the gases from the stomach, and become silent. Develop the effulgent form of your guru until he shines like the sun or the moon, and then communicate your sentiments or feelings to him. Like instant coffee, you will get an instant reply.

245

45

Guru as Psychotherapist

The psychotherapist and the guru both have important roles to play. Where the work of the psychotherapist finishes, the work of the guru begins. So, instead of comparing the two, let us connect them.

Of course, the guru can act as a psychotherapist, but that is not his primary motive. A psychotherapist is a person who helps you through a particular crisis in your life, but in the relationship with the guru, psychotherapy is spontaneous and ongoing. The guru's relationship with the disciple, his own personal life experience and his knowledge of the nature of the mind are such that after relieving his disciple of certain mental problems, he is then able to give him spiritual life.

That is why, right from the beginning, certain rules and regulations have been fixed. Not everybody can become a guru. In order to become a guru, you must first have had a perfect discipleship. How can you become a lecturer or a professor in a university unless you have been a student? If you have only read some of the yoga sutras and yoga books and attended a few seminars here and there, you should not think that you are a qualified guru. That is a very dangerous situation; such gurus need a psychotherapist.

If you treat someone's mind and then leave him at that point, he will continue to have problems. Of course, at a certain level sickness of mind has to be treated, but there is

246

no end to it. In my opinion, it has to be transcended rather than treated. The mind is a composition of the three gunas which keep on assaulting it all the time. Therefore, a disciple should develop new tools of knowledge and experience with which to deal with the problems of the mind.

Similarly, we cannot really equate satsang with group therapy, even though we often try to explain satsang in these terms. The Sanskrit root *sat* means reality, divinity and purity; it represents the Self or God. Satsang does not mean being in the company of many people; that is known as *sangha*, which means company or association. *Satsang* is being in the company of truth.

There are various types of satsang. You can close your eyes and practise satsang all alone. When you are reading a spiritual book which deals with the topics of reality, that is also a form of satsang. Satsang happens when you are with a group listening to the glory of the divine being or the ways of purity and self-evolution. Hearing about the lives of those people who have suffered or lived for the divine experience is also satsang.

In satsang you may practise kirtan or meditation, but these are not satsang, they are only ways of conducting satsang. In satsang the most important thing is the constant movement of ideas related to the ultimate reality, divinity or highest being.

There are certain groups that I have come across in recent years in which people join together to do some practices and to help each other. There is a very simple, scientific explanation of this. If you put a grandfather clock with many other small clocks, you will find that initially the movement of their pendulums does not coincide, but after some time all the clocks will be following the grandfather clock. This experiment has been repeated many times. Similarly, when you play a violin, all the other violins in the room begin to resonate. If you listen carefully, you will find that the vibrations from the first violin are being transmitted through the inactive violins. The same thing also happens in a group when people get together to help each other.

In India, there is not much need for these group sessions because the social situation is still very well organized. If a group of people live together in a joint family or in an ashram situation, they begin to understand the nature of human psychology. They have an opportunity to see where they stand with one another. They are able to assess their own minds, limitations and faults, which is rarely possible in the modern culture.

In the West, particularly in this century, group therapy has become an important phenomenon. In the eighteenth and nineteenth centuries the situation was different. There was a more compact and well-knit family and community life. But in the last one hundred and fifty years, the social structure has deteriorated bit by bit and hence the need for group therapy has arisen.

However, we must remember that the mind is not the ultimate reality; there is something beyond the mind. We only talk in terms of the mind because mind seems to be a barrier for many people. Actually, whatever we do in spiritual life is not done for the sake of the mind, but for the discovery of the universal spirit. Therefore, the path of psychotherapy can only be followed up to a certain extent; then there comes a point where it must be left behind. Psychoanalysis can definitely be of great use at a certain stage of development, but eventually it becomes a barrier and then you have to transcend it.

46

Guru is not a Policeman

To many, guru may appear to be a very authoritarian figure, but in my opinion gurus have to be very humble with all the knowledge they have. It is said that when the clouds are filled with water, they come closer and closer to the earth, and when trees are laden with fruits, they also bend towards the earth. Like this a person who has more knowledge and wisdom has to be more humble than others, rather than arrogant and egoistic.

Guru and teachers should not say, "I know" and "This is how it is." They should try to share with their disciples whatever knowledge and experience they have. The relationship between guru and disciple is a very intimate relationship. It is not based on superiority and inferiority and you should not see guru as the superior figure and yourself as subordinate. You are both built of the same stuff and there is a uniformity and similarity between you and him. Therefore, you should always try and feel the unity that exists between guru and yourself.

If there is no feeling of unity between guru and disciple, the disciple is always frightened of the guru and the guru seems to be egoistic about his achievements. And if he says, "Hey, you must do it", he sounds just like a policeman.

Many years ago I used to ask, "Is God a guru or is he a policeman?" because you know what we are taught about God and how he is presented in our Catholic, Hindu and

Islamic religions. He is like a policeman, a magistrate, a judge or a representative of the intelligence department – he watches and knows everything you are doing. He is also very partial – Hindu gods will not allow Christians to enter into heaven and the Christian god will not allow the heathens into heaven. You know all these stories very well.

Whatever we say about the guru-disciple relationship can also be said about the relationship that exists between God and devotee. Why should I be afraid of God? If I'm stealing your necklace or taking your money, I should not be afraid of him because he is my friend. He may not agree with what I am doing, that doesn't matter, he is still my friend. He is definitely not my boss or ruler.

This concept brings us closer to a view of spirituality and religion where God is not just a 'big brother'. The relationship you have with God should be just like the relationship you have with your girlfriend. I won't say with wife because there is a distance between husband and wife. With girlfriend and boyfriend there is a life of romance. That is how the relationship between God and devotee should be.

Look at the way many of the saints felt about God. Do you know the story of the Indian lady saint, Mira Bai? She was so mad about Krishna she demanded, "I want to see him. If he doesn't come, I'll die." Would you speak like that? That is how the real relationship between guru and disciple and between God and devotee has to be.

Remember that when we talk about guru here, we are referring to the external guru – me, he, anybody. This external guru is the way to the internal guru which is in you. There is no point in me telling you that the guru is in you and he is not in me, because you will neither get him nor me. You'll lose both. It is easy to say that guru is an internal reality, because he is, but before you can realize that internal reality, the relationship with an external guru has to be properly fixed first. You can understand his language, emotions, advice and so on, but you are deaf to the instructions of the inner guru. He may be speaking to you, but his language is Latin and you only understand Roman.

Before you understand the language of the inner guru, you must establish a positive and total relationship with your external guru. And in this relationship, you and guru must constitute one whole and not two. Just as there are two halves of the body, the right and the left, guru and disciple constitute one spiritual entity. And the same applies to God and devotee.

Often I used to ask, "Is God responsible for punishment?" because many Hindus, Christians and Muslims say he is. I don't think it is true, especially if we consider God and devotee as one spiritual entity. What business does God have to punish, and who does he punish? One half of himself? If God directs nature and he controls each and everything, how can you say that *you* are committing a sin? Can you commit a sin on your own? Is not God behind it? Is he not partially responsible? If I ask you to murder somebody and you do it, I'm partially responsible for that murder because I inspired you to do it.

So we have to make these things very clear, that God and guru are not policemen, and you and your guru or God are not two different entities.

47

Gurukripa hi Kevalam

The expression *gurukripa hi kevalam* means the grace of guru is absolute and is the only reality. For a disciple this expression holds good, because in his spiritual life and in the wild abyss of life to what shall he look? When ships approach a harbour, they are guided by a lighthouse. Just as a lighthouse is very important for a sea navigator, guru is equally important for guiding the disciple through the wilderness of life.

If you contemplate carefully, you will realize that you do not really know who you are and where you are. In truth, we do not know anything about ourselves, and if we try to dive deep in order to acquire self-knowledge, we confront frightening experiences. Therefore, in the darkness of life there has to be one lonely light in the hands of a traveller. That is why they say *gurukripa hi kevalam*.

My guru, Swami Sivananda, was a saint, not a preacher. Although he was the author of over two hundred and fifty books, he was not an intellectual. He was like a child, innocent and pure in intention, and he had many brilliant disciples with him. They served him with love and sincerity, and now, just as I feel his grace, I am sure they are receiving it too.

While I was with Swami Sivananda, I worked very hard in order to scale the wall. I had no intention at all of having ashrams and disciples and I never had any ambition to be promoted to guruhood. Even to this day I am not sure if I am a guru. Many times I try to find out, but I don't find any guru in myself. I find discipleship, of course. I never had any intention of being a preacher or a teacher. I just wanted to live as free as a bird, to move with the breeze and be tossed like the waves of the ocean. My ideal was to have nothing to do and nothing to accomplish; nothing to gain and nothing to lose; to be, that is all.

I succeeded in maintaining this standard of life from 1956 up to 1963. I never stayed at any place or associated myself with anyone. I lived like an ordinary beggar, like one of the thousands you find in India. And if you would have seen me, you would have pitied my lot. I used to spend my nights in the alleys and lanes, and drink water from any place. I slept anywhere, amongst all types of people. And I liked this life because there was a total and unspecified freedom. Nobody wanted me to follow a social code or a religion. Nobody talked to me about the so-called responsibilities of the society, family and nation.

Then one night in July 1963, I heard the thunder. It broke into the place where I was staying and I heard the summons clearly. And today I find that I am following it, not because I am honoured, but because he has chosen me. That is called the grace.

If he chooses me to suffer, I will accept it as his grace. Not only good things represent the grace; not only the positive and congenial situations in life represent the grace, either of guru or of God. The grace has a purpose even if we don't know what it is. Actually, my philosophical tradition is Vedanta and not yoga. I know more about Vedanta than yoga because I studied that subject for many years. However, I am preaching yoga and not Vedanta because he understands that everybody is suffering from infirmity of will and that yoga alone can help them.

When I lived in Swami Sivananda's ashram, it was difficult for me to accept anyone as my associate. I did not want anybody to depend on me. My one thought was always, "I came alone and I will go alone, therefore I must live alone."

253

But nowadays in the ashram, I find that everybody is too attached to me and people are always circling around my room and waiting outside my door. It is so unbearable for me because I am a different type of person. You don't see me coming to your room and talking to you, that is not my nature. Many times I have considered living quietly, but every time I think about it, I hear the thunder again – "Continue." Okay, I continue with the suffering.

Although I continue to be a disciple, gurudom is imposed upon me, and I must accept that heavy cloak. As a disciple, I don't feel I have any other choice. So when people ask, "Are you my guru?" I say "Yes." I would prefer to say, "I am like you. I am your elder brother, your senior friend." But I have to say, "Yes, I am your guru," because the grace of guru must be followed and the disciple should have no choice. If he has a choice, there is an iron curtain. Then the guru is on one side and the disciple is in the other and communication is not possible.

I have read the life stories of many great disciples and one of the most recent ones was Swami Vivekananda. How he was tossed by the grace of guru! Ramakrishna completely submerged him in his grace, and throughout Swami Vivekananda's short life, he lived in total dedication to the choice of guru. In the beginning he was a very negative man and used to say, "Oh, I don't like this sadhu at all." But Ramakrishna had made his final choice and once the guru makes his decision, the disciple has no other way to go.

Not only in India, but even in Europe, there is this holy tradition of guru's grace in the life of a disciple. Disciples exist today no doubt, but the disciples to whom the grace of guru is earmarked are rare. And often I wonder why Swami Sivananda chose me. I think it could only be for one reason. I had always been his very keen follower. Even an ordinary act in his life meant a great commentary to me. I noted each and every word and expression, I observed every movement of his life – what he ate and how he ate, how he slept and how much he slept, how he greeted people and how he treated them. There were times when I could predict what he was thinking, and on other occasions I could predict what he was going to do before he had a chance to decide anything. A disciple has to understand before the guru can decide.

In certain situations inmates of the ashram used to ask me what I thought Swamiji would do, and I was able to make exact predictions. When I stood beside him, I could see how his thought currents were functioning. Even now I don't believe that he is dead. Of course he is, but it is very difficult for me to feel that because when he lived, the body I perceived did not seem to be composed of empirical stuff. It appeared to be made of fine, divine fabric. Not just for a day, but for a full twelve years I saw his body like that.

During my life with Swami Sivananda, there was not one point where I was not in rapport with him. That kind of unity must be established between guru and disciple, then the grace flows automatically. So, the expression is *gurukripa* – grace, *hi* – indeed, *kevalam* – absolute.

I believe in God as many or most of you do, but what is there to think about him and how to think about him? What is he and what is he not? God is not a man, He is not just a little idol; he is the totality. How can I think of totality with this little mind? The mind is finite and God is infinite. Can you believe that a finite mind can ever visualize the infinite?

In order to experience, know and behold the infinite, you have to be infinity first. Therefore, I came to the conclusion years ago: unite with your guru, become one with him. Just as salt dissolves in water, sugar dissolves in milk and fragrance dissolves in the air, become one and not two. The water becomes salty and the salt becomes watery. They adopt each other's qualities. That kind of unity has to be achieved, then the grace of guru is always there. But no matter how much we talk, practical life is another matter. Mind is very hard stuff to crack, and we fail even if we know the truth.

QUESTIONS AND ANSWERS

Does guru represent God or divinity for the disciple?

Guru is a human being. In the human body he may have an effulgent spirit or he may be ignorant, but the disciple considers his guru as a replica of divinity. I think this is correct, but it is necessary to make certain amendments.

My guru was Swami Sivananda. I always regarded him as divinity and I still do, but I do not preach that he is God. That is the major amendment I want to make. The mistake here is that we consider our guru as God and we ask others to do likewise. My relationship with my guru is purely personal. Whether I regard him as divinity or as a monster, that is my personal opinion. Your guru is divine for you, I do not deny this truth, but if you want me to respect your guru as divine, I don't agree. That is where the confusion has come.

Divinity is inherent in every being. Some have awakened it and others have not. During my travels in search of a guru I met many souls, but I was searching for a guru in whom I could realize divinity. Of course, I knew that every guru is divine, but I could not see it.

The first saintly person whom I came across was Anandamayi Ma, a very venerated guru who has now left her body. I saw her when I was only ten, but at that time I could not see divinity in her. I don't say that she was not divine. She was, but I could not see it. After her I met many great men – Ramana Maharshi, Sri Aurobindo, Swami Ramdas, Meher Baba, but I did not see God in any of them. They were godly, but I could not see it due to my early education in a Christian convent. I had read the Bible and the library of Christian saints, so I had all those things in my mind.

I also lived with an old tantric guru for six months. He was a very simple man but a master of his science, and he loved me very much. I was nineteen then and he was sixty-seven. He wanted to teach me everything he knew, but I

256

thought to myself, "I don't see God in him. For me, he is a learned man, a good man, but I don't see anything more in him." So I left him.

However, on the very day I met Swami Sivananda, I started having experiences of lofty consciousness. I found in him the divinity personified, and as long as I lived with him I saw something behind his physical form. Whenever people asked me, "Do you consider your guru as God?" I used to reply, "This is my personal matter, just as a man's attitude towards his wife is a personal matter. So please don't ask me this." This is the fundamental thing which one must remember in relation to guru.

You must realize the divinity in your guru. If you are not able to do this, then he is not your guru. If there is petrol in a can and you touch fire to it, what will happen? Everybody knows. It is the same with the relationship between guru and disciple. The moment the guru touches the spirit of the disciple, there is an explosion. If there is no explosion, then there is something wrong. Maybe someone told you this is petrol, but it is really water. So, when you bring fire, nothing happens because there is no petrol. The relationship is not complete because fire cannot ignite water.

In the same way, when you realize divinity in your guru, there is the revelation. This is not intellectual; it is spiritual. You begin to hear sounds, see visions, do automatic movements. Such a man is your guru and such a man should be the replica of divinity to you.

What is divinity? It is higher existence, the totality of creation, an expression of God. God is divine. Now, guru is the incarnation of divinity. Divinity is without name and form. It has no dimension in which to exist; it is total. But human beings cannot comprehend its formlessness, so the subtle and transcendental divinity incarnates out of its own goodwill and descends in a gross form so that people may understand it. These incarnations are known as avatars or prophets, and to the disciples they are known as guru or God.

257

How does the guru guide the disciple after death?

When the guru dies and leaves the mortal body, he can operate from a nearby plane. The purpose of a guru is not to get liberation. After he has left the mortal body, he remains capable of guiding his disciples. It is true that whatever he has spoken also helps his disciples, but there is another very important factor which one has to keep in mind. The disciple's own spirit has to be receptive so that he can receive the transmission of his guru's vibration. Therefore, after death, although the guru is alive on a different plane, all disciples are not able to receive his transmission. In fact, gurus also make some choice. From that invisible plane they keep on guiding some of their disciples.

Gurus have different planes of existence. One is the astral plane. There is another plane of their existence, and that plane is the heart of the disciple. His spirit can come and swell in the heart of the disciple. The heart of the disciple is the spiritual plane. There are certain disciples who are very sensitive in this matter. They are so aware of their guru that the vibrations of guru can be planted in their heart. This means that the guru can simultaneously live on those planes, that is to say he can live on the astral plane as well as in the disciple's heart.

When the guru comes and dwells in the heart of his disciple, then the disciple need not be receptive. Guru controls his actions, his thinking process and everything else. This means his personal ego is replaced by guru. The body belongs to the disciple, but the mind has been replaced. The guru is there. So, this is a very important phenomenon. The body of the disciple, the mind of the spirit of the guru, this is a very important but rare phenomenon. And if this happens in the life of a disciple, then it is the second incarnation of guru. But this does not happen always. Usually, guru guides from the astral plane.

Now, there is a third phenomenon. Guru may or may not be on any plane, but a disciple has faith and he is very aware of his guru. Then his faith is restructured; his faith is cast in the form of the guru. This is called 'guru consciousness'. Guru is not there; it is the disciple's mind, it is his emotion; it is himself, but on account of his intense faith, he has developed a guru consciousness. Due to this guru consciousness, he develops within himself a higher state of consciousness. This is very easy, and it is possible for everybody who is able to develop faith.

Now, I have spoken of three possibilities. After the guru has thrown off his mortal coil, he guides his disciples from the astral plane. Or, at the same time, he dwells in the spirit of his disciple and possesses his life completely. Or, a disciple develops guru consciousness in himself and leads the spiritual life. The third one is very, very possible and everybody can develop this guru consciousness. The second is very rare.

Does the disciple come only once to the guru or is there a link from the past?
As far as your question goes, I have to reply in brief. I don't know about others, but I know about myself. I have been with many people in the past who are with me today as my disciples in the present life. I can know this at certain moments, but not all the time. This is so far as my personal experience is concerned. As for the philosophy, the relationship between guru and disciple is long-standing. It is not for the first time that one becomes a sannyasin disciple.

Ordinarily, you go to someone and take a mantra, that is different. But when you dedicate and surrender yourself, your personality and your material future, wealth, name and everything, it is not a small thing. A sannyasin disciple has made a very big dedication to his guru and that cannot happen unless circumstances from the previous life compel him to do that. It is not only changing your name, shaving your head, changing your dress, leaving your home and wife, selling your property and so many other things. What for? It is only possible if the destiny, if the circumstances from your previous incarnation, have brought you to this point of fulfilment, to this point of commitment. And,

259

therefore, for the same reason we should understand that the relationship between guru and disciple, especially a sannyasin disciple, is a long-standing one, a permanent one, a permanent union and a permanent commitment.

Often when I close my eyes, I see your face. Am I brainwashing myself, am I setting up an emotional situation, or is this the beginning of a guru-disciple relationship?
I think all three. You see, brainwashing is necessary, and an emotional situation is also very necessary in order to prepare for the guru-disciple relationship.

* * *

The guru-disciple communion is the most enduring type of relationship mankind has ever known. It transcends experiences and emotions and continues to work in its non-rationalizable way, even after death. Man, ruled by fear, passion and compulsion, cannot see it working as it propels his very soul to the heights of evolution.

48

Swami Sivananda

Swami Sivananda lived life in all its completeness: at once a great saint of the calibre of Christ; an administrator in the highest position; a sannyasin with total detachment from life; a man brimming over with compassion, love and charity, but living a life of austerity and dispassion; a bhakta and devotee of God, and side by side a philosopher of superior intellect; a man with discipline and strictness as well as loving kindness for every sentient and insentient creation of God.

Such a man can be an example to us all. Most of us are puzzled by the day to day problems of our life. We are swayed by passions and emotions and dejected when we face the ups and downs of our emotional life. Definitely, to sincere people the question does arise, "How is it possible for me, a person with so many limitations, to reach the highest pinnacle of life?" To such sincere people, who are disappointed and dejected by the cruelties of life, Swami Sivananda is like a beacon of light. To hear about him is a joy, to think about him is yoga and to discuss him is to invest the time properly. Even though he lived in the physical body, he was not a physical soul and his presence developed the inner awareness without any difficulty.

In one of the Upanishads there is a parable. A disciple asked his guru, "How does a man walk? How does a man move?" The guru replied, "In the light of the sun he moves

261

and walks." Then the disciple asked, "If the sun is set, how does he move and how does he walk?" The guru replied, "In the light of the moon." Then the disciple asked again, "When the sun is set and the moon is set, in whose light does one walk?" The guru replied, "In the light of the stars." Again the disciple interrogated, "When the sun is set and the moon is set and the stars are twinkling no more, in whose light does he walk?" The guru replied, "In his own light."

What is this light he is talking about? When the mind is swayed by passion, when the intellect is filled with confusion, when your own beliefs betray you, when your own concepts do not help you any more in life, then you will have to raise your own consciousness. You will have to awaken your own spirit. In order to awaken the spirit, it is very important that a satguru is sought. Such a guru was Swami Sivananda, not only in his own time, but even today when the message of his life and teachings is a lamp unto those who have yet to awaken their inner light.

The best of men

When you compare the life of Swami Sivananda with the life of other sannyasins and saints, you find that his was a different personality altogether. He did not behave like a miracle man, a great pontiff or a preacher. He just lived the life of a simple man. It was very difficult to change his human qualities. He was a shining example of all the great virtues that you read about in the books.

For me, it is more important for a man to be a man than a saint. It is easy to be a venerable man, a guru, anything exalted, but not a man. It is very difficult to give, it's most difficult to love, and it's impossible to understand. Today man has reached the point where he finds himself incapable of realizing his fundamental humanity. If a man can be a man, he can be everything, because to be a man he has to kill everything in him. Before you can play music on a bamboo flute, the bamboo must be hollowed out. In the same way, you have to empty yourself. You have to bear the kicks, face the criticism and live with the passions. You must end your fears and be prepared to be persecuted and abused. You should not expect to be loved or honoured; that is imperative.

Many times when people talk about love, I just laugh at them. I have never met any other person who I think knows love, but I can definitely say that Swami Sivananda was a man whose very being emanated love. Nevertheless, he was the least emotional person I have known – completely calm, quiet, unruffled and absolutely detached. He was the best of men I have seen in my life. I have never seen Christ, but I have seen Swami Sivananda and therefore I believe Christ must have existed. He was a man whose kindness and compassion knew no bounds. He was nothing but sweetness, nothing but smiling eyes.

In everything he did throughout his life, he maintained only one attitude – to do good to everybody. He was never a dictator and never interfered with his disciples. In fact, he used to touch the feet of his disciples just as a disciple touches his master's feet. Many times I made mistakes, both in my life and in the ashram, as an inmate and as an executive. I was always expecting to be called by him, but he never once called me. I thought that he would rebuke me or admonish me, or tell me what was right or wrong, but he never said one word. When I used to go to him, he would never raise the point. He would just say the usual things. He never recognized the mistakes in people. He always used to say that everyone had in them the spark of divinity.

His attitude towards people was unique. If anyone was concerned about being criticized, he explained very simply, "It is a divine test. When you purchase a steel rod, you don't examine it, but when you purchase a rod of gold, you examine it thoroughly. And if you go to purchase a diamond, you don't just pick up the first one you see. Likewise, when God is choosing you, he should test you. It is not your karma that is coming to you in the form of suffering. It is not your viciousness that is causing your criticism. It is the test of the divine, so that you may pass through it, and then you will be given the higher wisdom."

Give, give, give

Swami Sivananda started out practising medicine in the states of Malaysia. When he came to Rishikesh, he plunged headlong into spiritual life. He was so sincere and devoted that all the swamis who were living nearby were very influenced by him. Sometimes he used to collect a few chapatis from his daily bhiksha and keep them in a box. When he had a sufficient number, he would close his doors from the inside for a week and practise his own sadhana. Sometimes in the middle of the night you would see him chest deep in Ganga chanting, "Om,Om,Om".

With this sincere devotion to spiritual life, he soon became a darling of the swamis there. In reaction to this, there naturally developed a gang of rascals who harassed him and actually cause him injury as well. His attitude towards these people was superhuman. He used to say, "If someone kicks you, give him love," and he practised this every day. Later, when Swami Sivananda became very famous, he would give those very same people great respect and hold them in esteem.

He was very generous and gave people anything they asked for. His main motto was, "Give, give, give." Even if he had been alerted that a man had come to cheat him, he would not listen. He would say, "That is his karma and this is my karma." He freely distributed food, money, books, clothes, blankets and so on. If somebody told him, "Swamiji, this man is dishonest, do not give him a blanket," Swamiji would say, "God has given it to me for him. The money does not belong to me; the ashram does not belong to me."

Jnani and bhakta

Swami Sivananda was a sannyasin belonging to the highest order of Vedanta philosophy. This Vedanta philosophy holds

264

that "I am Brahman", and does not accept any lesser form of idol worship. It is a philosophy of pure monism in which the truth is formless and nameless and all the experience exists within the mind. This practical doctor then was at the same time a true jnani who spoke of the philosophy of the absolute, and also a bhakta, one who is devoted to God. In fact, he believed that devotion to God and repetition and singing of the name alone were enough to enable one to cross the barriers of worldly consciousness.

His faith in name was sometimes very unintellectual. He used to say, "Name alone can take you across the world." So in 1943 he started a wonderful program: continuous, unbroken chanting of the name. By that time we had built one hall and seven or eight of us had become swamis. In that hall a lamp was placed and every swami had to sing there for two hours a day, then another swami would take over the duty. So we needed twelve swamis and a few surplus, in case some should fall ill.

Swamiji decided upon the mantra which would be used: 'Hare Rama, Hare Rama, Rama Rama, Hare Hare. Hare Krishna, Hare Krishna, Krishna Krishna, Hare Hare.' This is a very ancient mantra known as the Maha Mantra, which forms a part of the *Kali Santarana Upanishad*, one of the one hundred and eight upanishads. Swamiji also decided on the melody. So, for twenty-four hours a day there would be a swami continuing the kirtan. In those days, whenever anybody came to the ashram asking to become a swami, I used to say, "Yes, please", and lead him in because we had to keep the program continuously running.

On the day of inauguration of the ashram, Swamiji said, "This kirtan will continue as long as the world lasts." We became greatly worried. I thought, "For one, two, three or four years, maybe, but as long as the world lasts!" And this was precisely the program of Swami Sivananda which became the nucleus of the whole structure that you find today.

265

An innocent mind

Swami Sivananda was a man who believed in everybody and never thought that anyone was bad. He was a man without ego and ambition who never posed as a great swami. Thousands of people came to him and were helped out of difficult situations, but his only comment was, "It is God's grace." They would all say to him, "Swamiji, you are a great siddha, you are a great master. On account of your blessings, my child has come through his crisis." He would say, "No, no, no. It is God's grace, and your prarabdha karma."

Swami Sivananda was not intellectual; he was purely a bhakta with a very innocent mind. If anyone came to him or wrote to him with problems, at once he would ask everybody to please sit down, close their eyes and repeat the mantra for that person's recovery. He had such faith that immediately after the mantra was repeated, he would have us write a letter saying, "We have conducted the mantra prayer for you and now you will be all right."

Unless you have faith, you cannot believe in this. We are all intellectuals. We know all the mantras, but we have no faith in them. If we practise a mantra for someone who is sick, we will not dare to write and tell him that he has recovered completely because we cannot be sure he got better. Whereas faith leaves no room for doubt, knowledge has fissures in it. I am not against intellect, but at the same time its limitations must be pointed out.

Faith is very innocent, but it is so powerful that the miracles you see in the lives of great saints are a product of that innocence. Innocence is not childishness; it is the blossoming of the purity in man's structure. To be innocent, you don't have to do anything or be anything. Rather, whatever you have acquired you have to throw away – knowledge, proceeds, wealth, power, status and political and religious background. You have to believe, "I am nothing." When this attitude takes hold within you, it becomes the centre of faith, and in Swami Sivananda I found this faith in absolutely living form.

Taking notes

At one time I was writing a commentary on the *Brihadaranyaka Upanishad*. I had a sound intellectual knowledge of Sanskrit and philosophy because my earlier academic background had been very bright, but nevertheless I had great difficulties in writing the commentary on this upanishad. From time to time when I used to go to Swamiji for clarification, he used to direct me to H.H. Tapovanamji Maharaj. He was not a disciple of Swamiji's and did not live in Rishikesh, but in Uttarkashi, a place on the way to the origin of the Ganga. He was a venerable swami, a master of the upanishads and a great Sanskrit scholar.

During his life, Swami Sivananda wrote approximately three to four hundred books. In the period I was there, he had already finished two hundred and fifty of them. But it was a very important part of his philosophy not to pose, even before his disciples, that he knew everything. You are deluding the disciple if you do not direct him to the proper authority for whatever he is trying to learn. Swami Sivananda could have also guided me by referring me to a few books here and there, but he was my well-wisher and knew that it was best to send me to a great authority like Swami Tapovanamji Maharaj.

So, whenever Swami Tapovanamji visited Rishikesh during the snowy winter, Swami Sivananda would say to me, "Swami Tapovanamji is here, go and study with him." So I would go to Swami Tapovanamji with all my philosophical queries and grammatical complications. I used to sit with him for hours discussing philosophy and when I returned, I always found Swami Sivananda waiting for me. He would call me to his kutir and question me: "What did you ask and what did he say?" I would tell him everything I had learned and while I was talking, Swamiji would be busy writing it all down. The next morning he would get these notes typed out and would develop a story, an article or a poem out of all those ideas I had received from Swami Tapovanamji and then narrated to him.

The humility of enlightenment

There are many people in this world who think that they know everything already and are not open to the positive effects of learning from others. If you tell them something you have just learned, they say, "Oh, I already knew that!" This is a peculiar characteristic of man's nature which represents his deep-rooted and inherent egoism, and where there is egoism there is bound to be ignorance.

All of the scriptures in Christianity, Islam and Hinduism say the same thing – that egoism is not a product of knowledge or enlightenment; in religious terms, one can say that it is the product of Satan. Where there is enlightenment, there is humility; the more enlightened you are, the smaller you feel. This is true not only in the life of a saint or swami, but also for an artist, a poet, politician, scientist or musician. The more enlightenment comes, the less you think about yourself, and when you feel that you are little, how can there be egoism?

Newton said about his discoveries that he was only collecting the pebbles on the shore while the ocean still remained untouched before him. A great man, a true man, an enlightened personality, is always open to every form of knowledge. Whether he learns from saints or sinners makes no difference because they are only social distinctions, categories and castes. For a mother, it makes no difference whether her child is a boy or a girl, healthy or unhealthy, plain or beautiful, a swami or a drunkard.

Saints never criticize and are never afflicted by prejudice or attachment. They interact on spiritual levels. Of course, to talk about saints is not an easy matter. They are like icebergs – you can see a small part of them above the water; the rest is hidden. Therefore, it is definitely not possible for me to make an accurate assessment of the personality of Swami Sivananda with whom I lived for only a short period of time, but who was also responsible for changing the whole current and concept of my life.

From shore to shore

In 1956, Swami Sivananda called me and he just said, "What sadhana are you doing?" In twelve years he had not asked me any questions like this. I did practise asana, pranayama, etc., but not at the command of guru, just as a matter of personal choice. The quantity of mantra I had practised was very great and at the same time I had practised karma yoga day and night.

I told him, "I do asana, pranayama, mantra japa", and a few more things that I did. He asked, "You don't practise kriya yoga?" I said, "No, I have heard about it but I don't know it." He took me to his room and in ten minutes he taught me kriya yoga. Or, to put it another way, in ten minutes I learned kriya yoga. Then he gave me one hundred and eight rupees and said, "Now you can go from here. This ashram is no longer the place for you. Keep moving and spread the message of yoga from shore to shore and from door to door."

According to this instruction, I left the ashram and kept moving. I was still young and it was very difficult because there were so many different movements and gurus, that a man like myself could hardly survive. I could never tell lies, cheat people or complicate matters. Nevertheless, I managed to keep moving for many years.

Waking up from within

In 1963, on July 14th I believe, I suddenly woke up from inside. I was in Munger at that time, and a vision swept across my mind. I was in Rishikesh, near the beautiful Ganga, and on it a ship was sailing across to the other side. Swami Sivananda was standing on the deck looking towards me with his hands joined in namaskara. Trumpets and conches sounded, drums were being beaten and bells rung. At one point, the ship moved very close to me and the current was so strong that the flywheel sprinkled water all over my head, throat and body.

When this inner vision was finished, I understood that it meant Swami Sivananda had left his mortal body and had transferred his blessings to me. Swamiji loved the Ganga very much; I cannot begin to tell you how much. During the rainy season when its water became so muddy, he would still drink it. When the Ganga rose high in rain and floods and his room became half-flooded, still he would refuse to shift to any other building.

That very same day I took my bag, went to the railway station, purchased a ticket and went to Rishikesh. And I was correct; he had already left. From that time on, even up to this day, at least once a year, I can wake up within myself. And that experience is as true, as real, as deep, as concrete as this one. It is not a dream; it is not hypnosis; it is not imagination. It has the same dimension as this reality. There I can find him and receive very clear guidance from him.

My life has been very exceptional, I've never had any difficulties, and therefore when I go to guru, I don't go with any desire in my mind. Many times I've thought I should try to pray for something, but I don't know what to pray for. He has given me everything and what he has not given me, I think I should not have. In my interaction and my life with Swami Sivananda, the discovery of self was the primary goal of the relationship between us. The period of twelve years that I lived with him was a time for me to polish my inner mirror. The ego had to be erased, the passions settled, the desires properly fixed, and ignorance erased. How can one do this unless he serves his guru?

QUESTIONS AND ANSWERS

What was Swami Sivananda's main teaching to his disciples?
Once Swami Sivananda told me that we are all instruments, we are all mediums. We have to love and serve everybody without passion and attachment, without expectation. We have to love God without asking anything from him. The purpose of our spiritual life has to be to have the vision of the divine. God has given us everything, we did not ask for it. Then why do we ask him for anything at all? He knows

270

what we need, he knows what we deserve, he knows what we should not have. So we must throw off the desires and just submit everything to the 'divine will'. Whether we are in pain or happiness, wealth or poverty, we are in his hands.

If you ever meet such a person as Swami Sivananda, then please let me know, and until you find such a one, keep on doing your sadhana. Unfortunately, today the world is devoid of such persons. I have been keenly and eagerly trying to discover if there is one such person around me. I find good speakers, I find very good people, but I don't find 'God-intoxicated' people. So, try to seek and follow, renounce and surrender to 'God-intoxicated' people.

Did Swami Sivananda have a particular philosophy?
In everything he did throughout his life, he maintained only one attitude – to do good to everybody. In so far as the spiritual life of Swami Sivananda was concerned, it was complete. The whole twenty-four hours he would remain immersed in the thought of his mantra. When he was leaving the body, a lady who was by his side asked him to give his last message to humanity. He took a pen and wrote, "God is real, all else is unreal." That was the philosophy of Swami Sivananda throughout his life and nothing else.

What was your greatest experience with your guru?
If you had lived with Swami Sivananda, you would have thought of Jesus Christ all the time. When Christ said, "God forgive them, for they know not what they do," I thought it could not be so, I thought that no man could possibly have been like that. However, in the lives of Swami Sivananda and Mahatma Gandhi, this was practised. This was a very great experience in my life.

How did you overcome the difficulties of your early days as a disciple?
When you have love for someone, difficulties are not difficult. You become aware of the difficulties only when you have no

271

one to love. If you love your guru, or anybody, even if the whole world kicks you, or criticizes you, you don't realize it. The personality of Swami Sivananda was so compassionate and peaceful that the diseases and sicknesses which I suffered from, I never felt.

When I look back on those years, I myself am surprised as to how that happened. Was I dreaming or was I under hypnosis? When you have deep and abiding love for someone, how can you be aware of the extraneous experiences? When you are in the warm embrace of a young boy or girl, you do not even notice the passage of time. When you are under the grip of passion, you do not think of anything else. So, when you are in the presence of your guru, how can you be aware of yourself?

Please explain complete renunciation in the light of your experience.

Frankly speaking, I don't want ashrams. I don't want disciples, and sometimes I get exhausted from all these surroundings. I want to give up the ashrams and go away into seclusion in a forest and just sit down there. I think, "When I have left my parents and property, when I have left all my relatives, why to have these relatives?" It is at these times that I always get a vision. I don't know if it lasts for long or for seconds. At that time I am transported into another realm of consciousness. I am no longer Swami Satyananda, and I hear very clearly, "No, keep on moving; don't withdraw yourself!" It is the voice of Swami Sivananda.

Renunciation has to be complete. Each and everything we are attached to should be renounced. My house has become old and I can renounce it. My robe has become old, I can renounce it. But how can I renounce the person I love? That is very difficult. Most of the time we practise convenient renunciation. We renounce those objects we dislike. But when you renounce what you like, that is real renunciation.

I know very well that, sooner or later, I am going to get out of this cycle. I wrote this short poem some time ago:

With nothing on the body,
And with nothing in my hands,
Let me roam on the banks of the Ganga
With the name of Shiva on my lips
And the thought of Devi and Durga in my mind.
Let me not even know that I exist,
And when I die, I will not know that I am dying.

This is the type of life which Swami Sivananda infused in me and I have to follow him now.

49

Guru Stotram

A selection from *Guru Gita* as given in the Uttarakhand section of the *Skanda Purana* in the form of a dialogue between Shiva and Uma (Shakti).

Gurubrahma Guruvishnu
Gurudevo Maheshwara
Guru Sakshat Param Brahma
Tasmai Shri Gurave Namaha

Guru is Brahma, Guru is Vishnu, Guru is Lord Maheshwara. Guru is verily the supreme reality. Sublime prostration unto him.

Dhyanamoolam Gurormurti
Pujamoolam Gurorpadam
Mantramoolam Gurorvakyam
Mokshamoolam Gurorkripa

The Guru's form is the object of meditation. Real worship is of the Guru's feet. The basis of all mantras is the word of the Guru. The bestowal of liberation is the Guru's grace alone.

Akhanda Mandalakaram
Vyaptam Yena Characharam
Tatpadam Darshitam Yena
Tasmai Shri Gurave Namaha

I prostrate to the Sadguru by whom the whole world, comprising unbroken consciousness, is pervaded and filled through and through in every moving and unmoving object. Sublime salutations to the Guru who is established in 'That' and who has awakened me to its realization.

Mannatha Shri Jagannathaha
Madguru Shri Jagadguruh
Madatma Sarvabhutatma
Tasmai Shri Gurave Namaha

My Lord is the Lord of the universe. My Guru is the Guru of the whole world. My Self is the Self of all beings, therefore I prostrate to my Guru who has shown me this.

Jnana Shakti Samarudhaha
Tattwa Mala Vibushitam
Bhukti Mukti Pradata Cha
Tasmai Shri Gurave Namaha

He who is established in spiritual knowledge and power, who is adorned with the garland of truth, the reality, He who bestows both liberation and enjoyment here in this world, to that Guru, sublime salutations.

Stavaram Jangamam Vyaptam
Yatkinchit Sacharacharam
Tatpadam Darshitam Yena
Tasmai Shri Gurave Namaha

Whatever is moving and unmoving and that which pervades whatever is animate and inanimate, to that Guru who reveals all these things, sublime salutations.

Chinmayam Vyapitam Sarvam
Trailokyam Sacharacharam
Tatpadam Darshitam Yena
Tasmai Shri Gurave Namaha

I prostrate to the Guru who has made me realize that essence which pervades past, present and future and all things moving and unmoving.

Chaitanyam Shashvatam Shantam
Vyomateetam Niranjanaha
Bindu Nada Kala Teetaha
Tasmai Shri Gurave Namaha

Prostration to the Guru who is eternal, peaceful, unattached, full of light and knowledge, beyond the stages of Nada, Bindu and Kala, and who transcends even the ether.

Glossary

Aghora sadhana – a tantric practice in which no rites are considered abominable.

Ajapa japa – spontaneous repetition of mantra.

Ajna chakra – the highest of the six psychic centres situated at the top of the spinal cord; the 'command centre' where the voice of the inner guru is heard.

Anandamayi Ma – twentieth century woman saint of Bengal.

Anushthana – a prolonged mantra repetition practice.

Arjuna – hero of the Bhagavad Gita and disciple of Lord Krishna.

Asana – yoga posture.

Ashram – a place of spiritual retreat and growth.

Atmajyoti – light of the soul.

Atman – the soul of inner spirit.

Atman anubhuti – direct experience of atman.

Atman samarpan – self-surrender.

Avadhoota Dattatreya – name of a great Indian saint who was a renowned tantric yogi.

Avatar purusha – an incarnated soul of divinity.

Avidya – ignorance.

Bhais – brothers.

Bhajan – hymn.

Bhava – inner feeling.

Bhavana – same as bhava.

Bhiksha – alms, offering.

Brahma – part of the Hindu trinity; creator of the universe.

Brahmachari – one practising sexual abstinence.

Brahman – absolute reality.

Brahmanishta guru – a guru who is established in the supreme self.

Brahmashrotriya – one who is well-versed in the subject of supreme reality.

Brahma Sutra – a collection of talks on jnana yoga by sage Badarayana.

Buddha – an enlightened sage who was born and lived in India approximately 2,500 years ago, after whom Buddhism originated.

Chaitanya Mahaprabhu – great Bengali bhakta.

Chela – disciple.

Chidakasha – the mind space visualized behind the closed eyes, inside the forehead.

Dakshina – offerings made to guru.

Devata – deity.

Devi – goddess.

Dharma – one's duty in life.

Dhoti – piece of unstitched cloth worn around the body.

Dhyana – state of meditation.

Diksha – initiation.

Durga – goddess, overcomer of obstacles on the spiritual path.

Dwesha – dislikes.

Ganga – sacred and longest river in India.

Geru – ochre-coloured dye or mud used for colouring the robes of a sannyasin.

Gita – short for Bhagavad Gita, the explanation of the twelve types of yoga.

Gopis – female devotees of Lord Krishna.

Gunas – qualities of the mind.

Guru – the dispeller of darkness.

Guru Poornima – a festival celebrated on the full moon of July, when devotees pay homage to their guru and the guru meditates on behalf of all his disciples.

278

Guru kripa hi kevalam – guru's grace alone is sufficient (for enlightenment).

Hanuman – great devotee of Sri Rama, half-man half-monkey, and a symbol of brahmacharya.

Hatha yoga – a form of yoga in which the two poles of energy existing in the physical body are brought into harmony by a systematic series of practices.

Himalayas – mountain range in North India considered as the abode of sages and saints from time immemorial.

Ishta – personal vision of God.

Japa – repetition of a mantra.

Jiva – the individual soul.

Jivanmukta – a liberated sage still operating in the world with absolute compassion for all living beings.

Jnani guru – a guru who imparts scriptural knowledge and emphasizes the importance of reflecting and contemplating on the formless reality without resorting to any external methods or rituals.

Jnana yoga – a form of yoga in which contemplation of truth is practised without the aid of any external forms of sadhana.

Jyoti – inner light.

Kabir – famous fifteenth century poet saint of Varanasi.

Kali – Shakti in her destructive form.

Kali yuga – present age of spiritual darkness at the end of which will come the Golden Age.

Karma – actions which determine one's destiny, life after life.

Kapali sadhana – a form of tantric sadhana in which a human skull is used.

Karma sannyasa – a form of sannyasa in which the aspirant evolves through the performance of social and family obligations by maintaining an inner spirit of detachment.

Karma yoga – a branch of yoga in which every type of activity is aimed at self-realization by inculcating a deep sense of detachment.

Kirtan – repetition of mantra to music.

Krishna – eighth incarnation of Lord Vishnu.

279

Kriya yoga – a form of yoga in which a series of practices derived from tantra are practised for the awakening of kundalini.

Kumari sadhana – a tantric practice in which a virgin is used as the basis for sadhana, but not for sexual intercourse or maithuna.

Kundalini yoga – an important form of yoga which aims at awakening the primal force and directing it to the highest pinnacle.

Kunjal – a hatha yoga cleansing technique for the stomach.

Lassi – Indian drink made from curd and water.

Lata sadhana – a tantric sadhana in which an adult female is included as a participant in the practices.

Laya yoga – yoga of absorption.

Mahabharata – a famous Indian epic symbolizing the battle between good and evil forces in the mind.

Mahavir Jain – a great sage, after whom Jainism was established, who practised intense austerities and was a contemporary of Lord Buddha.

Maithuna – union between two opposite poles of energy, commonly called sexual intercourse.

Mala – a string of beads used in mantra japa to count the number of repetitions.

Mandala – pictorial diagram for focusing spiritual energy.

Mantra – a sound or combination of sounds used for developing higher frequencies of the mind.

Mantra siddhi – perfection in the practice of mantra.

Maya – the veil of illusion responsible for erroneous perception; the great obstacle for an aspirant to overcome.

Meher Baba – twentieth century saint who carried the message of spiritual life from India throughout the world.

Mira Bai – female saint, born in the early sixteenth century in Rajasthan; a great devotee of Lord Krishna.

Moksha – a state of individual self when one becomes free from the association of ignorance produced by maya.

Mooladhara – the root chakra or energy centre which is the seat of sexual and spiritual energy.

Nadanusandhana – discovery of sound vibrations.

Neti – hatha yoga cleansing technique for the nasal passages.

Nirguna – beyond the three gunas.

Nirakara – beyond form.

Nirvana – salvation.

Paramahamsa – literally, supreme swan; one who has achieved the highest discrimination and wisdom.

Parivrajaka – wandering by foot.

Parvati – consort of Lord Shiva, symbolizing awakened divine energy through the practices of yoga and tantra.

Prana – subtle energy or life force.

Pranayama – an important practice of yoga in which the breath is manipulated for regulating the prana and improving respiratory, circulatory and nervous functions.

Prarabdha karma – that portion of one's actions which is bound to fructify in the present life and cannot be averted.

Puja – worship.

Puranas – ancient Indian historical epics.

Purascharana – set numbers of mantra repetitions performed over a period of time.

Radha – chief disciple and consort of Lord Krishna.

Raga – attachment.

Rajas – one of the three gunas.

Raja yoga – a form of yoga propounded by Patanjali, also known as the eight-limbed path.

Rama – name of one divine incarnation or avatar.

Ramakrishna – enlightened guru who lived in the nineteenth century and preached the universality of all religions.

Ramana Maharshi – twentieth century saint from Tamil Nadu.

Ramatirtha Swami – twentieth century Punjabi saint who visited America and Japan teaching Vedanta and Buddhism in the spirit of modern science and philosophy.

Ramdas Swami – twentieth century South Indian saint and devotee of Lord Rama.

Rani – queen.

Rishi – one who can see intuitively.

Rishikesh – place in North India, famous for swamis and gurus.

Sadhaka – one who practises sadhana.

Sadguru – inner guru.

Sadhana – a spiritual practice for inner illumination.

Sadhu – a spiritual mendicant.

Saguna – having forms or attributes.

Samadhi – formless awareness.

Samosa – savoury Indian snack.

Sakara – that which is manifest.

Samskaras – the seeds produced by karma, responsible for future incarnations.

Sannyasa – an order of renunciation.

Sannyasin – a renunciate.

Satsanga – meeting with spiritually minded people; literally, 'in the company of truth'.

Savikalpa samadhi – primary states of samadhi in which a trace of ego still remains.

Seva – selfless service.

Shakti – feminine aspect of inner energy.

Shaktipat – direct transmission of energy from guru to disciple.

Shaligram – smooth stone found especially in the Narmada river; symbol of Lord Vishnu.

Shankhaprakshalana – hatha yoga cleansing method for the whole digestive tract.

Shatkriyas – hatha yoga cleansing techniques.

Shishya – disciple.

Shiva – Lord of yogis; the supreme reality.

Shivalingam – psychic symbol of sahasrara chakra, representing superconsciousness.

Shivaratri – festival celebrated on the dark moon in the month of February-March, commemorating the marriage of Shiva and Shakti; a most auspicious time for tantric initiation.

Shoonyata – the state of darkness or void achieved in meditation just prior to enlightenment.

Siddhi – spiritual power attained through yogic practices.

Shmashana sadhana – tantric sadhana practised in the burial ground or cremation site.

Sri Aurobindo – contemporary saint from Pondicherry.

Sri Shankaracharya – an enlightened sage who lived five thousand years ago and established the Dashnami order of sannyasa.

Sutra – formula; abbreviated form of knowledge.

Swadhaya – study of the scriptures.

Swami Sivananda – an enlightened guru who lived in Rishikesh in the twentieth century; the guru of Swami Satyananda.

Swara yoga – a form of yoga in which a study of the alternating breath in the left and right nostrils is used as a basis for all practices.

Tamas – a quality of mind manifested by laziness and inertia.

Tantra – an ancient science incorporating innumerable practices for the expansion of mind and liberation of energy.

Tantric disciple – an aspirant who offers himself to guru to learn the practices of tantra.

Tantric guru – a guru proficient in the theory and practice of tantra.

Tantric yogini – a female yogi who initiates evolved souls into the practices of tantra.

Tattwa – subtle elements.

Tukaram – famous poet saint of Maharashtra.

Upanishads – most ancient literature containing intimate dialogues and discussions between guru and disciple on the nature of the absolute and the path leading towards it.

Vairagya – spiritual dispassion.

Vedas – oldest literature revealed to sages and seers in India, expressing the knowledge of the whole universe.

Vedanta – one of six main Indian philosophies dealing with knowledge of God.

Videhamukta – a sage who has attained final liberation.

Vishnu – part of the Hindu trinity; sustaining principle of the universe.

Vivekananda – one of the brightest sannyasins India has nurtured, who preached the spiritual truth throughout the world in the early twentieth century.

Vritti – changing pattern of the mind.

Yoga – well-experimented and scientific system derived from tantra for all-round evolution.

Yogananda Paramahamsa – great contemporary yogi born in Gorakhpur near the Himalayas, who took kriya yoga to America in 1920.

Yoga nidra – a technique of developing the state of deep relaxation.

Yogi guru – a guru who teaches raja yoga and hatha yoga practices for physical well-being, concentration of the mind, and samadhi.

Yogic kriyas – dynamic meditation practices related to yoga.

Index

— Notes —